MW00398916

BY **NOËL TOLENTINO**

bon

on the go-go

CHRONICLE BOOKS
SAN FRANCISCO

MANUFACTURED IN CHINA

Distributed in Canada by
RAINCOAST BOOKS
9050 SHAUGHNESSY STREET
VANCOUVER, B.C. V6P 6E5

10 9 8 7 6 5 4 3 2 1

CHRONICLE BOOKS LLC
85 SECOND STREET
SAN FRANCISCO, CA 94105
WWW.CHRONICLEBOOKS.COM

THANK YOU
To my Father, Mom, Jenny, Elyta, Caroline.

SPECIAL THANKS
Brian, Rob, Ray, Penny, Lee, Cosmic Tolentino Family, Ateolu, Fern, Antonio, Stereo Total, Jane Gainsbourg, Brigitte Bardot, The Who, Plastics IQ, Chocolate, Tracy & Breeders, Atelier Sci, Beach Boys, Velvet Underground, Go Mutantes, Warhol, Fauve, Riley, Fassion, Vorrorchy, Nesuchi, Nelson, Ramda, Wright, Godard, Antonioni, Kubrick, Qpon, Cornejoid, Courréges, Pucci, Twiggy, Roketo Ongaku, Bennis, Lovo, Plastique, Fanclub, Phillip, 330 Hitch, Bigfoot Lodge, Stockholm, Berlin, London, Tokyo, New York, Los Angeles, San Francisco.

MUCH LOVE
Jessica, Milna, Dana.

for
ALL THE BON BONS OF THE WORLD...

ARE YOU ready ?

LET'S

_go._

...UNDERGROUND

WHAT ARE YOU *into*?

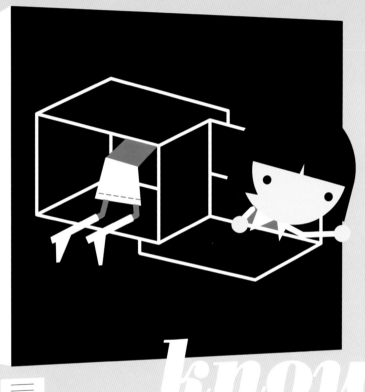

know

YOUR

OPTIONS

PRESS play

GET IN THE
groove

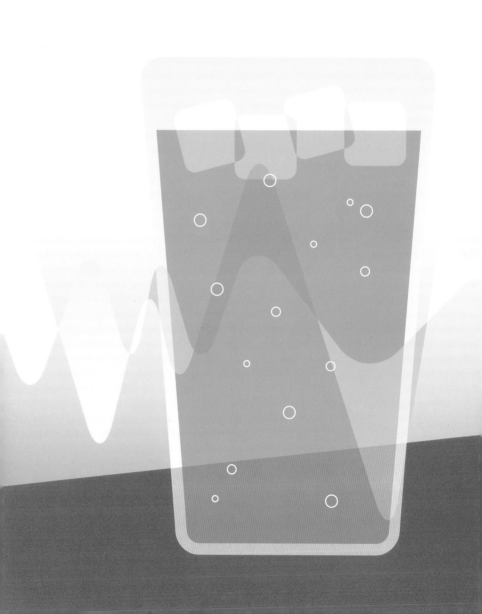

THINK *deep*

immerse
YOURSELF

KNOW
YOUR
true COLORS

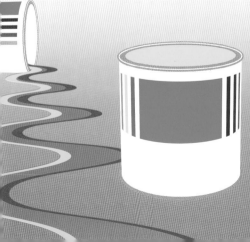

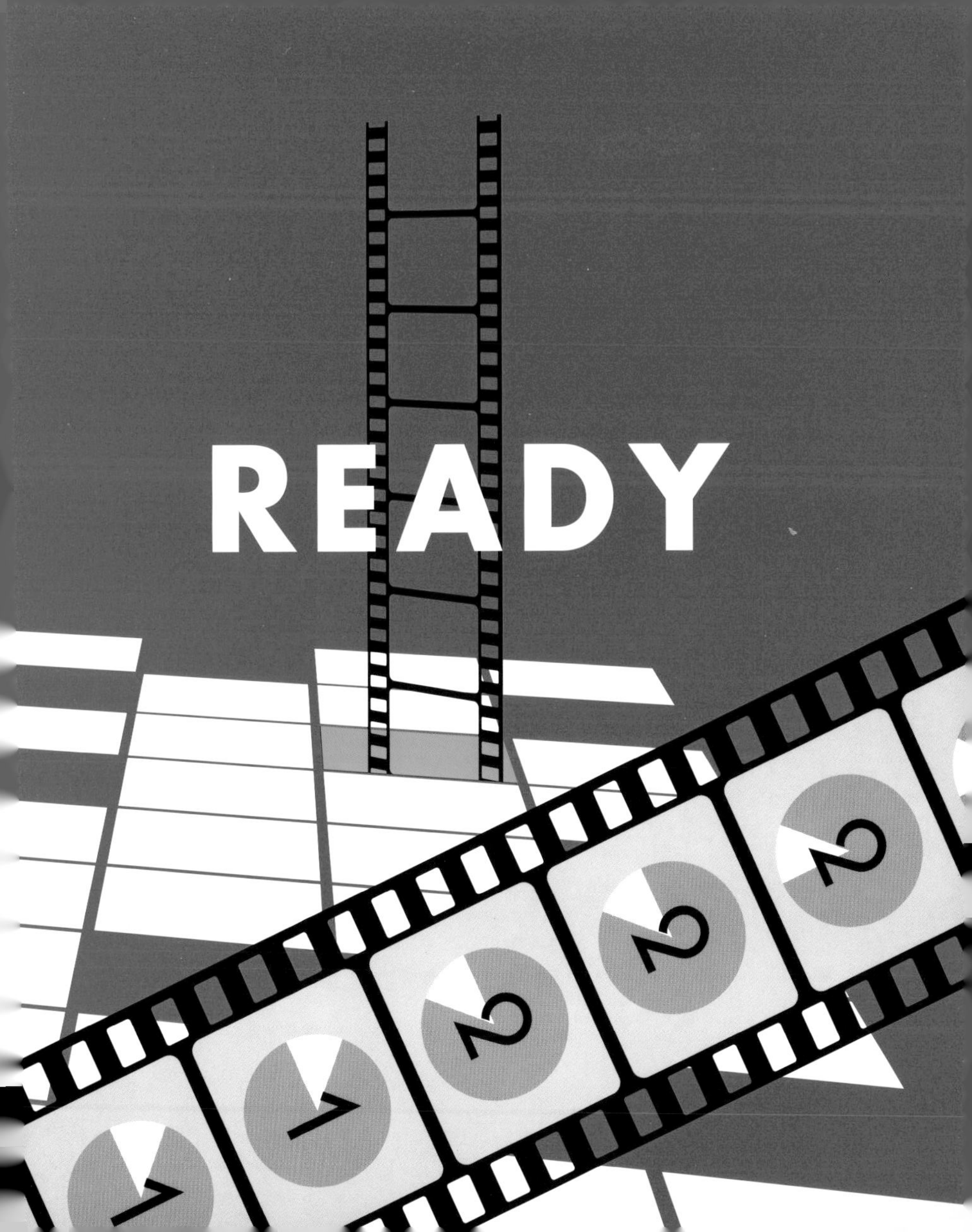
READY

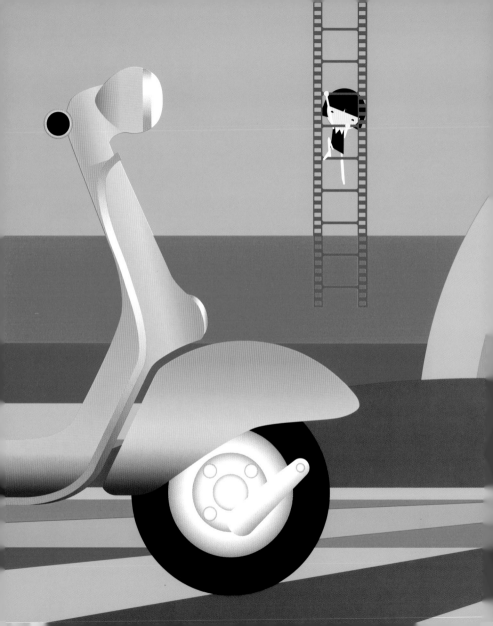

GET *in*

GO **out**
OF YOUR WAY

read
BETWEEN **THE LINES**

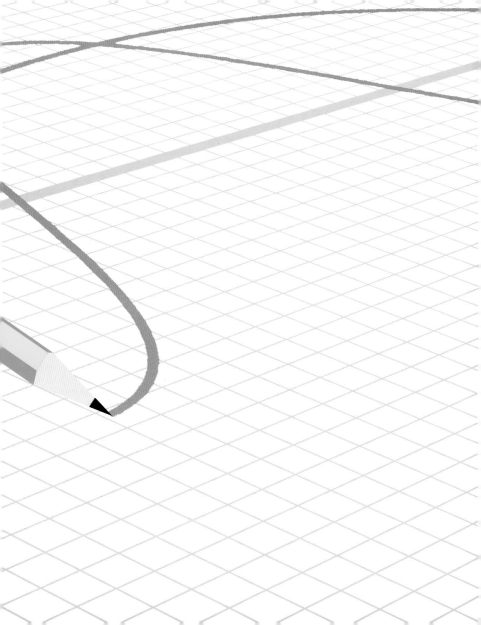

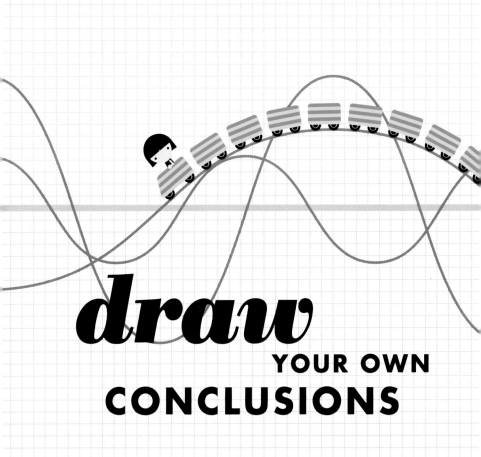

draw
YOUR OWN
CONCLUSIONS

expand

YOUR HORIZON

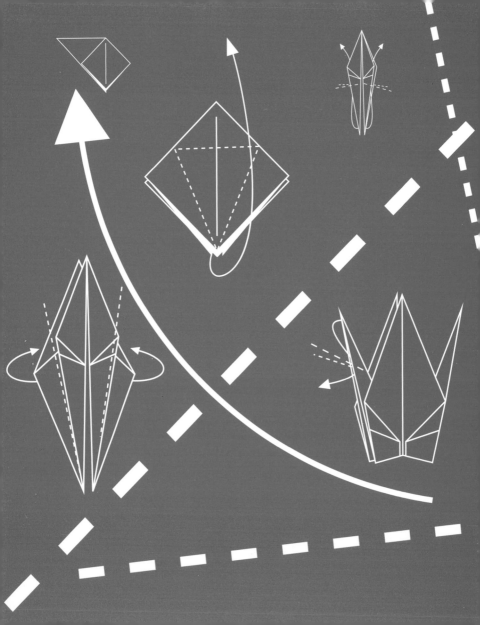

flyAWAY

FIN.

FRONTIER INVENTORY

NANCY HERTZBERG

SIMON AND SCHUSTER

NEW YORK   LONDON   TORONTO   SYDNEY   TOKYO

Simon and Schuster
Simon & Schuster Building
Rockefeller Center
1230 Avenue of the Americas
New York, New York 10020

SIMON AND SCHUSTER and colophon are registered trademarks of Simon & Schuster Inc.

Designed by Irving Perkins Associates
Manufactured in the United States of America

10 9 8 7 6 5 4 3 2 1

Library of Congress Cataloging in Publication data
Hertzberg, Nancy.
Frontier inventory / Nancy Hertzberg.
    p. cm.
I. Title.
PS3558.E7945F7   1989
813'.54—dc20   89-35211
                                                    CIP

ISBN 0-671-65864-6

I would like to thank the following people who helped make this book possible: Kate Aichele, Robert Asahina, Michael Chalfin, Nigel and Joe Poor-Dinmore, Bret Easton Ellis, Aurelia Hertzberg, David Scribner, and the entire community of BSI.

FOR MY SISTER RACHEL ELLEN

Those who had on earth believed, and those who had not, came to try and wire a message home.

—*The Blue Island*

PART I

Sleepy Hollow

Anthropology

YOU suppose everyone has a dream house. You don't mean an idea for a house, a place to live in at some future date, a place to hope for, like a farm or a condominium on the beach, someplace with a pool or a picket fence. You mean a dream house, a place you must return to every night when you are asleep.

The house in your dreams, and it has been there since you can remember, is a dark house. It has so many stories that you can't count them and they differ in every dream just as the people that move through the house are always changing. Sometimes the house is a high-rise building made of steel and glass. Sometimes the house is a cabin or a woodshed. No matter what the house looks like, you know it is yours, know that it is a place you must return to over and over again.

There is so much clutter in your dream house. You are always cleaning, rearranging; sorting through the many rooms trying to make some semblance of order.

In your dream house you are always packing a suitcase. You are never sure what to take with you to wherever it is that you are going. You try to narrow down the possibilities. There is always something to consider.

There is a subway station that runs underground. Sometimes when your dream house is as big as a city there are stores in it. The stores have things that you might want to have or things that you don't really care to see like mannequins that talk or various insects that adhere to your flesh.

There are people in this house. You can't always see these people but you know that they are there. When the house is empty you wait for the people to return, or you are looking for them, or you are hiding from people whose whereabouts you are uncertain of.

You may be alone inside your dream house and outside there are people trying to get in. No matter what precautions you take, what doors you lock, what windows you shut, you know these people will get into your dream house if they really want to.

There is a big yard that surrounds this house. In this yard there are mountains, meadows, swamps, streams with shiny rocks, but mostly this yard is dense forest. It is usually nighttime around this house, colors are muted, thick. If it is daytime everything looks as if it is being viewed through water; distorted, too big or too small, how your reflection looks in someone's eyes. Sometimes everything looks sharp and clear as real life.

There are animals in and around your dream house, cats and dogs. Mostly there are dogs, huge beasts with teeth as glistening and sharp as butcher knives. These animals are behind doors or appear at the end of dark hallways. They push at the door with a force you know you can't reckon with, all their weight slamming against the door. They are growling and clawing to get into where you are. At the end of the hallway these beasts will sit. All that moves is their glowing eyes and you can hear their breathing.

There is a beach. Always there is water in or around the house. The water floods the basement. There is surf crashing up onto the beach. Rarely do people swim at this beach, yours.

Sometimes the house is like a motel and there are people checking in and out of the rooms.

If you are tired of what is going on in any part of your dream house you can lie down wherever it is that you are and fall asleep. You will wake up somewhere else.

Sometimes people in this house scare you or are trying to scare you. Sometimes these people are trying to overpower you, something you never want to let happen. If you are violated in this house it is always someone trying to take what is alive out of you.

You make love in this house, maybe to someone whose face you don't recognize but you know them anyway, have known them for a long time. Maybe you just don't want to recognize these people, this person you are making love with, not yet anyway.

People get killed in this house. There are lots of wars in this house. There are lots of wars in the big yard that surrounds this house. You play lots of different parts in these wars; murderer or victim but mostly you are an accomplice to these crimes, letting things happen because you don't try to stop them. Sometimes you are killed in these wars, but you never really die and are all of a sudden just doing something else.

In this dream house or in the yard, or the mountains, or by the beach, you can fly. If you don't think about it you can fly as high and as fast as you want to. If you think about it, the recognition slows you, the weight of your body increasing, pulling you down.

There are no boundaries in your dream house. At times, flesh dissolves and you are running, flying, feeling that you can be everywhere and nowhere at the same time.

Mostly in this house people are constantly changing from one person to another, you are constantly changing from one person to another, or changing into something other than a person; people melting, becoming something that you are hard-pressed to name.

There are Holocausts in this house, and then there is nothing that anyone can do to survive the nuclear war or an invasion of an authority that is going to kill all the people who are different from themselves, all the people who don't believe as they do. No matter what, you never die. If you are killed you just appear somewhere else in this house, yours.

Occasionally in your dream house there are people that you know to be dead. From life to life we all must go, they say to you, or they say nothing extraordinary at all.

Often in this house you are looking for your parents. Sometimes you are making love to someone only to realize that it is your father. That feels good, normal. Your mother too, she may be naked and you are at her breast, eyes shut, floating.

In your house you are always looking for something. In your dream house people are always looking for something. You are trying to find a place to live. You will follow a man or a woman down a corridor that is flooding. These people will disappear before they can show you a place to live, will disappear just when you think you have finally arrived at the right place.

There was a time when the dream house was light and airy, a place to meet people, to fly, to embrace whatever it was that pleased you, a joyful place.

Will it be this way again?

In your dream house you think to yourself, say this to no one, you think to yourself that you must let go of the dead that are pulling at you.

In your dream house you are aware that you must not allow your imagination to be taken away from you. You are aware of this as you are aware also that you are attempting to destroy your body, attempting to escape.

This dream house, no matter what it looks like on any given night, is always the same, changing and transforming but still the house you return to every night. You know it to be the same by how you feel when you are there. It is smells really, sensation, walls, forest, surf, the environment embodying emotions, enabling you to recognize this place as your own.

If situations become unbearable and you are certain there is no way to tolerate what is happening, you say to yourself, I can't stand this dream anymore, I just don't want to be here. I must wake up, you say. You are never able to wake up. This is where you are.

In this house you are, whether you like it or not, connected to all that is. This place that can be inviting or hostile, lavish or crumbling, is your dream house. You must return to it every night. You keep returning to it because there is something in this house that you are supposed to find, or something in this house that will find you.

Snapshot

THEY are real veins; real blood veins and not the strings off a violin. You bolt out of sleep and in the dark there is whispering. Instead of turning on the light you sit in the dark and listen. Over and over you hear it, the sound of moving, the sound of making it stop.

Sometimes there is just one voice, then there is a roar, like a crowd or silence. An arm, the muscles taut, holds a weapon, and as the skull splits the muscles relax, that is the movement. The voices continue.

These voices batting around inside your head, knotted voices, garbled with or without your head under the pillow. Where are you? Heaving yourself back to flashes of June's leaving. Words that miss the truth about people's grief, an imposition of beliefs.

There is a poem; the last line of it before it happened is what? You are listening. What is being said? It is almost Christmas again. It is almost summer again. Please don't go away this time. It is dark. It is the same: the dream and being awake. Your sister June killed two people, first she killed him, and then she killed her. Can't someone see this, what has happened, what is happening?

You mustn't be afraid, June wrote. There isn't much time. You must come see me before it is too late. There were poppies, the postcard June sent was a picture of poppies. Wake up, Tracy, June wrote, you must come see me before it is too late.

Too late for what? June had nothing to say.

You don't know for how long you have been denying the truth, how long you have pretended that someone else killed two people, someone else and not your sister. You went to see June, you went home. It's all done. Grandma said, sleep, rest, we will talk about it later. You just wish that someone would tell you what it is that you are supposed to be doing. Waiting. You just need to know if you are really alive or not. Waking up.

When did it start? How did you come to know nothing at all, not dates, not that some things are important, not that there are certain things you must do.

This, then, your story is a binge for lonely hearts. It is about the space between people. It is about dreaming. It is about hiding. It is about being lost. It is about finding something only to lose it. It is about kamikaze daughters. It is about desert dads. It is about mothers who say yes, then say no, but not with words. Mostly it is about floating. If it was about resolutions then you wouldn't need a ghost to tell it.

You will start from the beginning since that will make it clear from the outset that this is your story and can be generalized only insofar as you can get one thing straight, your sister June she killed two people, she killed a young man and then she killed an old woman. This is what is.

You have to tell the story whether you want to or not. You say that you can't because you know that it has to be like making love. You are not sure what making love is. There is screaming but not sound.

It's because stories are important that you must tell this one, but it starts at the end, this story. Everything is already known, what happened and that there really are no characters, and that there really is nothing to be said that hasn't been said before in so many different ways. But it is what is beneath what was said before, or what is said now, what you say, that is important, what is underneath language or photographs, or a sleeping face. What is beneath all that isn't holding, this is what you have to understand.

You have to tell this story, you have to because you are lost and because once and for all you want to figure out where exactly it is that you are and what exactly it is that you are supposed to be doing. Grandma lives by the ocean in Raynes, North Carolina. Grandma lives alone.

For a while, for a long time, you stay in North Carolina. Your body goes through motions. You see yourself do things half out of your body as if you were a shadow riding piggyback on a body that is yours.

It's autumn and the landscape is sinking. Leaves fall, of course. Branches settle into themselves. Your lists. You have lost them.

Through the amethyst-veined night sky the moon probes discreetly. The moon, a fingernail clipping haphazardly placed. It's not asking to be stepped on, couldn't care if you found it there or not, the moon. This bed at Grandma's, this sky, your body itching into the darkness. You are not listening. Unable to sleep at night, you are aware of yourself as something less than sensation, a roundness, a dotty fullness pulsating beneath a sheet, how an ameba looks or anything smashed in a glass slide, two pieces of glass encasing something.

These eyes, this heart beating, telltale to no one, just alone. The feeling of transposing this self into this skin and this consciousness is what? You are not familiar with this feeling of wholeness? This consciousness, a chemical sensation that can go anywhere? Is trying to still the evaporating roundness of gray matter spreading, drying at the edges, these eyes that bolt about the dark?

It's hard to fall asleep with bronchitis, and your Grandma said she couldn't find the vaporizer, so tomorrow she will try to borrow one. But breathing is always harder at night, especially when you are sick, having to concentrate on each breath, each breath accentuated by your heart pounding everywhere in the room too loudly. Oxygen comes sparingly, rationing itself down congested pipes like water trying to incorporate into something denser than itself.

Be patient, and as long as you don't panic, the air does come, and when it does it is as if by someone else's strong hand. Grandma's fingers slipping smoothly through your hair.

You dream you are unable to wake up. In the dream you are trapped in your own flesh and you are unable to wake up. Wake up, you say to yourself in the dream. You are drowning inside something that is as heavy as concrete. It is your body that is this heavy. In your throat you are saying, help me wake up.

Outside, these trees here in North Carolina scratch against the window. You sleep. You wake up. The dreams and the waking reality are the same.

You imagine the air to be filled with screams, one guttural forehead-peeling scream after the other bursting through the roofs of houses, terror escaping from all the sleeping bodies of the world. The other half of the world is awake now. These bloodcurdling screams, a network of vapors trying to find each other in the darkness, floating through rooms, escaping first from the sleeping bodies and then escaping through roofs. This network of stress, of anger, of hatred, of passion, all this floating loose in the night sky trying to find itself drawing together to balance. Inside too, in your head all this.

Grandma is asleep. You are remembering how you tried to forget about June. You are remembering as far back as you can because this is what you can do now.

Everything is in between. What is happening, a grayness that shuttles you back and forth through space. In your dreams there is a dark well up from the depths of which comes a scream so persistent and painful that you have stopped hearing it. You know it is there because its presence is permanently fixed on every face that you have ever seen. It's in the eyes. Even when you are face to face with another person you can never be certain of what it is they are seeing. The dark well of living in the past is grayness. It just doesn't matter where you are. What you have to look at is what has brought you to this point where nothing registers but what has already happened.

What you are doing now is moving backwards and forwards at the same time . . . returning now to where your sister is. This is what you are doing because there is no stillness, only the trying to make things stop.

You used to wonder how you would reach the people you loved if you were to die, how to tell people you had come back as someone else in the same lifetime. You used to wonder this. You would say to yourself, it is about forgetting and there has to be a way to not forget when you come back.

At night is where it starts. While everyone sleeps, their dreams open up toward the constellations as if a great surgery was being performed, the skulls of the sleeping splitting from the stress of their dreams. You think that God is when two people dream of each other at the same time. Your sister June is in prison for life. You have to go back now.

The Rapture of Christmas and Summer

YOU felt like you should be helping.

You started it, really. Dad says there really isn't anything you can do. June's body is so small. Dad has got June down on the ground and is holding her feet. Dad brought her down first, because on the floor she is safe. Mom is straddled over June's stomach holding her head. June might bite her tongue so Mom holds her head. Homer is yipping around and around the living room, peeing a little bit and then yipping. June's eyes just rolled back into her head. June had a tantrum because of the roller skates. You said, don't use my roller skates because I didn't give you permission, no, June, I didn't say that you could use them. June is panting and crying on the floor and doesn't have any clothes on again. June was skating in the bedroom and then you asked her, who said you could use my skates? June said she wasn't skating, and all the marbles from your nightstand, and your kiddle dolls, and jewelry from Grandma in Old Saybrook and your rock collection that you and Mom found camping are all over the floor because June doesn't know how to skate and knocked everything over. And June said she wasn't skating but the skates were on her feet. You slapped her and pinched her hard. She got off the skates, took off her sundress and started jumping up and down on the bed. Up and down. June's eyes got angry. June's not four when her eyes get this mad. June is as mad as Dad when he threw his typewriter case against the wall and the white from the wall fell all over the carpet and the couch and some of the books, white in big pieces and some white powder. June is in a little girl's body but she is as mad as an adult. She is jumping on the bed. You lie about the skates, June is screaming. You grab her on the bed. You grab her arm first and then her hair. June bites you and you grab her neck. She screams louder and her eyes are wet and mad. You slap her and she won't stop screaming and then Mom comes and then Dad. It's Sunday and they were sleeping. Mom and Dad are in the room so fast. You back up against the wall quick and hold your behind so Dad can't spank you. You are against the wall and Dad doesn't come to you. June starts. She did this before. Her face is all red. She hollers and starts to shake. June's whole body shakes. June makes her hands into fists, then her arms are still, and then fists again. Everything is slow. Mom and Dad are rubbing their eyes. June punches at the wall, then jumps up and down. June scratches her arms and her face. June is jumping up and down. Dad grabs June first. June hits at Mom and Dad. You are against the wall. Nothing can stop it. It will eventually stop itself. June's body will stop shaking and then she will cry and Mom or Dad will rub her hair. It's just the waiting that is hard, the waiting and the scared look in Mom and Dad's faces. There are slices of sun on Dad's back. There is dust floating in the air in the slices of sun. You start to act innocent then. Can I help? you ask Dad, patting his back like how you might pat a dog that you aren't sure about whether it's mean.

June won't remember this.

June is very pretty even if she does have scratches on her arms and face now and her nose is all wet with boogers and her eyes are all red and puffy. June is very pretty and small and she looks like a doll. June has a big beauty mark on her pee-pee. You can see it. Dad's robe is open. Dad has hair around his nipples. Mom has Dad's big shirt on. Mom is naked under the white shirt. Their breath is bad. Outside the sprinkler has started and kids are yelling. The kids running under the sprinkler sound like you slapping June. There is laughing and yelling outside. You wish to go outside. June's beauty mark looks like a polka dot.

It's almost over, Dad says. Mom scratches her leg and looks at you hard.

. . .

JEWEL likes you to come over any time. Jewel is older but she likes you. You aren't supposed to go to Jewel's because she gives you things and your Mom doesn't know her. Jewel has long fingernails. Jewel has a picture of herself wearing a sparkling green satin dress with her arms around a famous person, James Brown.

Past the laundry room Jewel lives, and up the stairs that smell like pee. It's smoky in Jewel's apartment but she always has the air conditioner on. Jewel has two poodles, Miranda and

Amanda, but sometimes she calls them Randa and Manda or just Lady M or asshole. Sometimes Jewel brushes the poodles but mostly their fur is yellow where it should be all white.

Jewel sometimes lets you put on makeup or she will put it on for you. She has a table with a curtain of lace around the bottom, and a large piece of broken mirror is on the top of the table. Jewel says it's a vanity and isn't it pretty. You don't tell Jewel that it's not a vanity, that it is really a table with a lace curtain thumbtacked around the bottom, and that your grandma in Old Saybrook has a real vanity. There are lipsticks, red and pink and orange, on the table and a plastic container with a little bit of powder left in it, and an ashtray filled with cigarette butts. On Jewel's bed are lots of clothes, shiny dresses and a black leather miniskirt that Jewel wears to work, and fancy slips and stockings. Jewel doesn't like to clean much. On the floor are lots of little piles of clothes and lots of fancy high heels. Jewel says she steps out of her clothes and then she steps back into them. Jewel likes to brush your hair and she likes to give you presents. One time Jewel gave you a pair of shiny gold sandals with purple and green gems on them. When you came home from Jewel's, Mom asked you real loud where you got the shoes. You said you found them in the garbage.

Before here, at Grandma's in Old Saybrook, there was Grandma's rowboat in the harbor, and Grandpa's Doctor's office that is in the house because they are very rich. Mom says someday Dad will be very rich like his parents in Old Saybrook, but Dad says that he doesn't think that that is important. Dad says things like this and then he might reach around Mom from behind her and hold her so that she smiles and laughs the way a kid might. Mom's parents live in California and you have never met them.

Grandma in Old Saybrook makes special sandwiches. She cuts the crust off the bread and puts fancy colored toothpicks in the sandwich pieces that she has cut into thin shapes Grandma calls fingers. Grandma said, don't worry, Tracy, I will visit often, she said that when you moved because you wouldn't stop crying. Grandma rubs her hands that are cool and soft through your hair and says, don't worry. Grandma lives two hours away in a house that is big and white and the lawn is green in the summer and goes way back behind the house.

In East Hartford the projects are all brick, and Dad says, not long, he says we won't live in this place for long. Dad goes off to work early. He sells insurance for boiler companies. You are not sure what that is, insurance. Dad will explain it if you ask but it's hard to understand because you listen but it is a lot of words that don't go together right. Mostly you nod your head. People pay money and if something happens to their machinery we pay to fix it, Dad says. Can't people pay to fix things themselves? you ask Dad. It's like sharing, Dad says. Dad wears glasses. Your Dad is very handsome and has dark hair just like your Mom. Your Mom and Dad look like brother and sister.

Jewel says, come in. Jewel is in her robe. Jewel says, how is your father, did your father get his promotion? You didn't ever tell Jewel about your Dad before.

You tell Jewel that June had a seizure this morning and then you remember that Mom said not to tell other people the family's business. Jewel is OK to tell things to. Your Mom must be very tired, Jewel says. Jewel is smoking a cigarette out of a long gold holder and scrambling eggs on the stove for her dogs. Jewel wears miniskirts that are shorter than your Mom's. Jewel has very big tits like the ladies in the magazines you saw over at Teddy's and Tammy's house. Tammy's and Teddy's Dad has a big box of magazines that show naked ladies lying all over the place like they were food. You feel funny when you look at these magazines.

Here Manda, here Randa, Jewel says, but the dogs are eating already. The floor is dirty. Where the sun is hitting the floor by the walls there are hairballs sort of glued there. The dogs growl at each other to get to the part of the bowl where they want to eat. You are hoping Jewel will ask you if you want to stay and watch her get dressed to go out. Maybe she has presents for you.

I don't do this all the time, Tracy, Jewel is saying. She goes to the refrigerator and opens it. No I don't, she continues. Yesterday was a hard day, it was rough, she says. Jewel is pulling a beer can out of the plastic ring it's in. She throws all the now empty rings into the garbage, pops the beer open, rolls her head around on her neck, and moves her peach-polished big toe in a circle on the greasy floor. There is a hair ball on her other heel. Jewel goes back to the garbage and takes the plastic rings that held the beer cans out of the garbage.

Did you know, Tracy, that seagulls get their heads stuck in these sometimes, did you know that? Jewel says, and her eyes look like she might cry. Did you know, Tracy, that one should always tear apart these rings or cut them before throwing them away?

You were at the garbage dump once and there were lots of seagulls there. At the dump with Dad and June you brought all the carpet that Mom and Dad ripped out of the apartment. There are so many couches at the dump, and old shoes, and stuff that looks like it belongs in houses, not in a big pile outside. The sky is blue. The garbage is in mountains. There are chairs and couches and shoes and refrigerators and plastic bags that look like shiny pillows and sometimes clothes all mixed together outside. The man at the entrance to the dump gives you and June lemon lollipops. Dad gives the man some money to dump the carpet there.

You ask Jewel if she is going to go out tonight. Jewel is ripping the plastic rings with her hands. Her knuckles are white. She is chewing her lips. She takes a sip of beer and then puts the can on the top of the refrigerator.

Jewel tells you that Marvin is going to take her out to dinner tonight if his big rig makes it back from the city. Jewel laughs and sits down. Jewel's legs are spread and her feet go in at the bottom of the chair. Jewel continues to pull apart the plastic rings. Jewel has black underwear on. You look away quick so she doesn't know that you saw. Marvin has lots of pimples and lives next door to Tammy and Teddy. Teddy says he has been to Marvin's and that Marvin gave him money. You hope that Marvin doesn't come here when you are still here because there is something about Marvin that makes you afraid. Marvin just moved here last week. Jewel met Marvin in the laundry room.

My Mom doesn't care if I come here today, Jewel, you say, because my Mom is helping Dad paint some chairs. Dad is going to barbecue later. Jewel, it is all right if I am here. My Mom said to be home in an hour. Is it an hour?

When you left the apartment you didn't tell Mom or Dad anything. You felt bad about June. You just left. You didn't know any of the kids in the sprinkler and Tammy and Teddy weren't home. Jewel likes you to visit. Tammy and Teddy are twins. Jewel says that Tammy and Teddy are special and that it is an accident that they have the parents that they do. Jewel says that if she could she would adopt Tammy and Teddy. If she had the money she would give them a real home, love them. Tammy and Teddy's parents are just bad people, Jewel says. Jewel just says what she wants.

The first time you told your Mom about how pretty Jewel was, and that she was a dancer and had fancy clothes, Mom said, I don't want you to pester people. Mom said, Jewel is busy. Mom said, it's not a good idea to just go to strange people's houses. Mom said, I just don't know what kind of woman Jewel is. Then Mom just said, no, you aren't allowed to go there. Sometimes Mom says you aren't allowed to go places and you go anyway. Mom might forget she told you not to do this or that. Sometimes your parents just get frustrated and then they lay down the law. It's like how you want to pinch June when she slurps her cereal at breakfast and you just woke up, or if you slammed your finger in the door and everyone says, are you all right? Are you all right? and it hurts and you just want to swear like Dad. If Mom or Dad aren't there then you do swear. Sometimes you swear if Mom and Dad are there. If June is there you just want to hit her, make her cry.

It's just that Mom and Dad work. They say they are tired. Dad works in the day. Mom works at night. Mom works at the

Boeing factory where they make plane engines and parts for bombs.

Mom talks louder than normal people when she gets home from work in the morning. But she only talks really loud in the apartment. Outside your Mom is shy. Sometimes it is because she has holes in her pants, or sometimes it's because Dad just knows how to talk better, make people laugh. Your Dad is writing a book. The book is called *The Alley of Eden*. Dad says it is about paradise being smothered.

There is a knock on the door and Jewel stops filing your fingernails. She was going to paint them Luscious Red, just like her fingernails. Jewel likes to paint her fingernails a different color than her toenails.

Behind the open front door Jewel is pulled by a big hand and she laughs and makes mmmmm noises.

Jewel's air conditioner has colored ribbons coming off it.

Marvin is the one behind the door. You can hear them. You want to leave. You feel funny, like you should be doing something.

Jewel puts ribbons on the air conditioner and they blow around or just hang there when she turns the air conditioner off. Jewel sprays the colored ribbons with perfume. You go to smell them because behind the door Marvin says, baby, and Jewel says, mmm.

You pick a yellow ribbon. It smells like cherry but mostly it smells like the metal blinds for the window in your apartment that make your nose burn. The dogs are growling and circling each other real fast by the door.

Tracy, this is Marvin, Jewel says. Marvin smiles with one side of his mouth. You say, Hi. You don't want to be here anymore. Marvin is staring at you. He has one hand around Jewel and his fingers are on her tit inside her robe. Marvin's fingernails are dirty and there is black on his hands.

Yesterday, Dad and Mom's door was open.

Dad and Mom are naked. You have to go to the bathroom. Dad says, Hi Tracy. He says this from his bed. Mom is sitting between Dad's legs on the bed. Dad's hands are on Mom's tits. Mom says, good morning. Mom and Dad are naked on their bed. They talk to you but their faces look white because you are dizzy.

I was just fixing her nails, Jewel is telling Marvin. You know that Jewel won't do your nails now. Marvin smacks Jewel on the butt. Jewel's butt shakes under the pink robe. Marvin is staring at you. You want to be outside now. Teddy said Marvin gave him money. You tell Jewel that you have to go home. Jewel has brown-red hair that hangs down her back. Her hair isn't even on the bottom. In the sun the ends of her hair are split. Jewel is a dancer at a club and sometimes she shows you ballet.

Give me a kiss? Jewel asks you.

June is looking out the window and you wave to her. June looks like a doll and she looks like a small adult. June is four and she knows how to read already. June isn't smiling and she isn't looking at you and she isn't wearing any clothes.

Dad spanked you. It is because you were at Jewel's, or because you hit June and made Mom and Dad wake up on Sunday and then you went away.

No, Dad, no, you said, holding your butt and backing up from him.

Now you are in your room crying. There isn't an air conditioner and it's hot and you have your legs straight up on the wall and your back is on the pillow and the bed might just as well be anywhere, because you aren't going to leave it.

When June comes into the room you tell her to go away. You say, get out. Dad calls June. Dad says, June, leave Tracy alone now. The door is shut. You could go out in the living room. You aren't going to. You want to be at Grandma's house. Grandma would talk to you. Grandma would rub your head. Grandma wouldn't let you get this mad. You keep crying.

You cry. You wish that June would get spanked. You wish that June was crying now. You wish that Grandma was here.

In the bed once when you were sick for a long time you were

hot, then cold. You yelled for Mom. Please smooth the covers.
Please get the wrinkles off my bed, there are so many wrinkles,
you said. The covers look like huge valleys and mountains. You
can't leave the bed. Grandpa comes over to see. Grandpa takes
your temperature and gives you medicine. Grandpa's hands are
cold. In Old Saybrook, living next to Grandma and Grandpa it
was better.

You cry more. You aren't there.

You aren't sick now. Now you are mad and sad at the same
time. You have been in here for a long time. It's getting dark
outside. The covers are valleys and mountains. You can hear
Mom and Dad talking in the kitchen. They are talking about
you. You heard your name. There is light under the door. The
light makes straps across the blankets. You yelled, Mom. She
didn't come in. Maybe you didn't yell.

Dad says, above the sink. That is what you hear. It is in your
head, above the sink. It goes back and forth in your head. Mom
and Dad keep talking. It is loud and soft. It is not words. It is
whispers. Grandma has a big shell that sounds like the ocean.
Mom and Dad talking in the kitchen sounds like the ocean. Dad
said, above the sink. Rocks under water look big. When you
pick the rocks out of the water they are small. It keeps
repeating. Above the sink. Above the sink. Your knee is up.
The cover is coming down over it.

Above the sink, Dad said. You want it to go away. Above
the sink. Above the sink. Big voice. Little voice. You can't cry.

You want it to go away, Dad's voice saying this. When you
were sick you wanted the wrinkles out of your covers. In Old
Saybrook there was a bridge by your house. You could sit
under the bridge if you wanted to.

When you close your eyes you see lines. The lines are orange.
If you close your eyes tight the lines are orange or black or blue.
The lines beep or get hard. You want the lines to be one way.
The lines get big or small. You are floating. It is thick and gray.

You are supposed to be mad but you aren't crying anymore.
Under the door there is light. Dad knocks on the door. Dad

says, it is dinner now. June is on Dad's shoulders. June is holding on to Dad's hair. Dad likes June best.

The bricks against the side of the apartment are cool. The sky has pink marks in it. You move your fingers along in the spaces between the bricks. You like to finger paint. There are hot dogs on the grill. Dad is typing. Dad brought the card table out back. Mom is braiding her hair for work. June's got Mom's high heels on and is clack-clacking around the cement and then up and down the stairs. Dad types fast, then slow. Sometimes Dad says, that's it, and, yes. Over the fence a skyrocket sizzles, then explodes, then the sound of running.

Damn if I will, man. Someone says this walking by behind the fence. Mom turns the hot dogs and says, let's eat. The bricks are cool. You put your face against them. June holds her fingers spread wide up to the hot coals and says, one-two-three-four-five.

In bed June keeps pulling up the blankets. You keep kicking them off.

Dad is playing his guitar in the living room and singing. Dad never can sing like on the radio or on records. Mom says Dad is tone deaf. Dad can play the guitar as good as anyone. Dad can play the harmonica. Mom can play the guitar too. Sometimes Mom and Dad play together and Mom sings and sometimes you and June sing too.

Mom is reading. Mom reads before she goes to work.

You tell Dad at bedtime not to close the door all the way.

You hear Mom and Dad whispering.

The front door shuts.

Homer is out back. Homer growls when people walk by behind the fence. Homer growls, yips and barks. Sometimes Homer howls. Homer better stop because the man next door will start yelling and come over and tell Dad to do something about that dog or else. The man next door crashes things around in his apartment. One time he threw a plant through the window. You don't want him to come over and yell at your

Dad. Homer just wants to run. Homer likes to swim at the beach by Grandma's house.

June is snoring.

The airplane factory is down the street. The street is long. Your apartment is on one end of the street. The factory is way down at the other end of the street past the part of East Hartford where there are office buildings and the big grocery store where there is a small carousel that you and June can ride when Mom has quarters. The street is miles and miles long.

June says in her sleep, no rockets. June mumbles.

There is light from where Dad is.

Dad lets Homer in.

At the plane-engine factory Mom is polishing small parts that come down a conveyor belt. Mom sits in a chair in front of the conveyer belt and polishes piece after piece. It is loud. It smells like buses in the factory.

There are stars out the window over the fence.

June pulls the covers up. You pinch June hard on her arm. You wish you didn't. You move your legs closer to June. Where your leg is the sheet is wet. On the other side of the bed close to the door it is dry. There is no more music. Dad comes into your room. You pretend you are asleep. Dad looks at you and June for a minute. Dad goes away. The light in the living room goes out. Homer wants up on the bed. It's too hot. There is nothing under the bed. You check again, just shoes. The bedframe is metal. When you tap the bedframe it sounds like Dad's typewriter, or polished pieces dropping, or June on the back porch in Mom's high heels. Out the window the moon is cut in half. Jewel kissed Marvin. You didn't let Jewel kiss you today. Outside there are sirens.

Dad says, wake up. Dad smells nice when he is ready for work. You and June have to go to Mrs. Morrison's today. The tub is filled for June. Dad takes the wet sheets off the bed. June is in the tub. Dad soaps June, her arms and legs, her back. Dad washes June real nice and careful like she might break. Dad puts a wet washcloth over June's eyes and June holds the washcloth there so that when Dad washes June's hair he won't get any shampoo in her eyes. June splashes in the tub when Dad is rinsing her and she sings. When Dad tickles her on the stomach June laughs.

Dad never gives you a bath. You don't wet your bed. Mom gives you a bath or sometimes you take a bath with June at night and Mom washes both you and June. Sometimes when you take a bath with Mom you wash Mom's back. When you wash Mom's back she closes her eyes and says, that feels very nice, Tracy. When you and June take a bath, you play with the Barbies and Mom sits on the toilet and makes sure you both wash and don't just play.

Today you are going to wear the shoes that Jewel gave you. It's quiet except for June splashing in the tub. Mom is not home yet. Homer is on Mom and Dad's bed. Homer's body moves quick, then stops, and there is a sound in Homer's neck. Dad says that when Homer does this he is dreaming.

Dad dresses June in a yellow dress with flowers. You have one that is the same. Grandma bought the yellow dresses for you and June as presents before you moved from Old Saybrook to here. You are not going to wear your yellow dress today. You are going to wear a white dress that Mom made that has your name sewn on it in the front and red hearts. Mom likes to embroider on the clothes she makes. Dad says no to the shoes that Jewel gave you.

Mrs. Morrison is the baby-sitter. You don't like her because she never smiles except to parents and she squints her eyes all the time like she is very sick and she cleans up everything all the time so that none of the kids can really play. Some days she will wax all the floors and then all the kids will have to stay outside even if it's too hot and there's no swimming. Sometimes Tammy and Teddy are at Mrs. Morrison's but not very much. Mrs. Morrison goes to church a lot and only has coloring books with Jesus, either a baby or grown up, and farm animals. Mrs.

Morrison makes all the kids pray before snack. There are songs Mrs. Morrison sings really loud while she is waxing the floor or changing diapers. She teaches all the kids these songs and then you have to sing them all together with a record in the background. Stop and let me tell you what the Lord has done for me, Mrs. Morrison sings really loud, and most of the kids go lalalalala. You just hold your mouth together tight. One time Mrs. Morrison made you sit in the corner because you wouldn't sing. Mrs. Morrison has yellow teeth and arms that jiggle and she wears a cross around her neck that is as big as your hand and she says it has special water in it. Mrs. Morrison has hair that is cut like a man.

June was locked in the toilet stall by the pool and you could hear her crying. You didn't mean to leave June alone by the pool, with Mrs. Morrison just reading magazines and smoking. There are four big black girls. One of the black girls is standing in front of the door. She is holding June's yellow dress. You can see June's feet. Your heart is pounding and you say, Mrs. Morrison is coming. You say it again, because these black girls said that if they ever saw you by their apartment they would scratch your eyes out. You keep standing in front of the black girl who is standing in front of the toilet stall where June is. You aren't going to move. The black girl has lots of colored clips in her hair. The bathroom smells like pee. The floor is cold. The three girls behind you aren't behind you anymore. June is crying. The black girl holding June's yellow dress is not taller than you. She drops the dress. The sleeve on June's yellow dress is ripped. The black girls that told you not to come by their house ever made June take off her dress and the sleeve is ripped and they took June's bathing suit and towel. June is crying and crying and then she just stops and says, Tracy. You help June put her dress on. June is four and she can read and the black girls took her bathing suit. You say that you hope those girls get in trouble and that they die.

When June was born in Old Saybrook you sat in the back seat

34

of Grandpa's big car and cried and wanted to go home. Everyone else is in the big building, Mom and Dad and Grandma. In the car Grandpa hums, da da dum and you say, where's Mom? and then Grandpa puts you on his lap in the front seat and sings, bumpety bumpety bumpety bump as I was riding my charger. Grandma tells you this story when you ask her and the other one too about how when June was born your Dad was sure that June was the wrong baby because she was so dark and looked Mexican.

You let June get locked in the bathroom because sometimes June bothers you and you don't want to pay attention to her. Then you feel bad. You hug June.

You tell Mrs. Morrison about the black girls stealing June's towel and bathing suit. Mrs. Morrison just looks at you. You say that June can't go in the water naked. You say how come Mrs. Morrison didn't help June change, that June is only four. Mrs. Morrison calls for the other kids to get out of the pool. Mrs. Morrison smooths June's hair and tries to sit June on her big lap. June doesn't let Mrs. Morrison hold her and walks behind you. Mrs. Morrison doesn't like you. You don't like Mrs. Morrison.

One day Mrs. Morrison called you a brat and her face looked like she wanted to hit you. Mrs. Morrison said that your parents were too young and didn't know how to raise their kids. It's just kids raising kids, Mrs. Morrison said. You wanted to tell Mrs. Morrison that her daughter Dotsy was retarded but you didn't. Mrs. Morrison's fat daughter Dotsy is real slow. Dotsy gets beat up a lot. Big kids call Dotsy retard. The big kids and maybe some of the girls that stole June's bathing suit locked Dotsy in the laundry room before. Dotsy watches the babies when Mrs. Morrison takes the kids to the pool. Dotsy helps her Mom and doesn't have any friends.

The pool is dirty. Sometimes the lifeguard makes everyone get out of the pool because a kid might go to the bathroom there. You go to the bathroom but not the kind that makes everyone have to get out of the pool. You know it is safe to go to the bathroom because you don't see a red line after you pee. Mrs. Morrison said that if any kids peed in the pool everyone would know because of the red line and whoever did it would be ashamed. She said that the red line traced the pee and would follow whoever did it around the pool.

You can swim but not in the deep end. Mrs. Morrison says to take only one graham cracker but you take two and eat June's. Before Mrs. Morrison says it's time to go she pulls up her bathing suit straps and goes to stand in the shallow end of the pool to cool her fat red legs. You hate Mrs. Morrison because she let June get locked in the bathroom.

At 2:30 Mom comes and Mrs. Morrison tells your Mom that you and June are just wonderful. She doesn't tell that June was locked in the bathroom. She tells your Mom that she is washing June's bathing suit and towel because June had an accident. That's OK because you tell Mom later that Mrs. Morrison lies.

Mom says she is sorry. Mom says that Mrs. Morrison does her best.

After June was locked in the bathroom you decide never to leave June alone again.

Mom says that she loves you and June so very much. By the pool Mom kneels down. She holds you and June to her for a long time. She holds you both very tight. Mom smells a little like how Dad smelled this morning for work, and she is sweaty and warm. You feel nice here with Mom and June. The grass is brown and sharp beneath your feet. The grass looks like the sound of Mom's hands on your back where the white dress is.

. . .

YOUR father was sleeping.

You see Teddy out the window. Teddy is polishing his new bike with a blue washcloth. There is plastic fringe on the handlebars and training wheels on the bike. The sprinkler is not on yet. Mom isn't home. June says she can be a princess and she has Mom's shoes on again. June smells like the bed, like pee. June says she can be a princess if she wants when you tell June that she is not a princess and that she smells.

You rap on the window. Teddy looks at you. It's gray outside but hot. June can't go outside because she has a cold. You aren't supposed to go outside because Dad isn't up yet. You are just going to go out for a minute to see if Tammy and Teddy might want to come to your apartment for a while because they are outside.

Tammy is down by the pool. Tammy is pulling a big stick back and forth on the metal fence that is around the pool. The fence around the pool is too high to climb over. There is barbed wire at the top of the fence. Tammy is pulling the stick and the noise echoes. No one else is outside, just Tammy and Teddy. Tammy and Teddy are twins and they are seven just like you. If you still live here when school starts you will ride the bus with them to school. You don't want to go to school here. There are too many kids here that scare you and are mean and June is too young to go to school and will have to be at Mrs. Morrison's all day by herself. Tammy and Teddy's Dad has big parties at night by the pool. Your Dad plays guitar at these parties, and harmonica. Teddy and Tammy's Dad makes tattoos on people and he has three snapping turtles in his living room in a big glass tank. Your Mom drew a picture once of the turtles. Tammy and Teddy's Dad wanted to give your Mom a tattoo of a rose on her tit but your Mom just wanted to draw the turtles.

Teddy doesn't want to do anything but work on his bike. Teddy's Dad has a big motorcycle that he rides in a gang. Teddy thinks his bike is a motorcycle. Teddy is polishing the handlebars and polishing around the tires where it is already shiny.

Tammy says she will get her dolls. You come with her. Walking to Tammy's you sing the song that Tammy taught you that her cousin from Ohio taught her. It goes: My Mom and your Mom live across the street, 18, 19, Blueberry Street.

Every night they have a fight and this is what they say, Boys go to Jupiter to get more stupider and Girls go to Mars to get more candy bars. The song is really for playing jump rope, but you and Tammy sing it anyway. Tammy and Teddy's house is dark and smells like beer and the turtle tank. There is a man in a black leather vest sleeping on the couch. The man is wearing cowboy boots that are covered with grease. The man has a tattoo of a knife with blood on his arm. The man is bigger than the couch. Tammy says her Mom has a bad stomach flu since last night. Tammy says her Mom told her and Teddy to be quiet all day. Tammy says her Mom said that your parents are hippies. Tammy thinks your parents are nice.

Tammy's Mom has fifteen different kinds of salt and pepper shakers. She is in a club and she gets a different set every month. She keeps them on a shelf above the sofa where the man in the leather vest is sleeping. Your favorite salt and pepper shakers are a Chinese boy and girl with red hats that press up and down to shake out the salt and pepper. Tammy's Mom just uses all the salt and pepper shakers for decoration. Your Mom collects things too. Your Mom collects small things: dolls and animals and colored rocks. Your Mom keeps her collection on an old wine rack that is on one side of the record player.

In your house you and Tammy fill the green salad bowl with water for a swimming pool. Tammy has got five Barbies and one Ken doll and a GI Joe that Teddy melted the feet off of. You have two Barbies.

Sometimes you think that the dolls could be real. If they were real people and this small you would make them do things: dress and undress, sit in chairs, eat breakfast, touch each other. You pretend a lot of things. Sometimes at night you imagine that maybe there is a pretty lady hiding under your bed, pretty like Jewel. The lady is dressed in a beautiful green satin gown or with sequins. The lady is just quiet and you can touch her naked parts, the parts you aren't supposed to touch but want to. When Mom is naked Dad touches her. You want to touch this lady like how you have seen Dad touch Mom. If the dolls were little people you could have them sitting at the table and then make them swim. They would do whatever you told them to do because they are so small.

June has a Skipper doll but June doesn't want to play. June is drawing. June says that she is writing a book like Dad's. June's book is about a princess, a hand, and a cat. June makes clacking sounds with her tongue that she says is the typewriter. Sometimes Dad lets June sit on his lap and type on his big typewriter. Dad will show June which keys to hit for the words June wants. Mostly June wants to do her book herself on the paper she covers with words that she copies out of books.

June just copies the words. June can read some of the words. June sounds out the other words. Sometimes Mom and Dad laugh when June does the sounding wrong but then they both give June noisy kisses and hug her. June can almost read as well as you, Tracy, Dad says. You don't care about reading and writing. When you were first learning how to read there was a dream you kept having. It was a scary dream about the alphabet chasing you: letters with mouths and big teeth and everything else black and you don't know the order to put the letters in. You like to be read to and play and draw sometimes. June copies words. June can't connect anything. Just words. June is smart and pretty and small. June is like a doll but dolls can't do all the things that June can do.

Tammy says you could be a fashion model because you tell her to say this. Tammy has a fat lip she got from her Dad. He had to tell her too many times not to mess with his snapping turtles. She was feeding them cheese crackers.

Tammy and you want to be invisible. There are marbles on the floor next to the salad-bowl swimming pool. Ken and Barbie are walking around the marbles that are really magic stones that can make Barbie and Ken fly if they touch the stones, then lie down. Tammy wants to be invisible because then she could walk through the fence and wade in the pool and swim. Tammy and Teddy's Mom won't let them go in the pool ever because they don't know how to swim.

Tammy wants to go in the pool because she loves the water. Tammy said that one time she waded in a creek that had stones that sparkled like diamonds. You want to be invisible so that you can walk through walls and watch people. You want to see what Jewel does at night and you want to know where she dances. If you were invisible you could just float to where she was. Jewel is a mystery.

Tammy says she wishes she could live in your apartment because she likes your Mom and Dad. Tammy has orange hair that is curly just like Teddy's but long. Her and Teddy both have so many freckles. Their skin is white. When they stay out in the sun their skin gets red. You can see lots of veins on their necks and stomachs when you play Doctor.

The boards of the fence out back go up and down, not sideways. Above the fence is the moon. The moon has dark parts on it, dots like June has on her body, or the shadows on the hills of sand at the beach by Grandma's. When you put your hand up the moon is smaller than your hand. It is not all the way round, the white-yellow part, but where it's dark you can see the outline of the rest of the moon. Someone in a dark room.

You know that nothing lives on the moon because there is no air. In the dark the moon moves around the earth. Your Dad already told you this.

Dad has his arms around you and June and you are both sitting on his lap. Dad said we should look at the moon tonight and imagine that we are going there because tomorrow morning there will be men walking there on the moon for the first time. It will be on TV and you don't have a TV and you have to go to the baby-sitter's and you hope that Mrs. Morrison will let you watch it.

June says she can see people up there now.

Dad holds June's cheek to his. You put your cheek to Dad's but then you get up because it's too tight, the three of you on the chair.

By the fence you look at Dad and June looking up at the sky.
Mom can't see the moon at work, you say.

Dad's shorts are jeans that were cut off. Some of the strings
from the jeans are long and you pull them and the strings get
longer or come off.

Stars are pretty dots, sparkle jewels, I want to touch them,
June says.

On the TV at Mrs. Morrison's you get to see the first man
walking on the moon.

They're probably doing that at a movie studio, Mrs. Morrison says.

On the TV there is lots of crackling noise and inside a big
space suit there is a man you can't see. It's day and you can't see
the moon outside.

*What about what is going on down here? People are always running
away, going to new places to try and make a fresh start, forgetting that
no matter where they go they will take themselves along.*

People need to help themselves and others right where they are now,
Grandma says.

Summer is long. Grandma can't come because the doctor's
office is busy. Sometimes people step on glass down by the
water, and Grandpa has to sew them up. Grandma can't come
but she sends things in a package. Grandma sends brownies and
matching shorts sets for you and June that are green and white,
and coloring books with pictures of the beach and mountains,
and one coloring book with butterflies and moths that has
stories about each kind that Mom or Dad can read to you and
June while you are coloring or after you are done. There are
Barbie paper dolls and bubble bath that smells like cinnamon
and two special presents that are wrapped, one is for you and
one is for June, and you don't have to share these. Both small
boxes are wrapped in white tissue paper and tied with thick
yarn ribbon, the kind that Mom likes to put in your hair and in
June's hair when she fixes it. Mom has to fix your hair and

June's hair a lot because it is long and gets tangled. Dad won't let you and Mom and June cut your hair. Mom said we can if we really want to, Dad says this too, but he says he likes long hair. The yarn ribbon on your box is yellow and the yarn ribbon on June's box is blue. In your box there is a white sand dollar, a change purse that is see-through with three shiny pennies in it, and two dum-dum lollipops from Grandpa's office. In June's box there is a white sand dollar that is bigger than yours, a small change purse that is shaped like a fish and is blue and green and red with black eyes, and two dum-dums.

Grandma sent Mom some white shorts and dish towels with kettles and roosters on them. Dad got a book about marine life from Grandpa. His Dad sends books a lot because they don't talk much. Dad said this.

Grandma sent four milkweed pods wrapped in white tissue. You and June go with Mom to the brown lawn by the pool. You make wishes and blow the milkweed into the air.

. . .

MARVIN started it. You go with Teddy to Marvin's because Teddy says that Marvin gives away money to kids that want to fish for it. You can play with Teddy at Marvin's. Teddy and you play house. Sometimes Tammy plays but when they are together, Tammy and Teddy, you get mad. They are twins. You want to be a twin. You asked Mom before, didn't you have a twin and where did she go? Mom says, no, that it was just you born and she is sure of that. It's better when it's just you and Teddy or you and Tammy.

Marvin drives a truck. Marvin and Jewel kissed a lot for a while and then Jewel met someone she likes better who wanted to talk once in a while and said he had big plans for Jewel's dancing. Marvin doesn't like to talk much, just other things, Jewel said. Marvin has pimples. Marvin watches TV all day long when he is not driving a truck. Marvin doesn't have a rig like he told Jewel. Marvin drives a bread truck. You saw him in the truck. There is a picture of a blond girl biting into bread on the side of the truck. You saw the truck after McDonald's with Dad and June. You didn't say, there's Marvin, because Dad doesn't know Marvin. Dad knew you went to Jewel's but not Marvin's. Dad and Mom said, no you can't go to Jewel's anymore.

Marvin calls it fishing. Marvin fills up the bathtub and you and Teddy take off your clothes. Marvin says that this is fishing, and do you or don't you want money. Marvin puts coins in the tub. You and Teddy can keep the coins when you fish them up from the bottom of the tub: pennies, nickels and dimes. You have to close your eyes and get the money that way, you and Teddy. You don't want to be naked but Marvin says he isn't going to watch and he leaves you and Teddy in the bathtub and closes the bathroom door. Just make sure you don't peek, Marvin says.

You are looking at Teddy naked and there are coins in the tub. There is a dirty ring around the tub. The water is shiny and cracked on the top. Teddy touches your pee-pee and you touch his. Teddy has pointed ears. Sometimes Teddy scratches you when he touches your pee-pee because his fingernails are long and dirty. You let Teddy touch you because your pee-pee feels warm and tingly. Teddy and you or you and Tammy play like this in Mrs. Morrison's bedroom or behind the bathroom by the pool or in your bedroom. Teddy is the Daddy. When you play with Tammy you are the Daddy unless you are playing Doctor and then you are always the doctor and Tammy and Teddy are your patients.

You make Teddy and Tammy lie on the table or the floor and you do what your grandfather did to you on his doctor's table, only you touch everything. Your grandfather just looked in your ears, nose and mouth, and listened to your heart mostly.

Marvin says when you and Teddy are done fishing in the tub and have all the money, he says to sit in his lap. Marvin's eyes look wet and he is breathing funny and you don't want to be sitting on his lap. On the TV is boxing. You are getting scared

because you see that the bathroom door has a big hole in it and
that you can see in the bathroom even with the door closed.
Your face is hot. Teddy has a funny look on his face. Marvin
says, you cheated, Tracy, you opened your eyes in the bathroom. Marvin says this and he holds you tighter in his lap.
Beneath your butt is something hard like a big stick. Tammy
has a big stick that she carries and pulls along the metal fence
around the pool. Clack. Clack. The TV is fuzzy and Marvin is
moving the stick under you. Marvin is holding you too tight. I
need to go home, you say. Marvin pulls you and it pinches your
arms where he is holding. Marvin keeps moving and then he is
on top of you. You can't move. There are a lot of people
screaming on the TV, fuzzy and loud everywhere. Tammy and
Teddy aren't here. The TV is fuzzy and loud. Nighttime is
fuzzy and loud with your eyes closed. Marvin won't let you
move. The room is moving in and out. Marvin's eyes are
closed. Please get off of me, you say in your head to the pimply
face of the man that Teddy told you liked to play fishing.
Marvin is down heavy on your chest. You can't breathe.

What's the matter, cat got your tongue? Marvin says.

.   .   .

JUST do it, Teddy, you said. Come on, are you chicken? It's
cool down by the laundry room and Teddy is at the top of the
walkway. There is brown grass from where the grass was cut
before. The brown grass is in piles and mixed with lint from the
dryers. There is a lot of brown grass mixed with lint at the
bottom of the walkway. You move your toes around on a ball
of lint and grass. Teddy is at the top of the walkway. The dryers
whir. Hot air comes out from the laundry room. Your hands
are dirty and sweaty. There is a big black lady in there by the
dryers. She is sleeping.

You are leaning against the wall. Your feet are in the brown
grass and lint. Teddy is at the top of the walkway. Teddy has
pointy ears like an elf. Teddy has a big bruise under his eye.

Teddy and Tammy have bruises a lot on their faces and bodies. They get in trouble. Teddy thinks his new bicycle is a motorcycle. Here I come, he says. You know he won't be able to stop. You know that Teddy will crash into the wall behind where you are standing. You want him to crash. Teddy still doesn't come. You tell Teddy that you are going to tell his Dad about the fishing trip at Marvin's. You walk up there to Teddy. It's steep.

Teddy says, girls are just born with less teeth than boys. Always had them, always will, that's what my Dad says, Teddy is saying.

You and Count Dracula are the only boys with more teeth, you say to Teddy. Teddy keeps saying it and it's because your two front teeth came out. You push Teddy hard and he goes down the walkway. His bike goes down the walkway fast. Teddy crashes into the wall loud. Teddy's chin splits open. Teddy says, you are a witch. Teddy doesn't cry. Tammy is watching and she gets their Mom and their Mom comes pretty soon. Tammy and Teddy's Mom gets blood on her hands and on her face. You are hiding behind the black lady who is sleeping in the laundry room. The black lady smells like the bed in the morning when June wets. You want to stay behind her.

. . .

YOU told June to get on her knees next to you by the bed.

You tell June this in the dark because Mom and Dad already said goodnight. Grandma doesn't make you get on your knees. Grandma just likes you to say a prayer before you go to sleep at night. Grandma likes the sound of praying. Grandma says it is nice to bless the people that you love before you go to sleep at night. The night-light is on. The night-light is a seashell. Mom turned on the night-light. The shell is a scallop shell. Grandma showed you scallop shells on the beach in the sand. The night-light makes a fan on the wall. June doesn't know all the words but she God Blesses more people than you do after you say the prayer that Grandma taught you.

45

You say, Now I lay me down to sleep. I pray the Lord my soul to keep. If I should die before I wake. I pray the Lord my soul to take. You hold your hands together tight and close your eyes. You put your face into the blanket that smells like pee. You wish to God that you might be a big lady and pretty and soon. You ask God for these things. You aren't sure if God is a man who likes to do favors. You aren't sure if praying is just something to look forward to like when Grandma says she will visit or Dad says, K–R–S–K to Mom which means ice cream and is how you spelled it just to show Mom and Dad they can't fool you. Just in case God really does favors you ask for something awful to happen to Marvin. You ask if maybe Marvin could swallow his tongue and die. You say to God that you are sorry that you pushed Teddy down the walkway.

You tell June she can get back into bed now.

All of a sudden you think how sometimes you wish that June wasn't your sister so that it would just be you and Mom and Dad. You tell God that you are sorry for thinking this. You tell God these things in your head. June is special. June's eyes are brown. Not Mom's, or Dad's, not your eyes are brown, just blue. You say, I love you June. Loud after all the talking in your head.

What happened is that it was night and Tammy climbed out her bedroom window. Someone didn't lock the gate to the pool. There is a siren. You hear it. Homer is howling. June is sleeping. You are scared. Inside your stomach is tight, then hard. You are dizzy. You want to wake up June. You don't. Dad is typing and then he isn't. There are people talking, lots of noise and then screaming, because Tammy is floating in the swimming pool and her stomach is swollen. Dad goes outside. You can see this through the window. Dad doesn't know you are up and you go outside. Jewel is there and she is crying. Tammy's Mom is screaming and Tammy's Dad has red eyes and he can't walk straight and might fall down. Tammy was a twin. Your Dad picks you up and holds you to him and walks you back into the house where you can still hear the screaming for a long time. June is still sleeping. The sirens go away. The moon is full out the window. Nothing can stop how Tammy wanted to be invisible to swim because she was a twin.

It is this story, the one that you are in, the story that is being told for you or is it the one that you are telling? June is locked up for life because of what she did. You want to know where the story starts.

This story, it is the story that you and June are both writing, part to part, as if it might make a difference, as if there were reasons to always find an ending, as if it were possible to not look for endings, something concrete even though what you really want to do is float.

You are not sure if the story starts or ends with Tammy drowning or if the story starts or ends when you wanted to wake up June and didn't. You let June sleep even though you were afraid. People really do know what is happening deep inside.

June is sleeping. You don't wake her up. You wanted to? Tammy is already drowned. You didn't know she would drown then, but now knowing this it makes a difference, because now you can say, should have done, and what if. All this, does it make a difference now? These things to remember, to prevent from happening again?

People have to do what they really want to do.

Thoughts becoming actions.

. . .

IN your dream, a train is coming. It's coming fast. You are in a tunnel but it's the world you are standing on. You are standing on top of a globe. There is blue-paint ocean under your feet and orange and green continents. The train is so high that you can't see the top and there are sides that the train is pressed against. You can't turn around and the train is coming at you fast and the globe beneath you is spinning backwards like an escalator.

You wake up and June is drawing words on the wall in brown crayon; cat and hand, it says on the wall. There is dust floating in stripes where it is light. It doesn't matter that June is drawing on the wall because tomorrow you are moving to California.

If you keep moving there is nothing to leave behind, no attachments to be made, nothing to hurt any more than what you carry with you inside. If you keep moving there is always something to look forward to. Is there a finite number of places to go? When there are no more places to run to, then what?

There is no one to say goodbye to in East Hartford. Jewel moved away. One day she just left with the man who said he wanted to help Jewel do something with her dancing. After Tammy drowned, Teddy and Tammy's Mom and Dad sent Teddy to live with his uncle on a farm in Ohio.

Mrs. Morrison came by already with the boring coloring books and cookies for during the trip. You sort of feel sad that you never liked Mrs. Morrison but she is the one that made you sit in the corner and she is the one that let June get locked in the bathroom. The sky is gray but has lots of pink in it above the swimming pool.

Homer is circling himself fast and wagging his stump tail. Homer is a boxer and when he was a puppy he had his tail cut off. They have to do that to boxers, Dad said, because boxer dogs have tails as long as kangaroos. Mom and Dad say, it's a wonder Homer's butt didn't get cut off, because the stump tail is that short.

Mom is happy. She is wearing the white shorts Grandma sent and Indian sandals that she wraps around her legs and ties at the knees.

The van is all packed with suitcases. Everything else went into a big truck yesterday, the beds and books and the couch and kitchen table.

Mom brushes June's hair into braids and put the braids on top of June's head with barrettes. June, you look like a peasant now, Mom says. June says she is a princess. Dad says you both are princesses and picks you and June up. You can see your face in Dad's glasses. Dad is going to be a manager in California. Dad says he is going to finish his book there. Dad says the trip across

California will tie things up. Dad says it will be nice for Mom to be close to her parents. Mom says, Oh, Phillip, and wraps her arms around his neck like on TV.

Summer is a good time for leaving, Mom says. She says, it's good to move when it gets too hot. Dad says, Oh, Vi, it's all going to happen. Mom's real name is Viola but Dad calls her Vi once in a while and Violin when they are loving. You think your Mom and Dad look like brother and sister. Mom says that is what happens when people have been together for a long time.

As the van leaves the apartment you think about the swimming pool. It's not so much that Tammy couldn't swim it's that no one would let her.

Dad says there is a surprise and he spells out the surprise to Mom like he always does just to make you mad. You don't care this time because you know what G–R–A–N–D–M–A spells now, because you weren't born yesterday. You tell Dad this, then you and June play the alphabet game. You have to find the letters in words, on license plates or road signs and whoever gets all the way to Z first wins. June is only four but she wins. In Old Saybrook Dad drives past the house where you used to live before East Hartford. The house is down by the beach but not on the same block as Grandma's. This house is two blocks over from Grandma's. From this beach you can see the harbor where Grandma's rowboat is. You say please Dad, let's go to Grandma's now. Dad drives slow past the small brown house where you used to live and slow down to the harbor. There is a porch on the front of the house that is all screened in. You and Mom and Dad and June used to sleep on the porch in the summer when it was too hot. Dad doesn't stop because new people live in the house.

June is sleeping up front now in Mom's lap because you and June were playing and Dad was trying to drive and you and June were laughing so hard, almost screaming, so Dad stopped the car and June got up front.

Homer has his head out the window behind where Dad is driving. Dad drives slow down to the beach. Can we go to Grandma's now? Let's go. Let's go. Dad parks the van down by the water and turns off the engine. You want to scream because Grandma's house is only two blocks over. Dad is looking out over the water with the face that makes Mom say, don't bother your father now because he is busy. Dad keeps looking out over the water as if he was seeing something that you can't see. Grandma's rowboat is in the harbor and you say, look, to Dad but Dad keeps looking out over the water. You don't see anything but water and the island. Mom is looking out the window to where Grandma's rowboat is. June is sleeping.

Dad drives slow past your old house again, then faster.

Grandma's house, Grandma's house, you say, bouncing in the back seat until Dad stops.

Grandma and Grandpa are standing on the porch. The porch has big white pillars. Grandma's red sweater is what you see and you want to yell out the window but Homer is in the way. Grandma is waving and waving.

Homer is trying to get out through the window and barking and barking because Homer sees Grandma's big sheepdog, Buster. Dad says, down, Homer, and is getting mad. Buster is tied up by Grandma's garden and running around and around as far as the leash goes.

You say, let me out, let me out, and it takes too long for June and Mom to get out of the front seat to help you out of the van and Dad has to hold Homer.

You can't get out of the van fast enough.

Mom is carrying June to the porch. Homer is barking and jumping against the van window. Dad is taking the suitcases out of the back. Grandma smells like suntan lotion. The waiting room has magazines and books for kids. The stair rail is shiny smooth. Grandma's hands are cool and soft. How are you? and the you part sounds like a train whistle, and oh Phillip hurry up with that, and June says, where are we? and Grandpa shakes Dad's hand, and Grandma kisses Mom on the cheek, then June.

Buster is barking and running around and around. Homer makes the van shake back and forth. Dad just says Homer will calm down.

Dad tells Grandpa that you will all stay until Monday. Grandpa says there is a lot of business to take care of if Dad is sure that the house in Sleepy Hollow is what he really wants for his kids. For the kids, Grandpa says again. Dad says he has to take care of Homer and goes back to the van after he hugs Grandma.

Grandma fixed a big dinner. Mom says, what can I do? but Grandma never lets anyone help because she does things a certain way. June sits next to Grandpa and you sit next to June across from Mom and Dad. There is baked chicken and gravy and peas and fluffy potatoes and then lemon meringue pie because it is Dad's favorite.

Mom spills her water and Grandpa starts to get up but Grandma is already getting paper towels. You and June start to laugh and Dad says, stop it. Mom's face is red, then white. Grandma brings the paper towels and wipes up the water that is puddles around the candlesticks and on Mom's lap.

When it is bedtime you kiss Grandpa goodnight and Mom and Dad and June, but it is Grandma that tucks you in after you say the prayer.

Above your bed there is a picture. In the day the picture is OK. But at night the people in the painting move and are looking at you. It is Betsy Ross and George Washington. Betsy Ross is making the flag. All the eyes are yellow and glow in the dark and all the people have white hair that Grandma says is wigs. When you close your eyes you see yellow eyes that turn orange. Near the ceiling you are sure you see a ghost, an old lady, small and laughing in a rocking chair going back and forth.

Down the hall is Grandma and Grandpa's bedroom, past where Mom and Dad and June are sleeping.

Grandma is awake fast. Grandma's nightgown is white and shiny. It's toasty in here, Grandma says, pulling the covers around you up to your neck. Grandpa doesn't wake up and Grandma rubs your head until you fall asleep. Before you know it the sky is pink outside.

.   .   .

THE stairs creak in places. The stairs are painted brown, a brown that is not the color of wood but brown like a crayon. You step down the stairs with your body leaning on the railing so that the stairs don't creak. Grandpa said yes, go to the bathroom. Grandpa is watching TV and marking places on a map, places where he wants to hunt this year, hunt and fish.

You are in the kitchen now. The tall handle on the butter urn is smooth wood. There is a crack on the lid of the butter urn where you broke it by accident before. The clothesline is in front of Grandma. The clothesline goes from the house to the tree. There are white towels for Grandpa's office on the clothesline that go back and forth. Some of the wooden pins on the clothesline are upside down.

Grandma has a red sweater on. Grandma is bent over in the garden.

The garden is green with all colors in it, red and purple and blue and pink and orange; paint spots on the green. There are snakes in the garden and snakes under the house too. Grandpa shot a copperhead snake once that came out from underneath the house and he was lucky he had his gun then. Grandpa was lucky he had his gun the night he got out of his car in the garage and there was a fox. Copperheads are deadly poison, Grandpa says. You don't want any snakes to be in the garden.

Grandpa is upstairs. There are thumps across the ceiling. The channel changer clicks like teeth. The white squares on the clothesline go in and out. The clouds are big and white and look like faces. There is a cat cloud. Buster is white and brown on his head. Buster is lying down next to the garden by Grandma. Buster is like a baby and cries when Grandma goes to the store and won't eat unless Grandma stays right next to him.

Mom and Dad and June are at the store shopping for food for on the way to California, food and maybe a surprise, Dad said.

Grandpa said don't go into my office. He said that. You are standing next to June and Grandpa is in the doorway between the waiting room and the kitchen. You kids behave now in my house, Grandpa says. Grandpa has shoes on that are almost the same color as the rug in the waiting room, tan.

Grandma's sweater is red. The bathroom is upstairs. You told Grandpa you were going to the bathroom.

The knob on the door to Grandpa's office is cool and looks like a giant diamond. It is dark in the office and smells like medicine. The shades are down. The light on the ceiling buzzes, goes flicker and is blue in the middle, then hums.

There is new white paper on the table. Grandma tears off the white paper that the person was on. Blood and wet spots and hairs and crying get on the white paper. The paper gets wrinkled when someone sits on it. The paper is smooth and white. The paper that is not smooth and white goes in the garbage. Then Grandma pulls down more paper off the roll that is behind the table.

The table that the patients lay or sit on is white metal with a black plastic bed part, and high. There is a stool for kids to use so that they can climb on the table by themselves. Over the black plastic bed part is where Grandma pulls down the clean white paper. Grandma is a nurse.

The tools on the other table that is low are shiny and silver, sharp knives that are different sizes and scissors and other metal pointy things. Grandma arranges the tools on white towels. There are creases in the white towels where Grandma has folded the towels then ironed. Behind the tools are glass bottles some brown some clear with medicines in them. This table with the tools on it is on wheels and can be moved around on the floor.

Grandpa keeps dum-dum lollipops in the office. He gives the lollipops to kids. Grandpa gives shots and sews people up. In the summer people step on glass at the beach, or nails. Kids get lollipops.

You want a dum-dum. The file cabinet is gray metal and three drawers high. You need a chair.

Grandpa is at the door. Grandpa says he is sorry that you couldn't follow directions. Grandpa says you will have to learn to do what you are told.

Grandma is in the garden. Grandma's sweater is red. The sweater isn't on all the way. Only the top button is buttoned. The sleeves of the red sweater hang down Grandma's back. The butter urn has a crack on top because you dropped it before. On the clothesline are white towels waving.

Go in there, Grandpa says following you to the waiting room. You need to learn a lesson, Grandpa says. In the chair you are supposed to sit for ten minutes. Your face is hot. It is loud when you swallow. Grandpa leaves the waiting room. You could get up if you wanted to. You could go outside, to the well or to the barn where you aren't supposed to go, or to the garage where the fox Grandpa killed is hanging next to his car. You could sit in Grandpa's car. Grandma would say Grandpa is right. You keep sitting. The wood of the chair is sticky where your hands are. By the window it is hot. The window has white wood that makes two crosses on it. The tan carpet is not on the whole floor. There is wood floor all around the edge of the carpet. Some of the carpet goes under the couches but you can still see the wood floor by the walls and by the stairs. The sun is too hot through the window. You keep sitting. With your fingernails you can scratch up some of the brown orange stickiness. The butter urn in the kitchen has a crack on the lid. The chair seat you are in is made of pieces of wood glued together.

You can get up now, Grandpa says. Grandma's red sweater is folded over her arm and in the basket there are beans and tomatoes and yellow flowers.

Mom says, Grandpa just wanted you to do what you were told. Mom says this and holds both your arms and looks at you. Mom has blue eyes with yellow around the black part.

★   ★   ★

Out behind the well your mother took you and June.

Mom is going to draw.

There is a pile of dirt there that you and June can climb up. The dirt pile is scooped in the middle on top like a bowl and smooth.

June says it is a sand castle, a huge sand castle made special a long time ago while people were sleeping, a palace, June says.

No, June, you say to her holding both her arms the same way Mom holds your arms when she tells you it isn't fair for you to be snooping around in Grandpa's things. Mom says, Tracy, you can't just look through people's things that don't belong to you unless they want you to look.

No, June, you say, this is not a sand castle, it's dirt that a tractor put here. You have June's arms. June's eyes are brown, brown eyes that move back and forth fast when she looks at you. June's eyes are brown as smooth stones.

The bucket is too small to get into. There is no way to the bottom of the well. It's dark down there. You can hear the water when you drop something there. A lot of dirt dropped into the well sounds like rain.

June's head is right on top of the dirt mound. June is in there, in the smooth part that is like a bowl. June is busy and she doesn't see you. June is playing.

With a stick you scratch a house on the dirt road, one door, two windows, a chimney, and a sun above the house and a tree next to the house.

Mom is drawing. Mom looks up and down when she is drawing something.

June pooed in her pants. June took off her pants and is smearing them in the dirt. June says she is washing her pants. You and June are standing in the dirt pile that is a giant bowl. There are woods on one side and then the barn and Grandma's white house is smaller than your hand. June, this is bad, you say. June, this is not where you go to the bathroom. Clothes don't get clean in dirt, June, you say.

The dirt pile is a bowl. There is a wall of dirt around you that is almost as high as your stomach when you are standing. On all sides is a wall of dirt. The dirt is dusty like powder. Where June went to the bathroom the dirt is mud.

June, you are bad, you say. You grab June's arms and not where her hands are brown and dirty with poo. June just looks at you. Too tight, June says. Where you were pressing your fingers around her arms there are small brown-blue spots.

Mom is sitting behind the barn in Grandma's beach chair. Mom is drawing a picture of trees, the barn, and the well. June has no pants on. You take June to where Mom is sitting. Mom is drawing with black charcoal on a big white pad. The black charcoal scratches across the paper. Mom smears places with her fingers. On the white paper black charcoal is making trees, the barn, and the well. The trees, the barn and the well are in front of Mom. June is next to you and you are waiting for Mom to ask where June's pants are.

Mom looks up and down at the paper as she draws. Up and down. Mom says if you just look at the paper while you draw then you don't really see what it is that you are drawing. Mom says sometimes she wishes she were blind because if she were blind then she could really see.

SURVEILLANCE I

Grandma says, you come shopping with me. I don't know what you like to eat. It's been such a long time. I can't, Grandma. I can't go out there. You go. In the car. The sun on the car. Hot metal. The black pavement of the supermarket parking lot. Grandma why are women left alone?

What might happen while we are gone? We shouldn't leave the house. We shouldn't shop.

There is a little girl. This little girl is not someone you know. Sometimes you see this little girl in pictures, snapshots in other people's photo albums, mostly you see this little girl doing things, stuck in situations that you are helpless to do anything about. Always she is watching you. You know it is her by the look in her eyes, a hunger really like your eyes in the mirror. Or you know her by the way she holds her hands, touching something or picking it up.

The little girl, you see her in the parking lot of the grocery store. You want her not to be there because all of a sudden seeing her makes you dizzy, makes you feel as though you were spinning around and around. You want her to not be here now, you just want to do what it is that you have to do, shop.

I'll wait out here. I can't go in there, you say.

Always she appears like this, this girl, just when you think that everything is manageable. This is when she comes.

This little girl says, you can't forget about me, you can't pretend that I am not real. Look at me, she whimpers from behind her fixed gaze.

You want to know if other people are haunted by her, does she plead this way to others, an ache inside.

There is blue sky behind this little girl. The black cement of the parking lot and the blue sky behind this girl become a painting. You have likened this girl to a painting in hopes that she might go away.

Think of something else. The pain will go away if you think of something else.

You liken this little girl to a painting done on white butcher paper that has been torn, not cut from a big roll of butcher paper.

You are walking across the parking lot toward something, toward the store.

You walk in slow motion. Of course you are walking just as you always do. No one would notice any difference. It's just that inside you are walking in slow motion, inside is different than the way your body is moving.

The painting is a circle, the blue (no it's gray overcast) and black divided in half, blue and black, two halves on their sides one on top of the other fitting together because objects in a painting do that, fit.

You have to go shopping now.

The black pavement she is standing on, this little girl, extending behind her to meet the sky looks round and concave. It is the bottom of a glass behind this girl, and inside your knees have started to weaken.

No one knows this. The bottom of this glass has liquid in it, liquid quivering like someone's lips, someone who is excited or afraid or shy. The glass looks almost empty because the pavement has gotten longer, you have gotten farther away from the girl. You are seeing her over your shoulder. You aren't sure where you are.

The blue of the sky, no gray, is shorter now, the painting is no longer in halves, the proportions have shifted.

You are comparing this girl to liquid in a glass. This little girl, alone in a parking lot, a little girl in a green T-shirt, a little girl with brown hair that is long and unbrushed, a little girl holding a stick and dragging this stick along the pavement sharpening the end of the stick to a point.

You see this but you don't, because the glass you are thinking about is almost empty. Through the water behind the glass there are colors. In front of the glass is what you can't see anymore because it is all behind you. You must believe this. It is all behind you.

You are disoriented. What you really want to do all of a sudden is press yourself against this girl, smother her maybe. This is how it seems then, that you will have to kill this little girl somehow unless you want to be killed. To press yourself against her somehow because when bodies are close together the dizziness goes away and that's what you want because it is scary to float.

You could spin and spin, but it's the same, that you can't see what is in front of the girl, what is behind you in space. This space that is not the past. It is not the past (echo, like calling your name down a well) but the present.

You think of the space between people, the space that is real. You think about how this space makes you afraid. A space that is freedom? People really do go away and there is so much space between.

You think about how dizzy you get when you feel as though you are falling into someone's gaze. This is to feel alive? to float, to experience existence as a point in space where two people's eyes meet, any two people, where there is nothing to hold on to.

This helplessness that makes you want to press yourself against someone when this happens, the feeling of falling of having nothing to hold on to even in the midst of the most innocent conversation, because it's too overwhelming to feel this, too dangerous to be floating, to recognize potentiality and strength in not having definition. This recognition that where you really are defies everything that you have come to believe, what you teach yourself over and over.

This girl isn't there anymore. You can't see her. How she was, the sharpness of the stick against the pavement, her eyes looking intently at the end, the end that becomes memory.

Because you really do know inside that there is nothing to be afraid of.

This memory and another will start and stop and start again, the sharpness of memory, the clarity of what you make manageable, what you punctuate with fantasy.

What is real is lost now. The little girl is gone. Water glistens at the bottom of the glass.

The little girl. There are four parts, four variables, to consider, is she inside of you or outside of you and are you going to have to kill her or be killed by her? And what if the answer is all of the above, then what?

You are immobilized.

You try to figure it all out at once, rushing through space as if you weren't contained in a body at all.

No, that's fantasy, an ideal to forget where you are for a while, something to pretend away your immobilization that is real, that is now, that is a frozen still of the past and a future crushing in on you from the front and from behind so that you are flat, as flat as the stories people tell over and over again, that you tell over and over again because you are afraid, because you want to, no, because you have to believe that you won't die.

There is a grayness spreading outward, moving away from this body that has fallen into a state that can be likened to sleep but is not resting, is not calm. This grayness inside, a shadow that moves away, seeps out of the skin, seeps away from the grayness inside that is hardening, this shield against being in the present ever, against seeing the girl as she really is when she was there, against being in the future ever, this girl as she really is when you are here.

What part of you is it, the specific part of you that is crippled by and crippling the little girl that is inside and outside at the same time?

ART

That's it, what happens. His face is blank. He is a pallbearer. He is standing behind the coffin. There is snow on the ground. There are three other men holding up the coffin. But it is the one man, the man at the head, he sees you.

It should be OK, but it's not. In that coffin could be someone dear to you, but there isn't. That's it. You can drive by and his face is blank but his eyes follow you.

Grandpa is in the kitchen humming and sipping iced coffee. Grandma is asking you would you like red or green, and it's the toothpicks for the sandwiches she is talking about. Grandpa's eyes twinkle and June is saying she wants green. Grandpa lets June sit on his lap. Grandma and Grandpa don't know about the dirt pile and June pooing because Mom cleaned June upstairs and said not everything is Grandma's business.

It is before lunch. Grandpa picks June up and carries her around into the waiting room. Grandpa doesn't usually pick up kids or let them sit on his lap. Grandpa likes to do things that are small and take a lot of concentrating. Grandpa's hands are steady and cool because he washes them so much. Grandpa carries June into the waiting room and is telling her about all the doctor's tools that are in a tall glass case by the door. There is a metal thing that looks like a funnel and it is for listening to people's hearts before there were stethoscopes. There are pictures in the glass case of what doctors' offices used to be like; pictures of people with their feet in wooden vats with a big red thing on their stomach that looks like a slug. Grandpa says it is a leech and that they used to use leeches to bleed the poison and diseases out of people. Things like that don't scare June. June just looks really hard at things like she hopes they don't go away.

Grandpa sips his iced coffee and says aha but more like someone sleeping and not because the coffee tastes good. Grandpa says aha and his mouth is open, dark like the well. Grandpa does this because June asks him if the black girl with

60

the purple rag on her head that is in the picture that is in the glass case in the waiting room lives where we just moved from. June says, that girl stole my bathing suit and locked me in the bathroom. How come all black people look the same, Grandpa? you ask and Grandpa says that that's just the way God made them and they do look different if you are around them long enough.

Grandpa looks older than Grandma, maybe he could be her Dad though he really is your Dad's Dad. Grandma says he is not much older than her really. But Grandma does a lot of things like she was a girl and Grandpa sits a lot when he is not in the office. Grandpa sits and reads books or looks at the TV and sucks on sourball candy so that he won't smoke. Grandpa has short gray hair that is prickly all around. Grandpa keeps his hair short because it's clean and because it's gray.

Grandma said it's important to remember where you are and to always know what you are supposed to be doing.

Grandma is holding your hand and she is holding June's hand. Grandma is going to take you for a boat ride around the harbor. Grandma has her bathing suit on underneath her shorts because she might swim. Grandma has a basket and in it are towels and suntan lotion, swimming masks and three oranges.

In Grandma's garden there are violets and roses and sunflowers and tomatoes and herbs and snow peas and big yellow squash. Grandma picks a snow pea each for you and June. The snow pea is sweet and there are three peas inside when you bite into it. Grandma is not afraid of the bees and her hair is shiny in the sun.

Yes we can go to the well first, Grandma says. You want to go to the well with Grandma. Grandma holds your hand and June's hand so she is in the middle. The road is dusty. There are small rocks on the road. By the side of the road are bushes with empty milkweed pods. You go past the old barn to the well that is behind Grandma's house. You can look down the well and say Tracy. The well echoes back and Grandma says don't bend over too far. June says, me, I want to see, and Grandma holds up June and June yells bumblebee into the well and Grandma laughs. Grandma has two pennies to make a wish. You and June throw the pennies into the well. There is a wooden bucket that you can put down in the well by turning a crank. You wind the crank until you hear the bucket hit the water and then you turn the crank so the rope winds around and around on a big piece of wood and the bucket comes up.

Grandma's rowboat is tied up at the dock. It is white with two rows of seats that have two blue cushions on each wooden board. The boat has the name May painted on its side because that is when Grandma and Grandpa met. Grandpa gave Grandma the rowboat for Valentine's Day one year. Grandpa takes the boat out fishing. Grandma just rows, sometimes to good clamming spots, sometimes just to take friends out to talk, or to get therapy, Grandma says.

Grandma helps you and June into the boat and then she unties the rope.

Grandma's eyes are green. Grandma has her hair cut short because she doesn't like to fuss with it. It's not short like a boy's, it's short like someone in a magazine or in the movies and there are small pieces of hair pretty around her face under her big straw hat.

In the water there are stinging jellyfish. There are always a lot of jellyfish near the water's surface when the tide is high, Grandma says. The jellyfish have long tentacles that are pink. If they touch you your skin burns and itches.

Grandma rows first toward the sandy bank near the bridge. There, two horseshoe crabs are making trails in the sand beneath the olive-green water. Then Grandma rows the boat past the beach and out toward the island where people have summer cabins. Grandma wants to see if there is any clamming. Grandma smiles and winks about clamming. Grandma loves to be faster than the clams and scoop them out of the sand before they burrow away.

The sun is over June's head. Grandma takes her fist and measures from the horizon where the sun rises in the east, counting as she goes, and moving her fist, to where the sun is, and says it's 3:30. June is trailing her blue shovel in the water and Grandma is singing and rowing.

At the island Grandma ties the rowboat to a small pier. How about we dive for clams? she says. Grandma has green eyes. Sometimes you wish you could always live with Grandma and not just visit. The day after tomorrow you are going to California.

When you dive you wear a swimming mask. You hold your breath. Grandma says ready, and then you go under with Grandma holding your feet. It's like the wheelbarrow only under water, and you dig like that, upside down but only for a few seconds. Grandma is strong and can lift you and June up by the ankles, fast and high. June wants to go first but doesn't like it under water so she just watches after the first time. You all eat the oranges and then you row back to the harbor.

Grandma had a room that was just filled with shoes and boxes of hats. Grandma could be a movie star if she wanted to because she is that pretty.

Next to the room with all the hats and shoes right at the top of the stairs that go down to the kitchen, Grandma has her couch. This couch is made out of satin with small rosebuds all over it. Mom said, this is Grandma's couch.

When Grandma made dinner she all of a sudden got mad and said she had to do everything and that no one ever helped her and then she ran up the stairs. Grandpa went after her but not running. Dad said it was horseshit and he wished it was Monday. Mom looks at her hands that are folded in her lap. June is making bubbles in her milk.

Before bed when Mom is walking you down the hall to your bedroom, walking by the satin couch with the rosebuds on it that looks like a boat in the dark, Mom says, Grandma's couch.

Mom and Dad come back from Old Saybrook where they were saying goodbye to their friends. Grandma says goodbye and holds you and her lips shake. Grandma's arms are tan. Grandpa bends down so you can kiss him and then he stands on the porch with his hands in his pockets. Grandpa's eyes look happy sometimes. Grandma says goodbye. You cry so hard and can't catch your breath. June was locked in the bathroom. You don't want to leave Grandma. You didn't cry about Tammy and no one ever says, where is Tammy? again because Tammy is dead. You might have told Grandma about Tammy but you didn't have time. Grandma says no, all black people don't look the same, you think to ask Grandma this walking to the car. You say that you think black people are mean because mostly they just want to hurt people. Grandma says no, this is not true. You want to ask Grandma a lot of things now. And it's because Grandma isn't answering about when you will see her again and it's just like how Mrs. Morrison didn't hear you about the bathing suit.

. . .

YOU didn't like the trip to California.

Dad drives in the day and Mom drives at night. At first Dad has places he wants to go to because of his book, then he realizes that he and Mom just have to drive.

Your mother and father drove day and night to get to California where everything would be different, where your mother's parents that you had never met lived. Because the van keeps moving except for bathroom stops and eating, or a walk for Mom and Dad to stretch their legs you and June can sleep when it's light or dark outside. You like to sleep mostly in the day and so does June. Mom drives at night and makes up stories or tells ones from books while Dad is asleep.

There is the story Mom tells you and June about *The Legend of Sleepy Hollow* and Ichabod Crane. Sleepy Hollow is where you are going to live. Mom says big-nosed Ichabod just scared himself because he believed so hard in the headless horseman. Mom says that people can do that.

Mom takes Polaroid pictures on the first day. There is a

picture of Dad laughing with trees all blurry looking like they are coming out of his mouth because he is driving. There is a picture of June upside down on the black vinyl seat, and a picture of you with a mean look on your face. There are no pictures of Mom because she took all the pictures. After the first day Mom puts the camera away in her suitcase. You want to just get where you are going because it's too hot in the car and Dad yells. Mom sleeps in the front seat in the day or reads the map for Dad, her long fingers following the different-colored lines that wind over the blue of the map.

. . .

You are in the middle of the desert. The heat is melting your bodies into the black seat. You took off your clothes, you and June, but it's worse. You and your sister are going to die. Homer is panting at your feet. We are almost there, Dad keeps saying.

If one of us should die, you say to June, let's swear that we will find a way to come back and tell the other person where we will be, where we have gone. That way we can always keep in touch. With a safety pin you prick your finger and then you prick June's finger. The blood glistens like glass beads.

Through the windshield that is covered with smashed bugs the road shakes like plastic wrap. It seems like someone is standing over the edge of the world trying to shake the van off the road.

There are people that drive by all day long. You wonder if these people, the ones that look at you, will remember you, think of you sometime. For a trick you will see someone that you like the way they look, and look at them to try and remember what they look like after they have passed. You try to see how long you can remember what the person looked like. People just go past all day.

When you are moving it gets hard to remember.

THE walls didn't talk. You knew this.

At night it is so quiet that there could be an explosion. Your heart tick-tocking and when you put the pillow to your head it gets louder, your heart.

You are afraid to go to sleep, because you have bad dreams or because sometimes you are afraid you just won't ever wake up. In Mom's parents' house the shadows in the rooms and the tops of the trees out the window look like people with mean faces. There is a thin person bending over and you don't know who it is. Your heart pounds. The floor is moving. It's a sweater hanging on the doorknob. When there is wind, the tree branches make shapes outside. Sometimes a face, darker than Grandpa Green's room. You tiptoed there, past his room to the bathroom and his breathing sounds like a radiator starting. The faces in the branches look like screaming. Grandma Green is asleep in her chair with her feet up on the coffee table. There is smoke floating slow by the ceiling. Grandma Green has her teeth out and her mouth is into her chin. There are knitting needles and yarn and a purple and red square of knitting in her lap.

You want to wake someone up. Mom and Dad are sleeping in Grandma Green's bed. Grandpa Green is sleeping in his dark room. In the day Grandpa Green's room is still dark because he never pulls up the shades. Grandma Green will sleep in her chair all night. June is sleeping. You can't sleep because when you close your eyes there is your heart pounding in your chest, in your head, in the bed, in the room that is as dark as June's open mouth. Sometimes you put your head close to June's open mouth just to make sure she is still breathing. People die at night. Tammy's stomach white in the pool like a doll. People die at night. They go somewhere. Their body is lying there with the blankets and closed eyes, sometimes open eyes, but it seems empty, the sleeping bodies.

You tiptoe down the hall. You look at Grandma Green in her chair. Your shoulders are stiff and you can feel how fast your eyes move. There is a night-light in the hall that Mom bought and put there for you and June. It is not a seashell, it is just a little light bulb like a Christmas tree light, only white. Grandma Green makes a sound like choking. Snoring sounds like growling. There is a cat scratching in the box in the bathroom. Grandma Green has five Siamese cats.

Next week you are moving into a new house, a house almost as big and almost as white as Grandma's in Old Saybrook.

This hallway is too short. Everyone is sleeping. You have to wake someone up because something is happening. It's too dark, there are faces, and the walls of this house feel like they are pushing in then pushing out, like breathing.

You walk into where Mom and Dad are sleeping and tap Mom's arm and whisper, Mom. Then you get afraid that she will be mad. You stand there until your feet feel too hot. Mom and Dad are together in Grandma Green's bed that is really only big enough for one person. Mom, you whisper again then tiptoe back to your sleeping bag on the lawn chair next to June's lawn chair. Lawn chairs aren't flat like beds but they are longer than sleeping on the van seats. You try to sleep again. This is California. Where you are going to live is in a town called Sleepy Hollow.

You are afraid here. It's not like sleeping at Grandma's in Old Saybrook. You don't even know these grandparents. You know you should like them because they are Mom's parents but this house is dark and smoky and it seems like they don't like kids. Sometimes you are afraid at your other Grandma's, but then you are afraid in a different way. At Grandma's in Old Saybrook you are afraid of things like ghosts or the Betsy Ross painting, now you are afraid of something you can't describe.

You know that there is no such thing as ghosts or vampires but sometimes you wish that there was, something to define the night for you, something specific to be afraid of.

In Grandma's house in Old Saybrook you had your own bedroom because there were eight bedrooms. In Grandma's house you could wake Grandma up if something scared you. Here you are afraid to wake anyone up because everyone is sleeping hard and mean and like being dead. Mom and Dad and June are different here too, and the house is dark.

At Grandma's in Old Saybrook Grandma might fix you something to eat at night if you couldn't sleep. Grandma's skin is tan and warm and she talks of how nice the harbor will be tomorrow and about maybe going to Chattfield Hollow to get water from the spring there.

It's different here because this house is dark all day too and there are lots of plants but they are big like trees. Mom says they are rubber plants. These plants aren't shaped like small hearts and climbing the walls like at Grandma's in Old Saybrook.

June wakes up and it starts. Her hands are pins she says and she is sweating so much. You put a cool rag on June's forehead and you talk to June like how Grandma talked to you. You tell June about the new house and what she might get for Christmas. You aren't afraid for her when she goes to sleep this time because it feels better for her to sleep than for her hands to be pins.

Sometimes the lawn chairs fold shut in the middle of the night. You and June, your bodies bend head to feet and then giggles. June gets tonsilitis all the time and is constantly wetting her bed. Some nights you stay awake until it is morning, cooling June's hot forehead with a washcloth. June gets fevers and says that her hands are like pins and needles or that there is a man chasing her who has hands like knives. Other nights you stay awake until it is light outside because you are sure that there are evil spirits or vampires in the basement.

You would pick your nose until it bled and then you would have to go down the hall to the bathroom.

You were waiting for something. You were waiting to hear the creak of a door or the trees outside tickling the roof, or someone's voice, mean and tired.

There were trees scraping the roof or the windows and trees making faces in the shadows. You would crawl deep into the sleeping bag and stay there for as long as the stale air was bearable. Then you would be gasping for a gulp of air like water to something dehydrated.

June wakes up again and her skin is too cold this time. June says that they wouldn't let her out of the bathroom, wouldn't let her go home.

You dream that you are falling asleep. There is nothing that you can do to stay awake. No matter how hard you try to keep awake, in the dream you are getting sleepier and sleepier.

.   .   .

THE new house is big and white. June says it is a palace. Mom says it is her dream house. Dad has his hands in his pockets like his Dad and says it is just too good to be true.

Dad says here in Sleepy Hollow he is going to finish his book.

Mom says that here in Sleepy Hollow she is going to be a good mother, a good daughter, and an artist that people will know about.

When Mom and Dad say these things June says that she is going to be a princess in a special castle.

You want to have lots of friends at the new school in the woods. You want to go back to Grandma's house in Old Saybrook. You don't want to stay in Grandma and Grandpa Green's house for very long again. It's too smoky, smells of cats, and Grandma and Grandpa Green can make their faces mean if they want to.

The new house is two stories. The first story is a basement. Dad says he is going to turn the basement into a downstairs; a recreation room, a place to have an extra bedroom and a real study. Sleepy Hollow has lots of big houses. In Sleepy Hollow it is like being in a forest. From the main road you almost can't see most of the houses. In Sleepy Hollow there are lots of people that are very rich. There is one house that has a tennis court in the backyard. Lots of people have horses. Lots of people have swimming pools. Dad says, probably we will have a swimming pool too. You hope not for a while. You are afraid of swimming pools after Tammy.

June keeps saying the house looks like a palace because of the creek in the backyard and because of the colored glass window that is above the stairs that go up to the front door. You have never seen so many trees in a neighborhood. Mom says that one of the things she always liked the best about her hometown is that the trees are always green, no matter what time of the year it is.

Grandma and Grandpa Green live on the other side of Sleepy Hollow by the train tracks. They live about twenty minutes away. The new house is in front of a creek, the same creek that is by Grandma and Grandpa Green's house if you walk over a hill.

There is a big tree in front of the new house. It's not a new house really it's an old house. Mom says that old houses have character and are better because they can be fixed up. There are two orange trees in the yard, a lemon tree, blackberry bushes and a grape arbor.

There are new beds for you and June. Your bed is from Grandma. Your bed is the bed that was Grandma and Grandpa's first bed. Grandma wanted you to have it so you can think of her every night before you go to sleep. The bed is a wooden four-poster bed and big and has springs that creak. Grandma gave you the quilt that used to be folded up on the end of her rosebud couch. June has a brand-new bed. June's bed is a canopy from Sears and has white ruffles around the bottom and a white canopy that makes being in the bed like being in a tent.

There is a closet in your and June's bedroom that is big enough to walk around in.

In the backyard there is a playhouse. Dad says it used to be a chicken coop. To you and June it is a playhouse. There is a ladder inside the playhouse and you can climb up to where there is a small table and chair and a little window that looks out over to where the creek is and into the yard next door where there is a big swimming pool.

Dad sets up the dining room so that he can type in there. It's just a small table that he puts in front of the window that looks out to the grape arbor. Out this window there are purple flowers by the grapes. The purple flowers make the whole house smell like perfume. The grapes are green and don't have seeds. On the table by the window Dad puts his typewriter and his statue of Don Quixote, the man with the shield but no spear because the spear got lost and instead of the spear there is a pencil that June chewed some of the yellow paint off of. In the dining room Mom sets up her sewing machine and her painting easel. Mostly Mom paints pictures of you and Dad and June. Mom paints lots of pictures of the three of you naked but not always together. On the painting easel Mom puts a painting she did before you were born. It is a painting that you have never seen before. It is a painting of a baby-doll head, a broom, a rusty soup can and a picture of a man with no hands and no mouth that Mom says is her father.

On the big closet in your bedroom Mom paints a picture. She paints what you and June tell her to paint. First there is a harbor and boats with sails and a rowboat like Grandma's. There are fish under the water. June tells Mom to paint a cat. You say just not a cat like CoCo. CoCo is Grandma Green's cat that sits on her bed away from the other Siamese cats because it is so old and mean. Grandma Green said that CoCo will never die. CoCo can't walk and his eyes don't look like eyes and have pus. June says, paint two girls. Mom paints two girls and writes Tracy and June. Then Mom paints a castle on a mountain in back of their big brown cat. Mom paints a rainbow. It is a picture to look at all the time. There are birds and a princess and a ladder that goes up the mountain to the castle. On the picture June draws a person that is just a head with arms and legs but no feet or hands. You tell June this and then you draw a big lady with high heels and a purse. You get mad then because you can't make things look good and real like how Mom does.

You go to a school that is in the woods. Your teacher's name is Miss Purtle and she has lots of freckles and red hair and laughs really nice and told you that she was glad to have you in her class. She didn't seat you next to the twins though and that makes you mad.

The twins are Jennifer and Julie Knuckey and they look exactly the same except for Jennifer has a bigger head than Julie's if you look really close. Jennifer and Julie have hair that is longer than Jewel's was. Jennifer and Julie's hair goes down past their waists. They have long foreheads. When you are home you look in the mirror and try to pull your hair back so that your forehead looks high and shiny. Jennifer and Julie have brown eyes with eyelashes that are so long they look like they were bought at the store.

You don't cut your hair but it is different than Jennifer and Julie's. Your hair just doesn't get any longer and is not thick and shiny. Their hair is brown like beach sand and they always dress the same.

You can tell that Jennifer and Julie are happy to be twins. They always wear the same clothes and their favorite game is to trick people by pretending that they are the other twin.

You wonder if at night when they are at home, if they can talk to each other in their heads without saying anything out loud. You think that they must be able to do this because they look so much the same.

After school you followed them home, watched their hair waving in and out and back and forth. You tried to walk the way they did, how twins walk.

When you reach the playground you duck into the bushes quick hoping to catch a glimpse of them in their perfect house that is right next to the park and has a white fence. On their front door there is a brass door knocker that is a fairy with wings holding a cat with big teeth.

Their best friend is Cheryl Emerson. Cheryl always wears white blouses and there is never a speck of dirt on her clothes and her hair is blond and never tangled and smells like the purple flowers in the grape arbor or the first bite of gum. The three of them, Jennifer and Julie and Cheryl, go everywhere together at recess, to the bathroom, to the swings, to the drinking fountain, to Miss Purtle's desk. You think they do this on purpose just to make you mad.

There are always things to make at school. Miss Purtle likes to decorate the classroom. There are snowflakes to make in the wintertime by folding and folding any color paper, not just white. Miss Purtle says that this is California and snow can be any color. By cutting the folded and folded paper you can make all shapes of snowflakes to hang in the windows.

You like it best when Miss Purtle takes the class outside on hikes around the school, down by the creek and through the park, where there are redwood trees, some so big that your arms don't even bend when you put your arms around them but go straight like you were facing a wall.

In the park or on the hill there are lots of little paths for playing games after school like *Planet of the Apes* and *The Swiss Family Robinson,* games where you and your friends pretend you are living in another world, a world that is wilderness and you have to fend for yourselves. Not just playing in the park.

Behind the school Miss Purtle tells the kids to find flowers they like or leaves from different bushes and trees. Miss Purtle shows the class how to cut the leaves or flowers in a special way so that the plant won't be hurt.

There are scissors to bring on these walks in your lunch bag and paper and colored pencils to draw the flowers that can't be cut like the poppies.

Back at class Miss Purtle tells the class what the flowers and leaves are by showing pictures from a big shiny book. Then with wax paper and an iron the flowers and leaves are pressed together so that they can hang in the windows next to the snowflakes that Miss Purtle never takes down because she thinks the things her class makes are pretty and she wants everyone to see.

You didn't plan to do it. Cheryl was alone by the drinking fountain when it happened. You just ran over there and before you knew what had happened Cheryl's lip was bleeding because her lip hit the drinking fountain when you pushed her head, and then her white blouse is ripped and a piece of white blouse is in your hand.

In front of the whole class Miss Purtle makes you sit in the corner for the rest of the day and when it is time to go home she takes a big blue bow that she cut out of construction paper and pins it to your brown jumper. The bow says, Today I was bad, Tomorrow I will be good. Miss Purtle says you have to write, Today I was bad, fifty times on paper and then have your Mom sign it.

Right when you get out of class and you know that Miss Purtle can't see, the bow is off and you are running. You throw the bow in the creek.

Miss Purtle never even asked for the signed paper from your Mom. Miss Purtle likes you. People have to do things they don't want to sometimes because it is their job. Some days you go to look for the bow but you never find it. Cheryl is your friend now. The Knuckey twins say that you can come to their house. You just want to get them both in the chicken coop.

You tell Mom about your new friends at school. You tell Mom about how Jennifer and Julie look so much alike but that you can tell them apart. You tell Mom that Jennifer and Julie are your best friends.

· · ·

YOUR father always liked Christmas.

He holds you and June on his lap. He wraps your tiny hands around the red and green balls that he takes off the tree. Look at yourself, he tells you and June, laughing. Looking out of the shiny ornaments, your face wants to get out of the colored ball he holds in his hand.

Sometimes the balls fall off the tree and break.

There was the Christmas in Connecticut you and June had chicken pox so you couldn't go to Grandma's. You both were covered with little red dots. Your faces were wet and itching. There were presents but mostly the rooms moved and you just wanted not to be sick. Your nightgown stuck to you.

You see your face in Dad's eyes. You look and then you aren't sure if Dad's face is in your eyes and there is no one to ask this to. You hold Dad tight.

Do you love me? Dad asks.

Then Marvin is pressing his stomach on yours. There are people sitting around the tree here. These grandparents, your Mom's parents. Your Mom's brother and sister are here too and their kids, your cousins. The cousins are babies. You are sitting on Dad's lap. You think about Marvin. Dad strokes your back. Marvin's eyes were closed.

There was a park in Connecticut. The park is muddy. There is a stone water fountain near the entrance to the park. There are swings that hang from cold iron bars over the brown mud puddles. Dad lifts you onto the swing so you won't get your shoes muddy in the puddle. You said thank you. Dad looks at you the same as the time he zipped your stomach by an accident helping you into your snowsuit.

You can see yourself in Dad's eyes and then in his glasses. Grandpa Green says bless the children and then raises his glass. Thank the Lord that we are all together Grandpa Green says. Grandpa Green works at a big prison, San Quentin. He works there and guards men so they don't escape. Grandpa Green looks mean because his eyes look like he is trying to see something far away when he is looking at something that is right in front of him. Grandma Green's eyes look like this too.

It's not time for presents. Not until everyone is finished eating. There isn't snow here. It's not even cold outside. Dad said he heard on the radio that Santa is heading this way in his sled.

You get out of Dad's lap.

In Grandma Green's room there is a piano. Uncle Bill, Mom's brother, can play it without even looking at any music. He plays by ear. Uncle Bill is fun. He tells stories to all the cousins. He is the tallest man you have ever seen and he is an artist. There is a picture of Uncle Bill on the piano that shows Uncle Bill with a big piece of cake in his mouth when he got married. He married an Indian woman named Naheed. She wears saris that are big pieces of silk that she wraps around her body in a special way so that one piece of silk looks like a dress. She wears a dot on her forehead, a ruby or an emerald or a small black circle that she paints herself. Grandma Green has a box of candy bars next to her bed and a box of Christmas ribbons on her bed, the kind of ribbons that can just be stuck on a present. CoCo has his Siamese paw in the box.

In the room next to Grandma Green's is Aunt Sarah. Aunt Sarah is Mom's younger sister. Aunt Sarah is on the bed and there is a man with a cowboy hat who is holding Aunt Sarah's titties in his hands. Aunt Sarah sees you and pushes his hands away and her shirt comes down. My, Tracy, she says, that is a pretty dress you have.

Aunt Sarah is home because she didn't want to live in a tepee in Montana anymore with this man in a cowboy hat. Aunt Sarah's room is painted five different colors of purple. There are no lawn chairs anymore like when you and June slept in here. There is a big bed on the floor with lots of pillows. Aunt Sarah has lots of posters on her wall that glow orange and pink and green when she turns on this special light that makes the room really purple. Aunt Sarah also has a light that blinks off and on really fast and when you move your hand in front of you it looks like click click click. Aunt Sarah says sit on the bed and the man with the cowboy hat whose name is Coyote but everyone calls him Coy goes into the living room where it is noisy. The Christmas lights blink on and off and on. It is smoky in the living room and everyone is talking so that it sounds like Homer's stomach.

Aunt Sarah's room smells like wooden beads that Mom has a

necklace of. On the floor there is a big bottle that is covered with all colors of candle-wax drippings. The TV is on. Aunt Sarah says did you know that sometimes the people in there come out onto the floor? She says did you know that the people on the TV can hear what you are saying? Aunt Sarah says that if you don't want the people to come out of the screen you better wish real hard. You say you will because on the TV there are people running and something explodes and then they shoot. You would sort of like some of the people that you have seen before on the TV to come out of the screen because Aunt Sarah says that they are just small people.

There are so many people and you have to wait and watch while each person opens one present at a time. Grandpa Green passes out the presents and he goes around the room and that way you can see who gets more presents than who. June gets more presents than you. June gets a doll that has hair that comes out of its head so that you can make the hair long or short by turning a knob on the doll's back. June gets an etch-a-sketch. June gets five clothes. You counted because you only got three. June threw the doll on the ground and said it is ugly, then June is sitting on Mom's lap.

Before, Grandpa Green took you and June into his dark bedroom and said he had something special just for you and June. Grandpa Green gives you both a small brown paper bag. In your bag is a red plastic kazoo. In June's bag is a yellow plastic harmonica. You had hoped that the presents would have been something else. Grandpa Green looks happy to give you and June these presents. You feel sad all of a sudden. It's not the presents that make you sad, it's that Grandpa Green wants to give you and June something special and you don't like it.

For presents you got a blue hairbrush-and-comb set. You got a doll with dark skin like Naheed that is called a Sasha doll that Mom says is a good doll because it only has a belly button and not titties like a Barbie doll.

Mom is happiest about the dresses. You can tell that she is. These, Dad, Mom says, let them open these.

They are dresses Mom made.

You go outside and play, Mom said. I will call you when it is time to come back in. I am doing secret things, Mom said, you go out and play.

The pattern in June's dress is small purple flowers. The pattern on your dress is yellow flowers and small blue dots. They are the same dresses, puffy sleeves and a ruffle on the bottom. There are white aprons to go over the dresses that Mom says are pinafores.

Everyone says how *beautiful* the dresses are and Mom is smiling and Dad is smiling too.

You can take this with you. This is a picture you want to keep.

Grandpa Green burns you with a cigarette getting another present and you cry. It's smoky and Aunt Sarah is in her room with the man with the cowboy hat. Grandma Green talks and her words are like she just woke up. Then Grandma Green is crying because she can't believe that all her children are here together and Grandpa Green tells her to shut up and says that he is not long for this world, that he is sure that this will be his last Christmas. Grandpa Green burned you on your hand because you had your hand on your head and he walked by and there were sparks.

You wonder what the Knuckey twins are getting for Christmas. You don't think anyone burns them for Christmas or that their grandfather is going to die any day now. At the Knuckeys' there are probably all presents wrapped like how Grandma in Old Saybrook wraps gifts, with everything boxed and then wrapped and not some things in brown bags with already used ribbons on the bag. At the Knuckeys' there are two of each present for both Jennifer and Julie so that no one wishes that they got something else. The Knuckeys live next to the park and in each room of their house everything matches. In the bathroom everything is green and blue, even little soaps that are shaped like fish. In the kitchen everything is orange and white. In their bedroom there is a rainbow poster that is as big as the whole wall. Nothing is broken or old. Everything in their

78

bedroom is new and pretty like twins would have. You wanted to give them something for Christmas but you didn't have any money and from the way their house looked you didn't think they would like anything homemade.

Dad wants to play the guitar. Mom says, not now.

Grandpa Green is playing his records, an opera that is too loud over everyone trying to talk, and then he scratches the record and Grandma Green yells that the kids don't like his music. Your Dad says that the record is beautiful. Dad's face looks white and his ears are red. Grandpa Green yells that Grandma Green doesn't know anything, not anything at all. Mom's brother and sisters, everyone just keeps talking. Only you and Dad are paying attention about the records.

Uncle Bill says he will tell the kids a bedtime story, a Christmas story. Aunt Sarah has to come out of her bedroom so that all the kids can lie on her bed.

You lie next to June. She is already sleeping. June has a velvet dress on that is green, and white lace tights. Mom fixed your and June's hair in peasant braids but you took yours down because the Knuckey twins never wear their hair in braids.

Uncle Bill has big white sneakers on and his hair is in a long ponytail down his back. He turns out the lights and starts. First he tells about Santa and how Santa got lost in the sky because no one believed in him. Then Uncle Bill pretends to fall asleep to see if the kids are listening. Uncle Bill is your favorite uncle because he likes to do things with the kids like Crack the Whip in the park. Crack the Whip is where all the kids hold hands and then Uncle Bill holds the hand of whoever is on the end and all the kids start to run around in a circle around Uncle Bill real fast holding hands and Uncle Bill makes it so that the kids leave the ground almost, because he is spinning them so fast. Uncle Bill is tall and handsome and laughs at Grandpa when Grandpa says he is not long for this world. Uncle Bill knows how to get other people to laugh, and he doesn't laugh then so that he never gets caught when he is making fun of someone. Uncle Bill snores and then he holds his breath. You say, Uncle Bill, Uncle Bill wake up, and he shakes his head and lips and growls and then he tickles all the kids except June because she is still sleeping. Then Uncle Bill says he can't very well tell the story if all the kids are laughing. You try to stop laughing but he keeps tickling, pretending to sleep then saying he can't remember what the story is about.

The real story is about Rapture. Uncle Bill says it is the adventures of the dude known as Rapture. He is kind of a Christmas dude, Uncle Bill says. Rapture knows that Santa only comes if people believe in him but Rapture can't see so he doesn't know what Santa looks like and doesn't know what to believe in. Rapture lives in a land where there are pink trees. You ask Uncle Bill how could Rapture know if the trees are pink if he can't see. Uncle Bill says that is part of the story. Where Rapture lives people can fly. In this land people wish for things to happen, good things, and they do. It takes Rapture a while to realize this, Uncle Bill says. Finally one day Rapture asks Santa for glasses so that he can see. When Rapture gets to see he doesn't want to see anymore because all of a sudden the trees aren't pink like people told him they would be and people are meaner to him than they used to be. Uncle Bill doesn't end the story, he makes it so that you will want to hear more some other time. The other kids are sleeping now too. You pretend you are asleep.

Uncle Bill goes into the living room where Grandma Green and Grandpa Green are yelling at each other. Grandma Green is crying loud and going, oh, oh.

There is a loud crash. The Christmas tree lights aren't blinking anymore. The door of Aunt Sarah's bedroom is open and you can see Grandma Green and Grandpa Green holding each other but not like hugging because Grandma Green is pinching Grandpa Green's arms.

Your Mom is crying and Dad is putting his guitar in the case.

Surveillance II

YOU had this same thought over and over: that you were stowed on a ship in the cargo hold in a tightly sealed box. The box is not high enough to stand in, and it's not long enough to lie down in. In fact the box is square and you must sit in it for a very long time. You have to sit in the box and if you move at all the box gets smaller around you. Your knees are pulled tightly to your chest and each time you pull your head closer to your knees the box tightens. This thought just comes and it is on the back of your eyelids, or someone says, are you daydreaming? and their eyes are looking down at you. This thought is like someone else's voice in your head and it doesn't go away.

Weekends there is always something to do. Mom will pack a lunch. Mom and Dad just have plans and then you are at a place.

Look into my eyes, the man with his back to you is saying into the microphone. Look into my eyes and breathe in what they are saying. Sleep. They are saying, sleep. The man's voice is hazy and slow. His voice blends into the faces of the thousands of people that are attending this concert. His voice is blending into the back of Mom's long black hair. You are combing Mom's hair.

Look into my eyes, the man is saying. The sky is getting darker.

Can you see your Dad? he is up there on the stage, Mom says.

There are thirty people on the stage being hypnotized. They are in a green light like the light in the porpoise tank at Marine World. The people on the stage look like black crayon smudges.

Dark shapes standing on a stage in a green light against a purple sky.

There is a woman next to you. She is dancing barefoot on a quilt. Her feet are caked with mud. She is not wearing a shirt and her breasts are sunburned. Her long hair is tangled with dried flowers and bright-colored metallic stars. The woman dancing on the quilt is not aware of what is going on around her. She keeps swirling her skirt slowly around her legs. If she wants to, she massages her body: stomach, tits, anywhere.

Who's to stop this lady from dancing and touching herself like this?

There is a man. He walks fast and crooked. He just comes up to where June is lying in the sleeping bag and starts to unzip the sleeping bag to get into it. Mom says, please don't. The man says, far out, and walks away fast and crooked.

You can't move. It is night. The whole world is motionless except for the panting. You cannot move because the panting and groaning of your parents in the next room is crushing you like a dead weight. You are afraid that you will become paralyzed in this position. If you move you will be found out. Wide awake all you can see is blackness. You fell asleep with your head under the covers and now you can't move for fear of being found out. They are moving in there, fast and mean. The air beneath the covers is unbearable. The panting has become the cries of someone being tortured. Your Mom is moaning yes, then no. You can't help her. No one can help you not be here. The panting is so loud that you are becoming the panting. You are drenched in sweat, suspended in the darkness like the fixed gaze of a sleeping fish.

.   .   .

IN the chicken coop it is cool. The chicken coop smells like wet wood. You tell June to stop singing because you are trying to get the right angle so you can see the Davis kids next door swimming in their pool. June stops and says let's play house but that she wants to be the Dad this time. June says she is writing a book called *The Alley of Eden*. You tell June that is stupid because Dad is already writing that book. You say, it's time for bed honey and you and June take off your clothes and lie stomach to stomach and you move around with June on top of you until it stops feeling good between your legs. Then you tell June she stinks. And you put your clothes back on and leave the chicken coop and leave June in there singing.

You want to remember when it really started.

First you are afraid that someone will catch you and June when you are playing house and that because of being caught something horrible will happen to you. You don't think the Knuckey twins play house. You don't think that any of your friends play house. It just hits you, the feeling, and you have to make it go away by touching. There was the time when Pam Davis from next door came to the chicken coop. You hadn't been naked. You thought she saw and told her real quick that you and June were wrestling. She said, I know what you are doing, Tracy, me and my brother do it all the time. The chicken coop smells like wet wood. There are spiderwebs. Pam Davis has fat feet and says she does it all the time. June is soft and smells like a kitten. June is smart and can draw pictures of people that show the people doing all kinds of things and not just standing and staring straight ahead. June says she is going to be famous. Pam said she and her brother do it all the time.

You just want to know when it started, when it became clear that you were in a body, this one and not another one.

There are olive trees that line the streets in Sleepy Hollow.

. . .

YOU like to look at your shadow because it calms you.

. . .

YOU are back in the pantry again. The pantry is just off the kitchen. The door is shut behind you. You are wiping the dust from the shelf where your Mom stores the preserves: pickles

and jellies, jellies and jams and then pickles. You want to taste
the dust on the shelf. You put it to your lips. The dust burns on
your tongue. The dust is burning your tongue. The light caves
into the pantry. Your mother is there, half behind the door.
You are standing there in front of the finger-smear marks on the
shelf and you can feel her eyes on the smudges of dust around
your mouth. Your mother's eyes scare you. You push at her
like she is a door and run.

The creek behind the house is cold and there is ice over all the
leaves. The leaves look like they will always be frozen. The
leaves look made, like art. You break one off. Your bare feet are
turning blue, blue as June's face when she holds her breath. June
always holds her breath if the family is driving over a bridge or
through a tunnel.

You are running down the hill toward the creek behind your
house. You know the creek is cold. You are stumbling because
you can't see in the dark. You plunge into the creek and lie
down. The water doesn't cover your head. Steam is coming off
the top of your head. You get up and walk back and forth across
the slippery rocks. The shallowest part of the creek is right
behind your house.

You had stuttered that it wasn't fair. You said that you and
June needed to share a room. You thought Mom and Dad knew
about you and June. Dad said, wouldn't it be nice to have your
own room. You said that somehow you had been put in the
wrong family. You said that other kids' parents didn't do all the
things they did. You are dizzy. You are not really my parents,
you say, there has been some mistake. Your mother's eyes hurt.
Your father's eyes hurt. What will God think now? Your
mother says this but not to you. How can anyone argue what
is? Mom says. Mom says this because you tell her you want
different parents, want to live in a house where things match
and not here. You thought it was about you and June. Pam said
her and her brother do it all the time. When it is dark your Mom
says yes then no. No one can help you or her when it is dark.

You are not my mother, you said. Where's Grandma, I want

to live with Grandma, you said. I can't live here anymore. You said that, and then you are running toward the creek, running so fast because you said that to her face.

It's all you can hear, your mother's voice echoing in your head. Everywhere outside the pantry your mother's voice is a bass beat to other voices talking far away, saying this, saying that.

Your Dad says, yes, we want you to stay. Dad finds you and says yes, we want you to stay. Dad wears ties. Dad's eyes escape from the family when you are all together. Dad is writing a book called *The Alley of Eden*. Dad said it is about paradise being smothered. Dad said that his book is different from other books. Dad said that his book will make people see what they are doing, what they need to be doing.

You lived in a house but it was never like other houses because when you come home from school your mother would be painting and there would be loud music. When your father came home from work he would take off his tie untuck his ponytail and then he would type. Your parents would walk around the house naked.

You said, you are not my parents, there has been an accident.

Your mother wore high heels, but she never did say the things that other mothers said. She never did say, here are cookies. Your mother said that you could be anything that you wanted to be and then she looked far away, somewhere over your shoulder where you couldn't see.

Your mother wore high heels. Your mother's eyes would escape from the family when you were all together.

Your father came down to the creek.

Come back to the house so that we can talk this out like rational human beings, he says. Your feet are cold then hot. His voice is warm. You and June are old enough to have your own bedrooms, Dad says. Dad never says that you and June can't do that anymore.

There was panting and moaning. You couldn't breathe.

Dad says when you are back in the kitchen that he will fix up a new room for you that is nice, a room that you will like. Your Mom and Dad caught you and June holding each other naked and laughing hysterically. Dad laughed too. Mom just stands there looking at you and June like she is seeing a ghost. Mother? Father? Dad's hands smell like kittens. There is ice on the bedroom windows up here. Cold then hot, there is something squirming in your lap.

. . .

"If you sit on my lap June you won't be afraid." June's hair is smooth. June's body is soft. June is smooth and soft everywhere. You feel so tingly and nice to hold her in your lap. On the back of June's neck there is a small brown beauty mark. June's neck smells like your hands in the morning, sweet and warm.

You are in the pantry. You ran there again. Your mother's eyes are everywhere.

There was a time when you realized that you were called a girl, no, first there was a time when you became aware of the fact that there was a difference between people, that people's bodies didn't all have the same equipment, that not everyone had a hole between their legs, a hole for letting things in and out. Before this of course you realized that yes, everyone looks different and that some people are ugly or crippled or handicapped but all of a sudden what you realized was this one difference that marked you as a girl, a space between your legs just big enough to put things inside of, a space to hide things in maybe, your finger or a small round bead.

Mom and Dad are getting ready. It's a costume party at Jack's. You and June aren't going to get dressed up because this is an adult party and Mom or Dad will bring you home for bed or you and June will sleep up in the loft with other kids.

Jack is Katy's Mom's boyfriend. Katy was June's best friend. Jillson is Katy's Mom. Jillson will visit your Mom and say that the kids have to go play now because your Mom and I need to talk personal.

Katy and June aren't best friends anymore because Katy was afraid to spend the night at your house and June got mad and called her no fingers.

Katy has no fingers on her right hand except a thumb and stumps and on her left hand the fingers are bent crooked like a hook. Katy was born this way. Sometimes it seems like Jillson wishes Katy were different, sometimes it seems that Jillson wishes Katy weren't her child at all, because Jillson yells at Katy all the time and when Jillson is talking personal with your Mom she cries and says she doesn't know what to do because Jack says all the time that he can't stand kids, and Jack is always wanting to know why it is that Jillson can't figure out what to do with Katy when he is busy or when he wants to just be alone with Jillson. Jillson cries when she talks to your Mom and says that sometimes she wishes that Katy just wasn't so stupid because she is sure that other kids are not so needy.

It's not stupid what Jillson means though because in June's class Katy and June get all pluses on their schoolwork. But kids make fun of Katy at school and after school and everywhere and are always staring at her hands, adults too.

Katy steals things from the kids in her class, pens and books and jewelry, even money. Katy steals makeup from the drugstore for June and you too if you ask. Katy can steal anything and never get caught because in the stores people are so busy staring at Katy and then feeling sorry for her to themselves. Everyone is so busy being glad that their own hands are OK and their friends' and children's hands are OK too that they don't really see what Katy is doing.

Before Jillson and Katy came to live with Jack you never knew who exactly lived in the house on the hill by Big Rock. There would be big motorcycles parked in the street and dogs in the yard, always different dogs, but you weren't exactly sure who it was that lived in the house with the big porch and with the steps to the house that go up forever.

Jack has a big chopper and friends in motorcycle gangs. Your

Mom says the bikers are either from the Gypsy Jokers or from the Hell's Angels. Jack tells people that bikers are always asking him to be in their clubs, but Jack says he tells them he is a family man.

Jack has big parties, even bigger than the parties that your Mom and Dad have, with bands and people that paint on each other's bodies. When there is a party at your house you stay in your room. People that smell like beer and break things, the window in the bathroom once, or the time a man got on the roof and screamed, these people make you mad.

When Jack has parties there is more than one band and there are so many people it might just as well be a rock concert because people camp on the hill behind his house. At Jack's there is a light in the living room next to the stereo that blinks off and on fast so that everyone dancing is in a movie. The police never come to Jack's parties and tell Jack to turn the music down or that the party is over because Jack lives on the hill where no one comes unless they are invited.

Jack has a wolf, a real one that can't be let off its chain when Jack isn't home. Chilka's chain is long and Chilka can run up and down the brown grass hill where Uncle Bill takes the kids cardboard sliding if there is a party in the day.

Jack found the wolf when he was hunting, it was just a cub then, alone in the middle of a field where its mother left it to die. This is the story that Jack likes to tell about how he saved Chilka from a lousy mother. Even in the wild the mothers don't know what they are doing, Jack says and everyone laughs. When Jack laughs his teeth are as big as Chilka's, all black and yellow and sharp.

The neighbors know about Chilka, that it's a real wolf, but no one says that it's against the law. Jack drives around town with Chilka in the back of the truck and people stare out of the corners of their eyes. Plus Jack has a gun and sometimes he just shoots it off because he feels like shooting his gun on the brown grass hill behind his house.

No kids are to touch Chilka at the parties unless Jack is there because Chilka only likes Jack, not Jillson or Katy. Katy and June like to make Chilka bark.

There was the day when everyone was in front of Jack's house by the barbecue and you went looking for June.

June and Katy are out back just far enough from where Chilka is barking and jumping at the end of the leash. Chilka's teeth are snapping at the air and there is foam on his mouth. Katy is lying on the patio and one of the little dogs is licking Katy's pee-pee while June is throwing things at Chilka, a broken orange comb, and rocks, and Katy's sneaker with the sock still in it. That's gross, you said after Katy had stood up and put her shorts back on.

Katy and June and the other dogs that Jillson brought with her when she moved in with Jack are running fast and laughing. Jack's voice down by the barbecue is what you hear as you walk up the trail behind Katy and June. Not in my house you don't, Jack's voice echoes and then a lady laughing.

Where you are is at the bottom of Big Rock, in the woods where there are blackberry bushes and poison oak and tall shiny weeds that have small yellow flowers with yellow dust that comes off on your clothes and gets in your hair as you walk up toward the rock where June and Katy already are.

The two black dogs up on Big Rock look like small toys that hang above babies' cribs.

Big Rock is like a table once you climb up the side of the hill. Big Rock looks like a giant head from your house. And from Jack's house you can only see grass, not the shape of anything.

At first it was easy. You do what you did before, burning bugs, ants especially, with the plastic magnifying glass you got for your birthday from Grandma and Grandpa Green. But this takes too long and besides Katy has matches.

With the matches that Katy got out of her Mom's purse you each take turns lighting fires in the brown grass on top of Big Rock and then stamping them out. It is to see who can get the biggest fire, make the biggest burn mark, black circles on the grass.

It was you. You started it. It won't stop, the fire keeps getting bigger and bigger, shiny clear orange like water that is hot and crackling and then you and June and Katy are running down the street far from the party down the hill. You are running and knocking on doors, but no one is home at three houses and Katy is crying and June says she is going back because June wants to see them put it out. A man drives by and you tell him that there is a big fire and can he please call the fire department.

The fire is rolling down the hill toward Jack's house where Chilka is barking. Jack has already started to hose the grass behind his house. Everyone at the party stands behind him.

You can see this from where you are on the road. The people at the party can't see you or June or Katy.

No one asked where you had all been. The firemen ask you and June and Katy, who are sitting on the other side of the street on the curb, if you know how the fire got started. You tell the man in the yellow raincoat that it was boys, three of them.

Mom and Dad are going to the party dressed like straight people. It's Mom's idea because she has a dress that she would never wear in a million years to anything but a costume party. Grandma Hawkins sent the dress for Mom's birthday. The dress came in a shiny cream-colored box with a purple ribbon and when Mom opened the box there was lots of carefully folded white tissue around the dress. Mom opened the box and said very nice. You smelled the tissue paper, sure that you could smell Grandma Hawkins, a clean smell, spicy flower perfume, and laundry that has been hanging outside to dry.

You think it is kind of mean that Mom doesn't like the dress but Dad thinks that it is all very funny. The dress is short and blue and looks almost like one of Dad's work shirts except it has a white stripe just below where there is a rope belt that has a gold buckle shaped like an anchor. There are small red buttons on the dress and the material is fake silk. Oh, "polyzester," Dad says laughing.

Dad has his long ponytail tucked into his shirt just like he does when he goes to work anyway and he has his suit on but not like the ones that he wears to work. This suit is brown and green stripes and Dad keeps saying when do we golf, and where are the chicks at? Dad is carrying a briefcase that has in it a *Playboy* magazine and a sports magazine, a bottle of scotch and clear plastic cups and some underwear that is still in the package.

Dad and Mom are laughing and drinking beer. Mom drinks her beer out of a glass and Dad drinks his from the can.

What matters is the discomfort of their clothed flesh, and their eyes that twitch beyond the confines of a setting: your family seated at the kitchen table playing house, or white uniformed people in the hospital playing at healing.

First June said let's build something.

In the bedroom the mattress is off the bed and June is doing somersaults in the air by jumping off the bedframe where the springs are. The mattress is soft with all the pillows from the living room on it. You are being the spotter for June like how the lady in the gymnastics class spotted you. You only took the class once because Mom said there was no money for gymnastics.

You hold your arm out hard in case June might fall. It's easier to be the spotter if June does a back somersault starting from the mattress and throwing her body back. When you spot June this way you have to take all the pillows off of the mattress. It's really a back handspring this way and June has to use her hands. You are afraid to do this because you can only think of how you might break your neck but June wants to do more and more either from jumping off the bedsprings onto the mattress or with you spotting. Even when June lands on her head she doesn't get afraid. In the dining room Dad is playing his blues records and teasing Homer so that Homer howls to the music.

You do a couple of flips but mostly you watch June or spot. In the air when you flip you can't stop upside down or see yourself in the mirror, but when June flips she is tucked like she is sitting on the ground or the ceiling but she spins. You try to see her stopped in each place, upside down, sideways, but she goes so fast and mostly she is a blur.

June says, let's build something. Dad and Mom say it is OK as long as everything gets put back, but you know you won't have to clean everything up until tomorrow because it is almost time to go to the party.

In the living room you start by moving the couch away from the wall. It's going to be a city, you decided, and June said yes that it would be good to make a house so big that it is a city. Behind the couch and in between the wall is the main part. You stack the couch pillows over the top to the wall for the first roof.

Mom said yes it is OK to take the towels out of the bathroom and all the sheets and blankets off the beds and June does this while you get the chairs and small tables and the stepladder and the top part of June's canopy that never has a curtain anymore and arrange these things all around the living room, pushing Homer away, sweating and clapping to the fast song that Dad is playing in the dining room.

On top of all the chairs and the tables you and June put the sheets and the blankets. June's canopy frame is the center stacked on the stepladder and the short bookcase. Dad helps put a sheet on this, all the time talking to Mom who is in the dining room about what kind of crazy costumes Uncle Bill and Naheed will be wearing. One time Uncle Bill painted Naheed's naked body with gold paint that didn't come off all the way for weeks. Under plants and with books, and sometimes just by the way it is hung, the roof to the house is held.

The house covers the whole living room like how lots of circus tents would look from a plane, all colors.

There isn't time to go inside the big house that you and June made. There isn't time to play whatever game you and June might have played inside, beneath the blankets and sheets and towels and between the chairs and couch and under the canopy frame. It's time to leave, to go to Jack's costume party.

The last time you and June built a house like this one in the living room Katy was here. It was that day that June decided she and Katy weren't best friends anymore.

June is sitting humming to herself about how many beads she can get to fit this time. Not now Katy cries pulling the blanket down so that June and Katy are red ghosts under the blanket.

My Mom is home alone, Katy says crying. I have to go home now.

Oh, go ahead no fingers, just go and don't ever come back, June says.

The bead game was June's idea, not Katy's and not yours. Katy didn't want to play the bead game anymore. June got a bead stuck in her nose before and couldn't get it out. I don't want to be putting beads in my pee-pee, Katy says crying. My Mom is home alone.

The red blanket smells like cat spray, a smell that never goes away no matter how many times the blanket gets washed.

You walk Katy home because it is dark. First Mom called Jillson so that when you get to the long stairs in front of Jack's house Jillson is already halfway down the stairs to bring Katy home. Jillson has her hair all messy and is wearing a slip and Jack's big black boots and she says what is the matter cry baby, to Katy, and how come you are such a troublemaker?

Do we have to go to no fingers' house? June says. Dad says, that isn't nice June. Dad says everyone argues once in a while and that Katy will be your friend again June. June says, no way. Dad says, stubborn, but smiles.

Every day in the house June says, no fingers, no fingers, just loud enough for you to hear because you told June that it was mean to say that.

That's not very nice, June, you say but you don't like to look at Katy's hands because it gives you a stomachache if you are eating and Katy's mouth is chewing something and there is food on her chin and she wipes it away with her hand that is a hook, or the hand with stumps for fingers.

Give it back asshole June says, grabbing at the picture of June and Katy that you took off of June's dresser. In the picture June has blacked out Katy's face and drawn five overlarge fingers at the end of each of Katy's arms. Dad took the picture at the County Fair. It is of June and Katy just after they had gone on the basket ride, their faces almost green. June's eyes are crossed. The basket ride is spinning behind them. Faces and bodies a blur of colors in the spinning basket.

Here, take it, you say. There used to be a time when you could tell June what to do. Now June does what she wants, does things with Katy (used to do things with Katy), does things that don't include you.

Not that you want to play nasty games with June and Katy out in back of Jack's house or beneath the red blanket, things that you taught June, but not the bead game or with the dogs. June is your sister but mostly you are not friends.

You have lots of friends.

In school and at home are two different things.

Homer is barking in the window. It's not very far to Jack's house. It is windy outside and there are dark clouds moving fast over the olive trees. Mom and Dad look funny. Mom in the blue dress with a red sweater is laughing and telling Dad about the wonderful buys she got at Lucky Market. She has buttoned just the top button of the red sweater and not put her arms in the sleeves so that the sweater is like a cape like how Grandma in Old Saybrook wears her sweaters. You think that Mom looks really pretty. Dad is laughing at everything that Mom is saying about the supermarket and the bridge club and all the things she doesn't like. Dad looks funny with his bright-colored suit and briefcase. The family is walking down the street in front of the neighbors' houses that are quiet with people inside eating dinner.

Both Mom and Dad look happy and except for the color of Dad's suit and what is inside his briefcase and except for what Mom keeps saying and except for where it is that you all are going, to a costume party, and except for June who keeps saying, no fingers, no fingers, this could be a real family like the kind that other kids at school have.

June is walking on the curb balancing with her arms straight out, sometimes walking backwards.

From the street in front of Jack's house you can hear the music that gets louder as you walk up the steps. The windows in Jack's house are lighted different colors, red or blue or green, and then there is the white light on the porch that is usually in the living room that is blinking off and on really fast.

There are 630 steps up to the house, you counted once. June doesn't run up the steps like usual because she has already said that she is going to ignore no fingers.

There are tape recorders planted in the dark of the yard. One is playing howling and screaming noises. And one tape recorder that is coming from underneath the porch is of a woman screaming, help me, please, no.

. . .

You can see the wires that hold the arms and legs of the life-size wooden puppets, the wires that control their movements. The scenery behind the puppets is a drawing of a large house. The proportions of the house are all wrong. A door takes up the whole front of the house. A window floats in space next to the house. There are stairs that lead to the house behind the puppets. The stairs don't lead to the door. The stairs lead to just below the window that floats in space.

The life-size wooden puppets have eyes that are as big as their hands. All the puppets have weapons, weapons that are attached to their hands: knives, guns or axes. There are men puppets and lady puppets. It is hard to tell them apart.

June is sitting on your right. Dad is sitting on your left and Mom is sitting next to Dad.

The music is loud. The speakers are big black boxes as high as the ceiling of the stage. The music is Indian sitar music, not nice like when Mom and Dad play their Indian records on Sunday mornings. This sitar music is loud and you can feel it through the floorboards vibrating your seat. This music sounds like when someone is hoarse and screaming at the same time.

The eyes swing back and forth in the puppets' heads. The painting of the distorted house catches fire and is burning. A puppet with an ax and a bright red mouth is running around on the stage. The puppets aren't touching the stage but the clopping of their wooden feet keeps getting louder. You can see the wires that work the puppets. The clopping of the wooden puppets on the floorboards of the stage gets louder and louder, battling with the sitar music. You tell Dad that you want to leave. Dad says that it is almost over. June is staring straight at the stage.

You scrunch into the itchy green theater chair. There is a puppet holding a machine, a silver box with gears and knobs. The puppet with the red mouth and ax is flying toward the puppet holding the machine. The noise is so loud your ears hurt.

The stage is burning with red lights, then there is a light as bright as a doctor's office. The ax blade is sharp and needles of light shoot off its edge before it chops at the puppet with the machine held to its wooden chest. There is a headless puppet holding a machine and red liquid splattering everywhere. There is blackness. There is the sound of running water in the blackness. The audience claps and yells.

.   .   .

AT Grandma Green's in her dark house everyone is sitting around the television set: Mom and Uncle Bill, Grandma Green and you and June. Everyone is waiting for the news to come on, waiting to hear about what is happening at San Quentin. Grandpa Green is in there. There was a news flash, Grandma Green called to say, Please Viola, please come. The news flash said that the prisoners had started rioting, and that two guards had been killed. They didn't give names. Grandpa Green is in there.

The Alley of Eden

YOUR mother told you this one day.

Mom says that her maiden name is Green but that it used to be Greenberg. Her father, Grandpa Green, dropped the berg because he didn't want to be associated with his Jewish heritage anymore. Mom says, I think he did it during the war. I could be wrong, Mom says, maybe his father dropped the berg.

Mom is painting. Her brush scratches on the rough canvas.

Why wouldn't Grandpa Green want to be associated with his Jewish heritage? What is Jewish, Mom?

Oh it's a long story. Can you turn the coffee down please? I think it's boiling over.

What is true Mom? Please tell me what is true, where we are and where is it that we must be going. It just seems that something is missing all the time.

Not now Tracy, I'm tired. Not now Tracy.

Souls need to rest.

Is this where you begin to lose track of where you are?

In the dream you are trying to escape, get away from the people that might be spies. These people will tell on you if you aren't following the rules. You can't be sure who are spies and who your friends are. There are rules that you are supposed to be following.

You never can tell when they will come to your house. They are taking people away. You don't know who you can allow into your house.

There is a machine in the street. The machine chops people's bodies up and arranges them for the purpose of the authorities.

The machine looks like a garbage smasher. There are people that just walk in, don't seem to care that their body is about to be crushed into a million pieces.

There are traces of human bodies, hair, flesh, blood, adhered in places to the sides of this machine. Bodies are being tossed around like dolls. When this truck came to your house you knew that you had to get into the back, that you had to go into the crushing mechanism.

You are screaming please don't make me go in there.

You knew that there was nothing you could do, that you would have to figure out how to survive once the gears started and your body was pulled in.

People just refused to question the machine. Some thought it was population control.

Your legs are being crushed but you don't feel anything.

Just your legs, that's all that was crushed.

There is a man walking toward you with a machine gun. Please, just kill me, you say.

You will have to come with me, he says.

Up on the hill thousands of people are roped together like cattle. There are men with guns and bayonets surrounding the mass of roped-in people.

I am with them, I am, just let me go in there, you say.

The men just laugh.

You are in your house, you and the others, the ones that survived.

We will have to go, someone says.

As you are walking down the dirt road, there are people joining you, hundreds of people coming out of the trees, out of other houses.

The survivors.

The sky is ablaze with the smell of fires. There is smoke everywhere.

There are bombs going off, mushrooms of smoke exploding beyond the trees and the mountains.

People laugh or go to the bathroom.

*A small boy is coloring with crayons on a big piece of paper.
Everyone keeps moving.*

. . .

IN Aunt Sarah's room you and June were supposed to be sleeping.

Mom and Dad are away for the weekend.

Grandpa Green says that his brother had numbers carved on his arms, friends of his too, people to never see again, and they went away and there were people that he had lost touch with, had intended to get in touch with and then there is this war and it is really too late and intention made no difference. Grandpa Green doesn't say these things, he yells them. There is loud opera music on the stereo. The television is on but there is no picture, just fuzzy noise. Grandpa Green is yelling about numbers and then he smashes his glass against the fireplace. Grandma Green is just watching. You and June are each holding a side of the purple curtain and through the glass door you can see this. Grandpa Green and Grandma Green are drinking.

Grandpa Green says, damn if I can shower. All I want to do is get clean, to scrub and scrub at my skin, scrub it hard, he yells. How can anyone shower? The pipes, the water could be turned off at any time, gas might be pumped into our house. Shower they did, all naked, just eyes everywhere, seeing and not seeing. I can't even think, Grandpa Green yells. People sometimes, just like setting up a mousetrap. And my brother wrote operas, Grandpa Green yells, operas better than any of these, and no one will ever hear them. Do you hear me, Daphne, Grandpa Green yells. Grandma Green's teeth are out. Grandma Green has knitting needles and yarn in her lap but she is not knitting. Grandma Green is smoking. Grandma Green's eyes are barely open. Grandpa Green has his lips pushed out and his robe is hanging open. Grandma Green and Grandpa Green are both seated in their chairs, big chairs that lean back when the lever on the side is pulled. These chairs are on opposite sides of the living room. June is looking hard and you tell her to stop breathing so loud.

. . .

AT Girl Scout camp up in the woods behind where you live a counselor tells a story about a man who came up to a Girl Scout camp just like this one. He came up to the camp while everyone was sleeping, the counselor says, everyone was sleeping except for one girl. The one girl watched from behind the trees while all the other girls were chopped up into tiny pieces and zipped back into their sleeping bags.

There isn't anything to be afraid of, Mom says. When Dad is not home Mom sleeps with her bedroom light on.

. . .

DAD doesn't mean to do certain things if he knows someone might be watching. Dad's shirt is off because it's too hot in the house. It might be cooler except that June, who was the last person in the house this morning, didn't close the windows and the curtains like you were both told to do. The hot air filled up the house. There's no point in closing the windows now. It is hotter in the house than it is outside.

Dad is typing. Then he picks up the typewriter and throws it on the floor. He picks it up and throws it again. The fucking thing won't stop fighting me, Dad says.

You don't go in there because you know better.

June is in her room drawing. That's all June does some days is draw. June draws pages and pages of birds. June's small body is curled over a sheet of paper. June's pens scratch furiously at the white page until it's covered. June is never satisfied and keeps drawing. There are people sometimes, people running, people building things like space ships and boats. Mostly June draws birds.

Dad is sitting at the desk but his head is in his folded arms. The typewriter with a half-typed page is on the floor. Dad quit his job so he could write. Mom is working at a store that sells art supplies. There is one shelf in the store that has just big big blocks of wax on it.

. . .

I just don't know who I am sometimes. What am I supposed to be doing, just this, cleaning the house, selling embroidery thread and do-it-yourself craft kits? I am painting in a vacuum, Phillip. There are things going on. I need . . .

What can I do then, just tell me what I am supposed to be doing. Dad's eyes get wet when he says things like this, wet like leaves after rain, shiny.

Mom wants to fight. Dad picks up a half-typed page. This is it, Viola. When this is finished things are going to happen.

The whole house smells like the purple flowers in the grape arbor, a sickly smell when it is this hot. The smell of the purple flowers gets in your eyes, you want to hold your nose, the smell is on the roof of your mouth heavy as varnish.

You wish that you could tell them not to fight. You aren't supposed to be listening. You are supposed to be somewhere else.

You used to be afraid that you would swallow your tongue. Afraid that you would be alone when this happened and that no one could hear you cry out for help, because you had swallowed your tongue and couldn't speak. You used to hold the end of your tongue until the fear went away, until you could think of something else.

Your Mom and Dad try to keep their voices low. Then Dad just yells. Dad says, you wanted me to make money so I did. You wanted me to stay at a job I hated, so I did. Before, it was finish school. All I want to do is finish this book.

Dad is walking around the room. Dad is wiping and wiping at his forehead, pushing back his wild hair, then waving his arms like there are flies in the room. Mom is walking behind him, then she is standing at the window.

I need space. I need to go back to school, Mom says.

Please, am I stopping you? Do I prevent you from doing what you want to do? These dreams of yours, Vi. There isn't anything I wouldn't do for you, Dad says.

. . .

WHOSE voice is this? How do you remember? There is never really proof of what happened. There are monuments built or photographs taken. But monuments are built after the fact. Photographs might just be setups, complicated setups performed by highly skilled actors. Who are you anyway? Which voice is yours? You mother's voice is everywhere. Sometimes your father is just a dark figure like the shapes you can make on the wall with your hand held up to the light.

. . .

MOM said that when she first met your father she was only sixteen.

Mom says that when she first met your father she just knew that it was meant to be. Mom says that before you were born she was just empty inside. Mom says that she doesn't want to be alone and that she knows what alone means.

At night your Mom comes into your room and sits on the edge of your bed. Your Mom says, I love you very much, and whatever happens remember that I am in your heart. Your Mom says this and you think first that she might be telling you that tomorrow she will be somewhere else, she will just be gone.

Then you think of Tammy's Mom and wonder did Tammy go into her mother's heart after she drowned. You hold your Mom around the neck. If anything happened to your Mom you would die. You don't want your Mom in your heart. You want your Mom here and now. Mom hugs you tight and you keep holding Mom around the neck, tight so that your head is on her chest. Mom's heart beats beneath her clothes, behind her ribs that you can feel pressing into your cheek. Sometimes things like kissing goodnight, saying, I love you, just happen, keep happening over and over again so that they are like taking a bath or washing your face.

It is hard to believe that people really do go away.

You can't get out of bed. You can't face this. What has happened, what you must understand, your life in relation to your sister's, all this like folding a huge sheet of construction paper many times into a small matchbook-size square, a perfect compact entity that wouldn't under any circumstances unfold, and the creases wouldn't under any circumstance rip or tear in places.

This task of getting from morning to night and back again.

What is holding you?

. . .

At night you dreamt of you and June in the chicken coop. The chicken coop is on fire. You can't get out. The wood in the chicken coop is wet. You pick up the pieces of wood, soggy as wet papier mâché.

In your bedroom you have covered the wall above your bed with snapshots of your family and your friends. You put each picture up with masking tape, pieces of tape that you curled and put on the back of the pictures, sticky on the wall and sticky on the picture so that you can't see the tape, only the snapshots. When it is warm the edges of the snapshots curl and the tape loses its stickiness. Sometimes the snapshots fall and then there is just a space with a piece of curled masking tape still hanging on the bare wall between the rest of the snapshots.

There is a certain picture you want but can't find. You want a picture of the whole family together, a picture of you and June and Mom and Dad. There isn't one. There are pictures of you and June and Dad or you and Mom and June or June and Mom and

Dad. Someone always has to take the picture. There isn't a family portrait. Grandma Hawkins has pictures of the whole family.

. . .

JUNE reads Dad's books. You can't find anything you want to read in Dad and Mom's books. There are some books that you like but nothing to read, only the art books, pictures. One picture book is a massage book that shows hands kneading flesh, and bodies in all positions with hands kneading the flesh. There is one picture in the massage book of glasses lined up upside down all over a lady's back. The glasses are set on the flesh so that the flesh is rising up inside the glasses like mounds of smoothed dirt.

June reads a book called *Mein Kampf.* June says that in the appendix there are the good parts. June says that Adolf Hitler and Nazi Germany is something everyone should know about. June says, when you think about it, it's pretty goddamn funny that people don't know how to leave and go somewhere else.

You tell June that it is pretty goddamn funny that she is reading a book about such awful things.

No. What did you really tell June? You didn't really care what she was reading. You didn't even know who Adolf Hitler was. Just a name then, a person who made Grandpa mad.

SWINGSET

Not the chicken coop. Not June or Teddy or Tammy.

It's the moment; that it's dark, that the house is big and no one is here except for you and little Jamey. Who's to know? You don't even think about who's to know. You don't think. Something about the TV show, a man playing a guitar, his body pumping into the guitar, his face sweaty, his mouth open

wide, wet, saying, touch me. Sweaty and hot. The smell of
Jamey's mother's bed, a dark smell like yeast and wet wood.
Jamey's mother's water bed has the blankets and sheets pulled
back exposing the blue plastic, there is water sloshing around in
there. The trees tickle the side of the house. The house creaks
and moans. You have to go to the bathroom. You'd think you
were in a high place because of how badly you have to go to the
bathroom, in a tree or on a bridge looking down.

Between your legs is tingly. Between your legs says it's here
now.

Brush my hair Jamey, you say. He does this. His thin legs,
white flesh around the kneecaps. His hazel eyes obeying. The
smell of the house, the light in the kitchen flickering and
humming. You are dizzy to not be here or there or anywhere
where no one is home.

It's past Jamey's bedtime the clock says; a black needle
moving around a glowing dial. Jamey brushes your hair. You
are all wet between your legs.

Jamey's mother won't be home until morning. Sleep in my
bed, she said. Make yourself at home, she said. Help yourself to
food, she said.

Jamey says, at school they are learning about sand and how it
gets made. He says that it is ground and ground, big rocks are,
he says.

There is whispering around your head like a soft blue light.
The wind cracks the trees against the house. You are locked in
tight. Something is out there.

Jamey says, sand is so old. You ask him to sit on your lap.
His small body presses into your thighs, bone to flesh. Jamey's
hair is shiny blond, white at the edges. Jamey says he likes it
when you baby-sit.

Jamey has a swingset in his room. Jamey doesn't have a
Dad because his Mom just wanted a baby. Your Mom told you
this.

On your lap is a little boy. Between your legs is wet. On the
TV a man is singing and sweating.

Do you like this? you ask Jamey, rubbing his small shoulders. You move gently beneath him. The water is sloshing in the bed. The backs of your knees are numb against the wood frame of the bed.

Jamey says, did you know that in the spring there is a special day that you can take an egg and stand it upside down and it will just stay that way, upside down? My teacher told us that, Jamey says.

You pull Jamey tighter into your lap. On the back of your eyelids is a burst of green light, then nothing.

Jon tells your best friend Bridgette that he thinks you are pretty, that you and him should go steady. At first you say, no, and then you say, yes. Going steady is something to do. Something better than being at home all day where Dad is surrounded by typed pages. Mom never cleans the house anymore and you don't want your friends to come over.

Out back by the creek Bridgette and her boyfriend and Jon are waiting, they are waiting for you to kiss Jon. You have never kissed a boy before, not this way when it's for real. The branches of the trees that hang down over the creek look like ropes. If you kiss Jon you aren't sure what will happen. His lips are a hundred miles away. Hurry up everyone is saying, just do it.

Dad is getting skinny and his eyes are sinking into his head, his eyes peer out of black circles behind his glasses. Dad types all day and no one can come into the dining room. Mom is painting in the living room now. The house smells like beer and paint and Homer and sometimes like pee.

The garbage in the front yard gets higher and higher because after Dad drove through the front gate one night, it just stayed broken and every night dogs dump over the garbage.

Your house and the Davis's house are the dirtiest houses in Sleepy Hollow.

★   ★   ★

Jon says you are pretty and he presses up against you in his bedroom and you kiss each other for a long time.

Jon wears jeans and his hair is brown and long. Jon kisses you and you just stay there in his bed not thinking about things, just being there.

Jon doesn't have pictures on his wall. Jon's house is dirty and there is never anyone home. It doesn't matter. What matters is that you walk around town together or sit near the creek, always holding hands, or with your arms around each other.

In the mirror you sort of look like each other. In the mirror sometimes both your faces look like melting wax.

Jon catches a crawdad for you because you say they are good to eat. He reaches his hand down through the cold creek water and picks up the crawdad. His jeans are wet. The crawdad has blue and orange on its back. He kills it with a rock. He takes the meat out of its legs. Gross, you say, Jon, you killed it.

On the ropeswing straddled around the big knot you swing out over the creek then back. You look at Jon standing there with the crawdad with one leg pulled off. Jon looks sad then sorry. I thought you wanted to eat this, he says. The rocks under the moving water are shiny.

Jon kisses you with his tongue and you think about drowning.

.   .   .

It was because you told your friend who was also Bridgette's friend that you thought Bridgette's parents were alcoholics. Bridgette found out. She comes over to your house in the afternoon. You are watching TV in the living room, your right leg swung up over the back of the sofa. The doorbell rings. Bridgette just opens the door, her tall adolescent figure fills your head. You know what she is there for.

You're a liar, she yells walking toward you too fast. You pull your leg down over the puffy patterned upholstery, your calf brushing down over appliquéd birds and raised beige flowers.

You don't sit up fully, Bridgette's partially clenched fist and your nose crack like a shorted wire.

You hit me. I'm dying, you scream. Get out of here. Blood is pooling in your hand, the doorway is crowded with teenage girls watching Bridgette, teenage girls watching you, their faces fixed in these expressions like they had just seen an animal tied to a choke chain rush from a porch, its neck snapping, the creature dangling from the porch, a silenced mobile.

Don't you ever talk about my parents like that. Just keep your big fucking mouth shut unless you want more.

Bridgette grabs you again, clenching your arms, her face shaking, teeth tightly clamped. Your arms indent with crescents when she pulls her fingernails. She is raking your arms. She lets go, and underneath her long sky-blue fingernails is your flesh, like the white underskin of an orange.

Dad says he is sorry that it happened. Mom says what is important is that you are honest and no one likes the truth because it gets in the way. June says it served you right Tracy.

Bridgette was your best friend. You made a papier-mâché Buddha together in school for an art project, a Buddha painted with gold spray paint. It looked like a giant frog but you made it together.

Bridgette called you a liar. Bridgette let you show her massage that you learned from a book. Beneath your hands her developing breasts said touch me.

Bridgette's Dad slapped her at school. She said, come to see the Buddha we made, Dad. He stumbled across the blacktop and slapped her in front of the whole seventh-grade class because she hadn't made her bed.

In Jon's bedroom you lay together until it gets dark outside. There is nothing to be talked about with Jon. You just hold each other under the covers making the feeling between your legs go away.

. . .

DAD is out in the front yard. First he chops down all the blackberry bushes. Then he chops down the lemon tree and the two orange trees. Dad's hair is wild and his eyes are sunk into his head. His collarbones stick out too far. Lately Dad only types, day and night.

Mom is standing behind him. Dad is saying, What don't I do? You sleep on the fucking couch, he says. It's almost finished. I am on the final chapter. I am almost finished. I can see the end finally. You can't do this now Viola, he says. He is carrying tangles of blackberry bush and shoving them into the garbage cans. He is not wearing a shirt and the blackberry bushes scratch his arms, hands and chest. There are white scratches and veins of blood. Dad is crying. Mom's face is white.

Then Mom just starts in, saying things. Your hands sweat listening and you wish that you could figure out where to go.

You aren't supposed to be watching. You aren't supposed to hear what your Mom is yelling out there in the front yard. You aren't sure then where you are supposed to be. You live in this house and your parents are in the front yard. Where is June?

What are men for? Mom says. Dad is pulling at things in the yard again or cutting things, looking at what he hasn't already cut or what he has, walking around the yard, crying, walking like he doesn't know where he is or what he is supposed to be doing with Mom yelling and saying things.

You like me too much Phillip. I don't want to be adored. Go away for a while will you, then I might want you again.

You hear Mom's voice now from beneath you. She must be sitting on the front stairs. You can hear Mom's voice and see Dad moving through the yard. Dad's arms have blood on them from the blackberry bushes.

Cars drive by. People just like to look.

What do we do? Where do we go? What is anything for? I am afraid. Trap each other, that's what we did, prevented each other from doing anything with our lives. I helped you to escape, you helped me and here we are. Here I am this close to my parents again. Trapped.

Dad is standing in the ivy. Dad turns on the hose and rinses his arms.

You know that all the neighbors must be watching. You know that all the neighbors will ask you, how are things at home? You wish you could put a curtain around your parents out there in the front yard. Through the window.

Listen Tracy, June is saying, I am not just making this up. Their father, there was two of them, girls, and the father killed each one of them in the house, and no one found out about it until a dog dug them up in the backyard, half bones and rotting. Anna Lea babysits there and when I went with her once I heard it myself. Late at night you can hear them scream, no, Mommy, don't leave.

Then why would anyone live in that house, June? I don't believe you. There is no such thing as ghosts, you say wishing that Anna Lea would hurry up and come so that June would leave.

There are bloodstains in the basement, June says. I saw it with my own eyes.

All you ever hear about is the horrible things that men do. Fathers? There was a man in the park that followed you. There was a man in the car asking you for directions. A man in a car rubbing in his lap the biggest thumb you ever saw. You start getting dizzy.

June has her leg swung up over the back of the sofa. Her eyes look black. She moves closer to you, leans so that the whites of her eyes show underneath the black. Her forehead is wrinkled.

You stare back at June and don't look away. She doesn't look away. The house is quiet except for the sound of your breathing and June's breathing and your heart beating so loud that you hope she can't hear.

I move into you Tracy. When a person stares at another person with the right power they can move right into them. It happens every day, all day long, people looking at each other, merging.

JUST give me one good reason why we can't make this work? Dad says.

I can't, Mom says.

There is a loud crash and then another. There are three loud crashes. Dad says, this is all I ever thought of these goddamn books.

You have to pee but you don't want to go out there. You wait. You can't go back to sleep.

In the hallway you can see Mom picking up the book, dusting the books off, and putting the books in neat stacks on the floor. Mom does this carefully. Mom looks like a little girl. The metal bookcases are still on the living-room floor making a grid on the carpet.

In your dream there is a library. In this library people aren't reading books. In this library people are accusing each other of lying, of committing violent crimes. Everyone is guilty except for those doing the accusing. Then the chase starts. The chase always ends at a racetrack where people are watching oily black engines drag people around and around the track until someone blows up.

Dad is staying in a motel.

Mom said, if you don't like it then you can leave.

Mom's eyes are hard, like thumbtacks. Mom says, there is the door, if you don't like it you can pack your bags and leave too. There is no one stopping you, Mom says. June left. You slam your bedroom door. The hallway shakes.

Dad got an apartment next to the freeway. June went with him. It's dusty in there, dusty and sad. Dad's statue of Don Quixote looks out the window to cars. Dad doesn't have a real bed. Dad and June sleep on the couch that pulls out into a bed, a mattress through which the springs and support bars can be felt.

Dad put his book in the basement. Dad put all the pages in boxes in the basement. Your father and I don't love each other anymore, your mother says. Dad didn't say this, Mom did.

At night you can hear the panting and moaning, Mom crying out, yes, then no.

You just stand there in front of the open door. You are looking at Mom standing in front of the open door. Her hair is braided. The braid comes over her shoulder like a snake. She is carrying a painting under her arm. The painting with the blue-and-gray background. It is a painting of a woman with teeth like a vampire and no eyes.

.   .   .

It doesn't matter how old you are. There is just that time when you realize that it is you in this body and not another one and that there is no one to make anything just go away.

If not now, then when? Dad I can't breathe, you said.

Dad I don't feel like I am in my body. Dad I am dying. You say this to your father and he is sitting on the couch because Mom is at school. The TV is on and there is this lady sitting next to Dad, this lady who Mom says is going to help you and June take care of the house because your parents are going to go away for a few days. You know that she is really going to watch you and June, a baby-sitter.

The lady looks at you and her face is like hard wax, pale, a half-smile just fixed there. She wears a long skirt made out of jeans that have been cut up and sewed back together. She wears a peach-colored gauze shirt. She wears a small gold cross around her neck. She wears clogs. She has pimples. She doesn't know anything. She just came here. She doesn't say anything. She just sits there.

Dad is sitting on the couch waiting. The lady with the face like wax who is going to watch you and June even though no one ever watches you really is sitting next to your father on the couch waiting.

You start. I went out for a walk today Dad. You are talking but your voice doesn't sound like your own it sounds far away. I was walking through the town and up the street. I can't explain it Dad. Your hands are sweating. Your stomach feels like you might throw up but it is empty. All of a sudden Dad, you say. All of a sudden I just had this feeling that I wasn't in my body that I might just disappear and I was trying to make this feeling go away, trying to not feel like I was dreaming but to feel real, awake, solid, and not all fuzzy. I was trying to make everything feel normal. I was trying to make the olive trees look like olive trees, be olive trees and to know that it was me walking on a street in front of this house. Dad keeps sitting there. He is looking at you with his hollow eyes like he is trying to pretend that nothing is wrong. The baby-sitter lady looks like wax. Daddy? You walk toward him on the couch and hug him and it's as if you were hugging the couch because he doesn't let you melt there in his arms. He is here, you are here, there is a big space between. Dad pats you on the back and you can smell his neck. You press your nose into his neck and he keeps patting you on the back. You just want to lie on his lap and cry, and you aren't crying. You can see your face in Dad's glasses when you look. Where is June? June is your sister. June doesn't live here anymore. She is in her room now because Mom and Dad are going away somewhere. People say one thing and then they do something else. Your throat is tight like a fist. All day you felt like you might swallow your tongue and you counted your breathing in and out. All day you feel like you can't wake up.

In the shower through the curtain, through the steam and water bubbles hanging on the plastic you can see your parents in there. They are standing in the tub. Shut the door. You can't.

Your Mom's legs are wrapped around your Dad like a baby's. You shut the bathroom door but you still hear it, the water running and running, your Mom crying and whimpering like Homer when he wants to go out. Your Dad's butt is squeezing tight back and forth. There is grunting.

There is nothing to hold on to. Your Mom's arms in the bathroom, in the shower pushing at the walls and the curtain then at your Dad's back, pulling her legs around tighter.

Mom and Dad are going away to try and work on some things, Mom says. Dad just looks pale and cold.

Dad says, it's OK Tracy, it's OK.

Mom says, There's the door. And so you leave and walk through town and then up and down the street in front of your house like you are floating in water. You feel as though maybe someone has hypnotized you and forgotten to snap you out of the trance. Other kids aren't walking up and down the street. They are inside where their parents have everything set up for them to be just kids and not this.

June is in her bedroom. June lives with Dad now. June says she couldn't care less, one way or the other what Mom and Dad do.

June is sick with tonsillitis.

You think you might be dying.

You try again. Dad, why do I feel this way? Why do I feel that I could just disappear? The lady who is going to stay with you and June has her head tilted and you would like to just push it right off.

You tell Dad about the olive trees, about how they look just put there and fake, how they line the street like the plastic plants in the lizard tank that June had.

June left the lizard tank outside and forgot about it. There were just lizard bones, June said. The plastic trees stayed until June threw them over the fence into the Davis's swimming pool.

Dad doesn't say anything except that everything will be OK. The corners of his mouth twitch.

Out the window you can see the olive trees. There are

shadows beneath the trees, long shadows that point away from the street.

For a minute you keep looking at the olive trees, at the shadows pointing away from the street. Your breath makes a round fog on the window glass. Outside the sky is the color of apricots over the trees at the edge of the blue. The sky that doesn't go up and up but looks like a lid. Apricot. Olive-green. Blue.

In the bay tree a family of squirrels lives. One is very big and the other two are very small. The concrete around the bottom of the big bay tree in front of the house is erupting in slabs.

All of a sudden you are dizzy and remember that Dad doesn't really live here anymore. You are talking to Dad but you can't remember what it is that you were talking about. Mom has a new boyfriend just like that. He has red eyes like Bridgette's Dad and kissed Mom under the bay tree.

In the shower there were hands and pushing. Something being caught and something trying to get away at the same time.

You are dying and there is nothing you can do about it. You can't go to sleep because that's when you might disappear. You can't stay awake because then you have to figure out what is happening to you.

There are things that are supposed to happen, a plan that is going on. What makes you mad is that people just do things and you can't always be sure if they like what they are doing. You can't always be sure what they are thinking, like with Bridgette, like with Mom. People just do things and inside of them it's something different than what they are doing.

June is in her bed just lying there. In June's bedroom that used to be yours too, June is lying in her bed with the covers up to her neck. Her brown eyes move but that is all that moves. June looks like a mummy under the covers. June is scaring you and she knows it, moving her eyes back and forth.

In June's room you can hear the bees in the grape arbor, a hum like a chain saw being used far away. There are people that keep bees and never get stung. If your mother gets stung she can't breathe.

At first Dad said he would take down the grape arbor so they wouldn't come, the bees. Mom said, no, she said it wouldn't help. Later she screamed at Dad and said why didn't you take them down?

June says she can see the bees working. You tell June, no she can't because she isn't looking out the window. June says she can and then she closes her eyes and moves her eyes under the lids back and forth.

June says that when she gets better she is leaving, leaving Dad's, going somewhere. Why, June? Don't leave. I am afraid. But you don't say that. You just think that: a voice in your head that isn't yours, like how you felt looking out the window at the olive trees, and how you felt talking to your father.

There is splashing in the pool next door. The Davis's house smells like diapers and is dirty. Next door there is just a mom and four kids. Mrs. Davis works all day and when she comes home there is yelling. Sonya, Pam's big sister, baby-sat once, but she stole some of your parents' records and drank beer in the house and then told people that your parents had drugs and orgies. It doesn't matter what people say about your parents. The neighbors talk to you no matter what. You know that you are different from your parents, that sometimes kids get accidentally put with parents that are wrong.

June says, don't move Tracy, there is a shadow on your face that makes you look like a devil. June, her brown eyes in a white face with a dirty orange blanket up to her neck. The blanket moves up and down as she breathes.

The mural Mom painted when you first moved here isn't pretty anymore. You and June scribbled all over it with lipstick, crayons, felt pens, dirty fingers, snot. It just happened slowly, then Mom said go ahead, draw on the closet but nowhere else.

On the wall in your room are snapshots; pictures of the

family on trips (but not all together), of the grandparents, of you, of June, lots of little faces looking out.

You ask June if she wants a washrag for her forehead. June says No she doesn't want a washrag for her forehead.

Big Herb is Mom's new boyfriend and he is in the hospital. Big Herb is in the hospital because he broke his neck. Big Herb broke his neck falling off his motorcycle right behind your house on the other side of the creek like an omen. It is like an omen because your Dad is the one that saw Big Herb walking down the street all covered with blood. Help me, Big Herb said to your father. Your father didn't know this huge man, covered with blood, had kissed your Mom under the bay tree. Now Big Herb is in the hospital with holes drilled in the side of his head because he is attached to weights that keep his spine still.

Your Dad found Big Herb. First your Dad was at the house because he was getting his book that is in boxes. He was putting the boxes in the van and then he saw Big Herb with a broken neck. Mom visits Big Herb at the hospital because after your Dad took him there then it all made sense.

Mom is in the living room now and you think to run out there and tell her that she is a slut and that you don't care that Big Herb is in the hospital and that you would like to know when Mom is going to tell Dad about kissing Big Herb under the bay tree. Instead you go out and tell Dad in front of the baby-sitter with Mom standing by the door, you tell Dad that Mom was kissing Big Herb under the bay tree. You scream that she is a slut. You don't do this at all. You are standing by the window looking out at the olive trees and Mom says, how long are you going to look out that window? You are dizzy. Sometimes people look like dolls and their faces are poses like their mouths and arms were being moved with invisible wires.

You go to your room.

Mom is saying that June is fine and needs to have her medicine in an hour. June is not fine and neither are you, but you just whisper this to the wall of tiny faces, eyes.

Dad is writing a book and it is about growing up in America, it is about love and how people can make so much out of nothing, Dad said. He says, someday you can read it but not now. You want to read it now because you want to know.

The last time you were in the basement looking for the book and looking for the love letters your Mom and Dad had written to each other that your Mom said you could read someday when she was dead, you found a letter your Dad had written. It was a letter to the insurance company saying he couldn't work for them anymore that he was sorry but he needed to write only and that he hoped they understood this. The letter said that he was sorry but he felt like finishing his novel would be a greater contribution to his generation than what he was doing. He wrote that he just couldn't go on anymore. The letter was written like he was writing to his father, personal, not like a letter written by a man in a suit and a crisp white shirt. What your father did.

The baby-sitter comes into your room and asks if you would like to talk. She says your room is pretty and that she likes how you have decorated. She sits carefully on the edge of the bed. Her eyes look wet this close. She tells you about God and believing and how she is saved now. She tells you she wants to take you to church with her.

You say yes, you want to go.

Tracy. Tracy. The baby-sitter is shaking you and there is an ironing board in front of you. I wasn't going to wake you up, she says. She is talking really fast. You want to know why you are standing in the living room in front of the ironing board. It is dark outside. She is talking really fast and her face is white:

I watched you come from your room, go to the kitchen and I called out your name but you didn't answer. You got the ironing board from behind the refrigerator and then came out with it and you looked at me but not like I was sitting here, and you set up the ironing board and smoothed the cloth and kept smoothing the ironing board cover and kept staring at me and then you closed your eyes but kept smoothing at the cover. I was trying to wake you up. They say it is dangerous to wake up a sleepwalker.

Your head hurts. There were olive trees and then Dad is in the living room, first he is in the orange rocking chair and then he is on the couch. June had a blanket up to her neck. Mom said, you can leave. In the shower there were drops of water on the clear plastic curtain. Mom kissed Big Herb. Big Herb is in the hospital. Sometimes people's faces are wax. Sometimes people's eyes are wet and not from crying but from kindness. There are no bees but crickets. The baby-sitter put away the ironing board. She wants to take you to church. You want to go.

. . .

It doesn't matter what you are fighting about. It's the fighting, who is stronger. While you were doing things with Jon, June has been learning how to fight wherever it is that she goes.

There are dirty dishes in the sink.

You are a fucking bitch. Bridgette should have killed you that time, June says. You are a goddamn hypocrite and a liar.

You have June by both arms. She has the butcher knife.

I'm going to kill you.

The knife falls on the floor and you kick it.

You told June that you know what she does, where she sneaks off to at night when your Dad is at work. You told June that you were going to tell Dad and that he'd have her put away. You told June that you thought that her boyfriend who is almost as old as your Dad is probably a rapist or a pimp. You told June that she was too young to be hanging out in the Canal, that prostitutes and drug addicts hang out where you saw her and Anna Lea. She said, go to hell. She said, if you only knew what I do. You said, it's your turn to do the dishes. She slaps you. You slap back. There was screaming and then she had the knife.

You and June are fighting on the kitchen floor. Homer is

locked in June's bedroom, jumping at the door and barking. The floor is sticky. June has your head and is banging it against the cupboard under the sink. You have your hands not near June's gnashing teeth, but on her stomach. You want June dead. She won't get off you. Her stomach. Her teeth. Metal. Wood. June is pushing your head farther into the sink cupboard. Her stomach. Her breast. Your teeth go into her breast. The flesh breaks.

The screams are so loud that Pam Davis is in the kitchen and some man who pulls the two of you apart, stubborn as an oyster, bodies filled with adrenaline, separating two sisters.

· · ·

In the kitchen Mom was sitting on Grandma Green's lap. There is a cigarette burning, the blue smoke rising in a straight line to the ceiling. Grandma has her arms around Mom. Mom is crying into her hands. Grandma's mouth hangs open like it won't ever shut. Her eyes look like she is stuck on something, a geometry problem. When she sees you standing in the doorway she says, you're never too old to sit on your mother's lap. Her cigarette, her hands that have sores that never stop itching. You're never too old, she says.

· · ·

When Susan drove up in her yellow bug you were shuffling around under the olive trees.

Mom said, where are you going? You told her church and she laughed. Church with lonely crazy Susan, she said.

Susan takes her Bible off the seat. There are dots of oil on her nose and pieces of her bangs are stuck on her forehead. She says, I am glad you wanted to come.

Susan had told you that her church was a place of miracles. She had said, sitting on your bed, that if you pray maybe God will bring your parents back together. She said that when she

120

turned to Jesus she knew that eventually Jesus would give her everything she needed.

Susan has scars on her wrists that show under her long-sleeved blouse. She finishes her cigarette and lights another one.

Scars are something to believe. To see the sacredness of life in skin that is pinched together in places like piecrust or the lip of a ceramic vase, to see this skin on a person is to realize how difficult it is to make anything go away.

Susan has a yellow ribbon in her hair that is the same color as the car. At a red light Susan looks at you and says she has been thinking about you. She looks at you funny. She swallows hard and her eyes glisten. You just have to believe, she says.

You aren't sure what she is talking about. Mom was laughing.

The church looks like a doctor's office from the outside. You see your reflection walking toward the glass doors. You remember Mrs. Morrison and how she lied about June's bathing suit.

Susan picks up a little girl in pajamas that are safety-pinned together in the front where the zipper is broken. The little girl's eyes are dull blue. The little girl's fingernails are dirty. Snot is dried on the little girl's nose.

See in there is the playroom, Susan says. Through a glass window that small hands have smeared near the bottom you can see: red plastic steps for climbing on, some broken dolls and one with no head, and a diaper-changing table with a blue checked cover on it. Susan says, there is a speaker in there so whoever is watching the kids can hear the service.

There are people in the room where the service will be. People standing in front of white folding chairs on the gray shiny floor. The chairs aren't in rows.

The little girl is in Susan's arms, then Susan puts her down. The little girl is sitting on the floor.

There is a lady in a green-and-orange large triangle-patterned dress. She moves a white chair to sit next to you. She says, you are in the right place that is for sure honey. She laughs. Her teeth are brown and crooked. She rocks back and forth in her seat. Her fingers are yellow. She smells like rotting food. During the service she smiles at you. During the service she takes your hand and holds it. You look over at Susan but her eyes are closed. The lady in the green-and-orange dress holds your hand tighter. Susan's face starts to look like wax again.

The voices in the church aren't just amens and thank you Jesuses anymore. The voices are getting weird. You feel like you have a fever. You feel dirty and that you should shower. The preacher is looking straight at you. The lady is squeezing your hand. Susan is moaning. The lady squeezing your hand is mumbling. The lady's eyes are rolled back into her head and her eyelids are fluttering. The lady screams. No one looks at her. The voices in the room sound like panting and moaning: Hear me Jesus, Oh yes, Your way is my way, I am yours. You shut your eyes for a second. With your eyes shut you feel like you are in a hole being covered with dirt.

Susan has her eyes shut.

The preacher says everyone hold hands.

You tell Mom that in church everyone holds hands in a big circle. Mom says, that's nice. You don't tell her that everyone in church looked sick and scared, dead. You don't tell Mom that the two people's hands that you held in the circle were sweaty and slippery.

. . .

So you had to say it. Go away Dad, just go.

You swim every day. Not with Grandma Hawkins like in Old Saybrook, but alone. Blue terry towel, uncracked books, your head getting harder and tighter. It was since you had seen your reflection in your father's eyes. It was since you forgot where you were. It was since you have come to believe that the only thing that matters is getting from one place to the next without having to think about anything specific.

There are voices in your head that don't go away, other

people's voices. At night you dream of wet toilet paper clinging to your fingers in gluey strands. You are supposed to be making something?

You think you remember how it started. Dad comes back. He says, lets play a game of twister on your multicolored dotted dress. It's a dream? You say no we can't now. Lips are like lids. Dad's hands have blue veins that tickle. No, we can't? People do things different than what they are saying. You knew then even better than you know now, that sometimes things that are uncomfortable to look at come out of your skin, small white, pus like clots, hard and persistent as sand.

There is Mom. There is June. It's OK, you can touch them if you like. They are just breasts, your Mom says.

The nipple is hard and big like June's toe when you bit it once. Mom's nipple is brown and you rub your hand on her breast and so does June.

In the dream again.

Which is awake?

This.

Will you squeeze this? your father asked. Spreading his legs as wide as possible on the bed you lean forward so he can see the inflamed blister on your shoulder. You want to wake up and can't.

Do you love me? your father asked.

Why is that always such an impossible question?

You have resolved, the blister still pulsating, a dull pain that is something to focus on, to pursue simple things, so you remain half-curled in pale green sheets for the rest of the summer; sheets as cool as words when Mom told Dad she doesn't love him anymore. Words. Sheets.

You told your Dad that sometimes you think that from between your legs you will lose your mind and his Daddy voice said: What can I do? I want to help. Just let me know what I can do.

You tell him. Screaming, but not to anyone's face. This. Screaming across a desert. Your throat is dry.

The sheets are an opiate. When the window is open wide and the curtains are flicking across your legs, you can imagine that Grandma Hawkins's house is floating through space clean and fast, a light-speed journey that no one has to know about. If you just forget about what happened it will go away.

Even though the humidity is as thick as shortening you prefer the rosy lavender sky this way. The rosy lavender sky that is all ribbed with orange neon. No, I am not angry, you say.

You are just not thinking of it anymore. You are not thinking of the charcoal rubbings you and June might make of all the chafings between people's legs, your legs. You are tired of thinking about making those rubbings.

Lying in the sun, your body contracts with heat. You wipe the sweat from your forehead; feel it running down between your breasts, water oozing out of every skin crease and pore. Melting.

Is it always summer then?

And then you are there again because you have to remember. You are trying to get out but your head is still pressed against his chest. Marvin. Your father?

Nothing but images in your head that join and separate, like how a story can be told with a film strip, frame by frame.

A man's stomach pressing hard against your back.

Whose?

Which is love?

If you touch me I don't understand, you say in your head, you say in your head, not remembering. You are trying to get out but your head is still there, pressed against his chest.

Your father's hands were stroking your shoulder blades. His eyes were closed. Your face in his glasses, looking down at your belly button. Skin on skin.

You can't tell anyone what it is like because you don't know.

When there was an earthquake, the furniture shook and you were certain because you had heard this once, you were certain that the tube inside the TV would break and suck all the air out of the room. The room was shaking so you went to the TV and held it steady.

When your Dad was on June you could see the black hairs
that ringed his nipples.

Do you love me? your Dad asked.

Your father's hands were stroking your shoulder blades. His
eyes were closed. Not Marvin, Dad. People are somewhere else
when their eyes are closed. Your face in Dad's glasses looking
down at wide open eyes.

You couldn't tell anyone what it was like then. Now, wrapped
again in another summer, your belly weighted with emptiness
like a rope-netted fishing buoy of olive glass, now you have to
speak.

Marvin. It felt like right before you are going to throw up,
him on top of you, or getting beat up by your best girlfriend.

You know how to make yourself throw up now. And
afterward, your face in the mirror, reflected backward of
course, a smeared otherness until you remember that it is you
there purging up all the wrong things for no one.

*These things that make you so angry, so angry you are numb. To
make your flesh disappear, this is what you wish, to make desire and
anger go away.*

*There is a soul that screams into the night, tears at the flesh of the
bodies that try to engulf it, because you don't allow yourself to seek
solace, be comfortable at all in this body, your own house.*

Water drips from your red eyes. The corners of your mouth
twitch. Your lips are hued blue. Your face is pale. It's a helpless
feeling of satisfaction. Control. You alone in the bathroom,
standing over the toilet. You look down at the bowl where
strands of saliva in slippery swirls like hardening glue weave
slowly around masses of partially digested food.

You try to hold still.
Sometimes remembering is like trying to stir muddy water clear.

. . .

OUT past the fish house a swimmer slices through the green-gray water; arms splitting an undetected pattern in the murk. It is happening again, as urgent as your blister, as marked as the olive trees that line the streets where you live. That swimmer gliding unseen. You are going to scream. You are delirious to tell someone what that swimmer is doing out there alone in the ocean. No one is watching.

Forgetting.

You can hear the swishing of the swimmer's arms digging and pulling through the water. Sperm makes that sound as it shoots through the dark, so does the splitting of the nucleus of an atom. You hear it. You'll remember that motion. The increasing whir amplifies in your ears. Then you smell the tar of black asphalt, the laundry-room walkway rushing toward a head that momentarily becomes the size of a pin on impact.

Let me go, you said to Marvin, but not loud.

Your forehead bulging furiously in your father's eye.

Mom, tell her I'm going to give her a boatride. You raise your head. The swimmer is gone. The voice, a sing-song, is coming from the girl, Tammy, that lives next door to your grandmother. She is half submerged in the water. She is struggling to drag her little sister into the lake.

Dionne, the mother's name is Dionne.

Donna the little girl with blond hair is the one that Grandma likes, the one Grandma says there is hope for if she can leave Raynes by some stroke of luck. You pretend you are asleep. What do you have to say to this family, this family that is a home for the devil, in all their ignorant ways? Two little girls that go to an all-white Christian academy two towns away from here.

Dionne was born in Raynes, Grandma said.

Where is there to go?

They will have to leave soon, because there is a baby turning red on a blanket next to Dionne.

Leave her alone and please find a way to entertain yourself, says the girls' mother, a large woman in a floral print housecoat.

She is reclined in a lawn chair that is on the edge of the lake. She is wearing a straw sun hat and smoking a cigarette. Her toes are dipping in and out of the water.

The baby, what about the baby?

Every time you raise your head Donna is looking at you.

Donna, now alone in the water, turns from her mother and sister on the shore. She is standing waist-high in the green water, a clear plastic tube around her middle. She is suspended there like something in formaldehyde.

You have a body that grows, a body that you remember being different. There used to be no hair between your legs. You remember this.

You remember wondering when you would grow up. Now you have a body that is mature, that is marked for nurturing life. Yet inside you still feel the same, the same as before you knew there was this reason for this body.

Inside you feel the same as you always have, long for something you still name. You are looking for something you can't seem to find because you don't know what it is. You remember looking before.

This longing and the longing you remember and the longing you see in others. It has not changed as your body has changed. Now there are just more names that you know of, names that pretend to describe what is inside, names to place on the longing.

This longing, what it is to be alive? And the names you have for the longing, what is inside that doesn't change as your body changes or the names to show you who you are: rich, poor, black, white, male, female, Catholic, bored, afraid, angry, sad, loving, loved, God? These names don't change the longing, the names are just a choice someone has made and you can change the names if you want to.

. . .

IT was August. There is no one to make it stop. Alone most of the summer, you and June. Dad is not here. Mom is in school.

You are lying in a hammock. The rust-colored hammock is attached at one end of the house. The other end of the hammock is attached to the bay tree. The tree is older than the house.

The scratchy weave of the hammock is indenting warped graphs around your half-naked body.

It was a Sunday when your Father hammered that hook into the house. He stands on a ladder and drives the iron nail into the graying wood. The wood seems to groan from underneath the curls of white peeling paint. The wood of the bay tree is soft and the hook went in easier.

This hammock hanging from house to tree holds you. If you hold your breath it remains motionless. There is no breeze. It is hot.

It hits you that there will be a time when you won't be here anymore, gone, and you wonder again like you wondered before how you would go about telling people where you had gone. You don't want to just die. You want to make sure that someone knows where you are. You wonder if you would know that you were the same person from life to life, and how you could leave yourself signs to know this. You would first want to reach the people you loved if you were to die. You would want to tell these people if you had come back as someone else tell them how to find you. You think it is about forgetting. There has to be a way to not forget. You think about your body as a costume. It is so hard to find the people that you really belong with.

You wish to be dead for a while so that you would know what it was like and not be afraid.

The next thing you know lying here in the hammock is that you can't remember why it is Wednesday. You can't remember why you are here. You can't remember why there is this constant clicking in your ears like fancy earrings. You aren't wearing earrings. This clicking like so many snapping fingers makes your skin cold. You start breathing fast. You are not getting air. You lunge toward the side of the house. Your face flashing slow motion in the dark basement window. Your back

curving in spasms. You retch violently. Nothing comes up.
You crumple. The dirt smells of cat shit. The brittle geraniums
poke at your legs.

Your mother's hands have these big blue veins that climb up
her arms like heavy cords.

I'm sorry it hurts, she says.

. . .

MOM was standing in the driveway, her arms to her chest like
she was holding something. She looks hard at Dad. They don't
say goodbye.

Mom said, it will be special to go on a trip just you and your
father and June. How lucky you are, she said, I never got to go
on special trips with my Dad.

What is Mom doing that she can't come? Big Herb has a
broken neck. The garbage is spilled. Mom kicks at the garbage,
drags her feet through the gravel like she is walking on a beach.
A can rolls under the fence where the blackberry bushes used to
be. She keeps her arms to her chest.

June is tapping at the van window. June is singing, Let me
sleep all night in your soul kitchen. June's voice is gravelly.
Where Mom is standing on the pebbles by the garbage pail there
is a swarm of gnats moving back and forth. The air is still and
hot. Homer is running around and around the bay tree, his
chain dragging on the cement then pulling taut.

Dad sits at the wheel about to say something. Still with his
eyes closed, Dad sits at the wheel.

Mom scrunching through the pebbles, shuffling garbage
around with her arms to her chest, Dad still. You just want to
go there, to Disneyland or wherever.

We're off, Dad says. Damn right, June says. Can I smoke?
she asks, lighting her cigarette, then putting the match out on
her tongue.

Déjà vu, June says, everything over and over again.

★ ★ ★

June is back from a special school. Dad got her back. She called Dad from the school and said there was a man there that was coming into her room at night. She said the school was no good, couldn't she just come home and try again. It's not the things that June said that got her there, what Dad says is genius and everyone else says is crazy; that June tells people she can see the future and knows what is going to happen to people before it happens. The court suggested June go to this school. One night June stole a car and drove around Sleepy Hollow. She beat up the Chinese man in the 7-Eleven, called him a chink, smashed the window. She didn't remember doing these things. She blacked out, she said.

She was put in the school to reform her and get her off drugs.

Dad went to get her, told the courts he would take care of her, that it wouldn't happen again. One more chance, they said.

June was in school for two months.

June wrote to tell you that at the Cherokee River Reform School she had devised a language so that she could talk to the other girls there without the staff knowing what it was that they were talking about, what it was that they were planning.

There's something wrong, June wrote. There's something wrong with all of us being here in this school because there is nothing any more wrong with most of us in here than there is wrong with the people that put us here and keep us here.

The language I have devised confuses them, June wrote. It baffles them how we can contort ordinary language and can understand each other. The staff can separate us and still we do things they don't know about. They are the outsiders.

What things do they do? What language?

You don't write back to June. You are too busy.

When it was her birthday, you and Mom and Dad drove there to see her. Mom and Dad didn't talk to each other the whole way.

June just smoked, opened up her presents and glared at you and Mom. She said, Tracy, you always have been Mom's favorite, that's very nice, isn't it. She told Dad she didn't need to be in this school anymore. She wouldn't do drugs, she said, and if she wasn't doing drugs she would know what she was doing all the time. She told Dad she didn't need to be here any more than anyone else. She said, this therapy is horseshit. They don't even have families. They're queer or divorced or still living at home themselves. The therapists need therapy, she said. Fuck, the whole goddamn society needs therapy, she said. It's such a lot of lying, hell, the therapists are shaking, have sweaty hands all the time, smoke too much, their offices filled with books. They tell me about how nice their little families are and you know it's horseshit. They tell me I just need to follow the rules, change my behavior, take responsibility for myself, behave myself and behave like them. Dad you got to get me out of here. Behave like who? Am I supposed to act a certain way so that I can have a nice pretty nothing life, have a nice husband, have nice babies. Is that all there is? The world is such a fucking nice place isn't it. Dad's eyes are wet. Mom is fidgeting. June is smart and mean. You just want to hold her but June hates you.

It's a lot of crap, people have everything hog-assed back-wards, June says. June snuffs out her cigarette on the gold-foil wrapping paper that she tore off the hair dryer Mom gave her.

June says, did you ever stop to think that all these people driving by, each one of them, thinks that what they are doing is important? June is chewing on her fingernails. Did you ever stop to think that no one really cares about the next person really? Think about it Trace.

Dad is trying to get a radio station.

You think about Old Saybrook, the hammock, the blisters, about how Grandma Hawkins is probably swimming in the harbor. Grandma makes things smell nice; she always hangs the laundry outside to dry and it smells like wildflowers, something clean and white, smells like hugging. You unstick yourself from the vinyl seat. Grandma has a big garden. Grandma cleans Grandpa's Doctor's office, the shiny gray-and-white floor with something that smells like lemon.

I can't wait until I get my own car, June says.

Grandma, something could happen to Grandma, she is so far away. All of a sudden you want Dad to stop the car, here on the highway heading toward Southern California, here in front of this big wooden plank fence in front of the drive-in movies. Now, because something is wrong, something that should be figured out before you go any farther. You are dizzy and there is ringing in your ears. A drop of blood moves down June's arm from where she picked a sore. People miss each other somehow, these people driving by in cars, why won't you ever know that young man who just drove past or that old woman sleeping in the backseat of that white Cadillac? You wish June would stop humming. You want Dad to cry at least or scream, his eyes beneath his glasses so dark. His hands bony.

This feeling, too much adrenaline, nothing to do with it, like being all alone at night in a dark shifting house. The sun goes through the windshield, June picking at the scab inside her arms, needle marks and bruises, Dad moving his lips occasionally to mouth something he must have wanted to say to someone before. In front of a fruit stand you wish Dad would stop the car, but what reason would you give him?

Last night you dreamt of Dennis, blond Dennis who used to excite you; hands to thighs, hands up the skirt, under the desk in junior high school. In the dream you and Dennis were in the corridors of the high school. The corridors were empty, just rows and rows of metal lockers, no doors anywhere. Dennis appeared.

You talked for a long time about how much fun the carnival was, about how he was going to be a great drummer and you the lead singer in a band. Then you realized the corridors were dark.

There was water rising up around your ankles. Dennis touches your face and his hands are cold. You realize that Dennis is dead and that you too must be dead because here you are talking to each other. There is water up to your knees.

Orion, he said, look for it. You woke up. The tiny faces of all the snapshots on your wall looking down at you.

At the county carnival you had seen the whirling rides, neon colors against the night sky behind Dennis's head. You are drunk, you had said to him. But I am having so much fun, he said.

Two days later on a blistering hot Saturday, the street in front of Hanson's funeral parlor was crowded with somber faces of people waiting to squeeze into the chapel to say goodbye to the wax body of Dennis, the high school Principal's son.

Two weeks before school is going to start again.

Is summer over yet.

Dreams.

Through the windshield the heat waves flicker always the same distance from the front of the car. The heat waves like a calm surf moving onto the beach. The highway disappearing into a point.

June was at the County Fair. Strange, this one night when you will see Dennis for the last time, except in dreams. You and June laughed, went on rides together. Did it really happen?

Despite the 100-degree temperature thousands of people are at the Fair. There are 45-minute lines to wait in for some of the rides. In the Red Cross tent all the cots are full of people suffering from heat exhaustion. There is dust everywhere. There is dust on all the merchandise that people are selling, and on the arts and crafts, and the jars of canned goods with prize ribbons. Up close there is mud on people's faces where the purplish dust has mixed with sweat; a gritty film of purplish dirt on people's legs and arms. There is dust in the corners of everyone's eyes. There is dust on the hot metal of the rides and on the tops of the tents along the Midway where people are playing games, shooting darts and throwing balls to win dusty stuffed animals.

When a rare breeze moves through the fairgrounds, causing small twisters of purplish dust to swirl about all this activity, people close their eyes and just keep moving.

The air-conditioned Civic Center building is not being used this year. Everything at the fair this year is under tents and when it rains the dark green tents are zipped shut after everything is secured inside, making the fairground; the arts and crafts booths, look like an army barrack in the midst of a carnival.

You spot June standing in front of the Right to Life booth. There is a cigarette dangling from her lips. Her eyes are squinted, not because of the smoke going up into her face but because she is looking like she does when she is about to say something nasty.

June is walking toward the overweight woman who has put the fan down on the ground, pointing it up toward her dusty legs. The people with the sandwich boards are moving slow, back and forth in front of the Right to Life booth at the County Fair. Pregnant? Let us help, the sign above the booth next to the one June is walking toward says.

Hi June. Where's Dad? What's up? I haven't seen you in a long time.

June keeps looking, acts like she doesn't hear you. The focus of June's attention is an overweight woman seated in a lawn chair holding a portable fan to her sweating face. Two jars with human fetuses are in front of the woman on a card table.

There are women, men too wearing sandwich boards and handing out pamphlets to people that pass by, pamphlets about God and about the rights of all humanity. The sandwich boards and the posters on the inside of the tent behind the woman in the lounge chair are photographs of fetuses. The captions on the posters and the sandwich boards say: This could have been another Albert Einstein, and, Abortion is Murder, and specific quotes from the Bible.

What makes you think of Anne Frank all of a sudden is that you know what June is about to say and it won't really matter in the end. The bristles of the hairbrush June has in her back pocket are sticking out through the faded denim. In between your toes is dirty and itches, and there is a blister where the sandal strap cuts into your heel.

Five pages comparing Anne Frank to Huckleberry Finn. This was never an assignment in high school.

During the last week of school at Sleepy Hollow High news reporters came to interview students about a freshman who had been beaten up by students who claimed that they were members of the KKK. They said this was only a warning and that the rest of the punks at school better take this as a warning and stop dyeing their hair and wearing outrageous clothes to school.

Nothing makes much sense, except for the blood on the ground by the bike rack, except for June telling the lady with the portable fan that there were many reasons for a woman to not have a baby, especially for a teenage girl to not have a baby, and that the best reason of all was to save a human being from having to suffer through an existence with people as ugly and evil as her.

The woman says, How dare you speak to me like that? The men and women with the sandwich boards are still moving slowly back and forth between where you are and where June is talking to this woman.

June tells this lady that she wishes with all her heart that she could help this lady to end her suffering. June doesn't yell, she talks. You can always hear what June is saying if you want to.

What about your friends and the things that you do that are apart from your family? It is hard to remember anything that is not about June, except for other things that hurt, what grates between hopelessness and possibility.

Listen Tracy. I don't have anything to do until later tonight. Want to screw around, go on a couple of rides?

June is younger than you are so how come now when you are remembering how come you see her as if you admire what it is that she has done?

If you want, Mick can give you a ride home later.

Mick is June's boyfriend, a twenty-seven-year-old man who has been in jail for assault and battery.

June wants to pass the time. June has been in jails, psychiatric wards of hospitals where she was put in straitjackets. June has been in schools where the girls there carve initials into their flesh with sharp objects.

In school you are so busy you don't realize that you are learning how to pretend people like your sister, people like the self inside of you that stays there, you are learning to pretend that these people don't exist.

You learn this on the sidelines of a basketball game, kicking your legs in a skirt that horrifies your mother. You learn this when you hear yourself telling the newscaster that you think the situation concerning the hospitalized freshman is awful and then hear yourself giggling. Your face is covered with stage makeup for the play you are in. A play about two sisters, one a scientific genius and an outcast, the other crazy. It is hard to tell in the play which sister is crazier.

He's after me, you scream in one scene, telling your best friend who is playing your character's mother about a nightmare you just had.

I think it's just awful, you said to the newscaster.

Let's go in here. There's hardly a line, it must be a real attraction, June says.

Inside "The Devil's Domain," June clutches your T-shirt from behind as you bump your way through the humid darkness.

Where are we going? June asks grabbing your hair. Boo, she says laughing, her breath on your neck causing goose pimples all along your right side.

Cut it out. It's scary in here, you say for effect. This is stupid. It's just dark. What kind of ride is this? You lead now.

Pressing up against each other in the narrow hallway you trade places.

I can't see anything. It's too fucking hot in here. June turns around and lights her lighter, holding it down below her face. Oh my God, how do we get out, there's no way to get out alive. June keeps the lighter on. There is silver electrical tape on the floor to keep the blackness in. There are cigarette butts and graffiti all over the walls. Hilda's cunt is as big as a house, it says on the ceiling in pink lipstick. Next to where June is standing it says, You never git out alife.

Let's keep going June.

There is a loud crash up ahead. Help me up. John, you have to slow down, a little boy says.

You and June edge your way to the voices. The tunnel is so narrow you have to go sideways.

There is a dream, something that is your own couldn't be someone else's that links you to the past, your own past. It has always been there, this dream, when you are asleep and when you are awake. It is a feeling remembered.

A flash of green light illuminates the faces of the two little boys. The light flashes again and over the boys, on the left of the tunnel there is a red devil with a pitchfork and a missing hand which you see on the floor when the light flashes again. In the devil's wrist where it should be automated, probably to wave the pitchfork up and down, there is a grinding noise.

The two little boys are petrified against the wall in front of the broken devil.

We're right behind you kid, June says, grabbing a small hand and pushing the boys forward.

The two little boys are holding hands. You see this as the light goes on again.

Once outside the little boys run toward the ticket booth. They are both wearing shorts and the purplish dust is caked on the back of their insectlike legs.

Against the nighting sky, the colored lights of the carnival rides whirl neon streaks above where June is standing.

Check this out June says, pulling her sleeve up. A blue-green heart is tattooed on her upper arm.

There are needle marks and scars on the inside of June's arm that look like small red zippers or a prehistoric sea fossil.

Not a lot of retards in lovely Sleepy Hollow, June says.

In front of June moving through the crowd between the

circus concession stand and the double Ferris wheel is another heavy woman, this one with a long greasy ponytail, and her butt squeezed into black leather pants. The woman is pushing a black stroller with rubber wheels and a canvas awning that is ripped in places. In the perambulator sits a cherubic-looking child with curly blond hair, rosy cheeks and dull blue eyes and dirty cheeks (as you get closer), sucking at a candy apple. The child's fingernails are dirty underneath and there is a swarm of gnats around its diaper. Next to the woman and child, a skinny girl in a metal leg brace that bows her legs out is wobbling along with the same dull stare as the child in the stroller.

No eyesores today. We keep unmentionables hidden thank you. Well, on occasion, sir, one does escape, but we send out our men to clean things up, lickety-split. I should be a barker for a freak show, June says, continuing her monologue. And here ladies and gentlemen is a Right to Lifer, yes look at her, folks, funny isn't it, such an accident of God's thinks she has the right to procreate.

You always want to scream don't you? Never are sure if you should agree or disagree with what is being said, if you too should have an opinion about what is being scrutinized. You can always see both sides. It's hard to filter noise. Sometimes everyone talking sounds like silence and other times one person can be talking to you and it's as if they are screaming from many different sides of the room all at once. You worry that you are crazy, schizophrenia is what it is called. What happens is that dreamlife consciousness starts to invade waking reality. This is what they say about the people in hospitals and under special care. You aren't under special care.

There is a young man perched at the lever that operates the double Ferris wheel. He shakes his hand to the music coming from the basket ride as if he were conducting an orchestra. He makes a fist and slowly pulls his hand down to his grinding hips. He pulls the lever and the top Ferris wheel descends, the people in their seats yelling and laughing, some just white, their eyes and mouths shut.

The man kicks his leg to the music and continues to gyrate his hips, his mirrored sunglasses reflecting darkness spackled with the moving colors of the carnival lights.

Up along the midway barkers are yelling.

A woman in a black T-shirt that says His on it leans out over the green plywood enclosure of the poster stall.

Fifty cents a dart, the poster is yours. Come on honey, she says, touching your shoulder with the sharp red feathers of a dart. Girls can play darts too, she says.

You give her a dollar, survey the poster collection then throw the darts. Two posters you get. One poster in black and white, shows a large-nosed man in a suit and tie, is captioned: I Am Your Father. The second poster in fluorescent colors for a black light is a cartoon drawing of a nude Barbie doll–looking figure with huge breasts and a tiny waist holding a bouquet, eyes downcast. The Burden of Life Is Love, the caption reads.

Do you want these hideous things or am I going to dump them? you tell June.

I'll give them to Mick.

In the back of Mick's truck on the freeway June jokes about the possibility of your facial features permanently shifting due to the force of the wind.

It's a good thing we aren't clams, you say. Can you imagine moving about the world by your mouth? Lick, lick, lick.

June thinks this very funny. Her hair is whipping into her face. She looks like your Mom all of a sudden and then your Dad, the resemblance shifting back and forth not because of how June is holding her face in the wind but because of how you are seeing.

. . .

HYSTERICAL laughter, how you first came to know that how you could cope with what you didn't understand, was to laugh. You didn't need to think about it, the laughter just poured forth.

I'm sorry you don't understand this historical film Miss Hawkins, the English teacher said in front of the whole senior class. Some of us don't understand an important work of art when they see it, he said. He said.

To your laughter, he said this. The ominous voice of learning.

In the room or wherever it is quiet for too long that's when parents know that something is going on.

Out in the living room Mom and Dad were entertaining your Father's boss.

Just do it June. Just do it Tracy.

Whose idea?

Laughter hysterical.

Tracy and June are naked. Stick your finger up your butt, stick your finger up your butt, the two little girls chant in hysterical singsong. They are running around the living room, sometimes with their fingers or their hands pressed between their legs or into their butts. They are dancing crazy like wild Indians, their faces red, their skin sweaty, not from the summer heat but from their hysteria, from their laughter. There are the shocked faces of the boss and his wife and Tracy and June's father shoving, pushing, spanking Tracy and June back into their room.

Their mother's face is pale.

Stick your finger up your butt.

The mother had read a book called Summerhill, *a book about raising children. The mother had read this book when she was pregnant with Tracy. The book is about raising children that will be free and independent and know how to think for themselves.*

Stick your finger up your butt.

Tracy and June had somehow gotten the notion into their innocent heads that they might entertain their father's dinner guests.

June laughs and laughs. Lick, lick, lick, she says, say that really fast. You both say it as fast as you can, a garbled sound mixed with the laughter. The sounds you are making gurgling through the warm night air, the sounds of your laughter as if you were at the bottom of a pool trying to talk.

When did you say goodbye to Dennis? Saying goodbye without knowing.

It's true, it's true. Two days after the County Fair was over, when the traveling caravan was packing up to move on, the trailer used for the Devil's Domain burned down. The newspaper said the causes were of suspicious origin.

Was this some sort of warning of things to come? You always think of yourself as a murderer of sorts, an accomplice to the crimes that get committed because you never do anything to try and stop things from happening.

June is your sister.

Who causes these things to happen? There are violent thoughts that you have and can't seem to wish away.

Are you dead or what, Tracy? June says.

Dad finds a radio station, country. He says it is nice, the three of us together. He says this enough so that maybe he is believing it. His hands grip the steering wheel so that his knuckles go white.

You used to pretend that you were Dad's wife. Now you are driving past fruit stands, fast-food drive-ins. Alone with Dad you used to hope that the people in other cars driving past would notice that there was a man and a wife in the van. Now you hope people don't see June sprawled in the back seat picking at her arms.

Maybe the San Diego Zoo, maybe Tijuana, we'll just play it by ear, Dad says.

There are machines in the fields, large metal structures, some painted with eyes, so that the metal structures look like giant insects. These are oil drills. Up and down, all day, these machines dig deeper and deeper into the earth to find oil.

At Dennis's funeral you wanted people to notice how much you were grieving, wanted to tell people how much you two had meant to each other. Under the desk and then dead. When people grieve they want people to see how much.

In the rearview mirror you turned so that you could comb

your hair, June has the paper dolls out. They are the paper dolls Mom made for Dad that June found in Dad's desk. Only you know that June has them. She raises her eyebrows to let you know she is aware of you seeing the paper dolls. Hide and go seek, June says. Dad, what about we go to that big wax museum in Hollywood, get a look at something important, June is saying, the paper dolls on her lap. The paper dolls on her lap, a naked man and woman face to face, flat, the drawing side sandwiched together so that on June's lap there are just two white shapes laying on top of each other.

People get things made after them if they do what they do and do it good, June says, ripping slow at the sandwiched paper dolls.

Your hands sweat. You think about secrets and what people should know and don't, what they might know and can't.

There are telephone wires. You count the connecting pole for a while for no reason really. There are ditches on the side of the road for miles and miles, ditches that irrigate the crops. This water for these crops comes from northern California, Dad said. You don't think it comes from the dirty green lake where you swim every day, Dad says, it comes from the mountains. The van is zooming past orange trees. Fields and fields of agricultural wonders, everything so carefully arranged as if one day rows and rows of orange trees just appeared out of nowhere. Every row flashing sharp green and brown and orange rays of diagonals out of the corner of your eye. You want the van to stop, freeze for an instant. This is a movie.

June is tearing the paper dolls into tiny pieces. There is an envelope with the paper-doll clothes Mom made still in Dad's desk at home.

There is a poem June wrote that Mom taped to the refriger-ator a long time ago. It went:

> A secret is something that nobody knows
> A secret is something that grows and grows

A secret could be happy a secret could be sad
But wouldn't it be better if it was happy not sad?

This poem is going over and over in your head.

This is the grapevine, Dad says. Man I've been up this road a
lot, up and down. When your Mom and I first met and I was
stationed in San Diego I used to hitchhike on leave to see her.
Get a ride with truckers plugging up this road, high-tailing it
down. Dad's voice cracks. His knuckles are white on the
steering wheel. We are not far now, Dad says. Dad has his hair
in a ponytail.

June has needle marks on her arms. There are bruises and needle
marks all up and down the inside of her arms. Dad said, baby,
to June and held her and said, no more please. He stroked June's
bleached hair that used to be brown and soft. June lies to Dad.
Dad never doubts what June tells him.

The lights of Los Angeles dot the darkness like a giant Light
Brite toy. The city of angels, Dad says.

It's not quality, Dad says, but if we stay here we can do more
things.
    In the motel there is a bed you can put quarters in and the bed
will vibrate. There are pubic hairs on the sheets. People sure
leave their marks here, June says looking at the sheets. The
bathroom is dirty. There is a white piece of paper around the
filthy toilet that says, sanitized for your protection. You tell
Dad you won't sleep here, not in this bed. It's just one bed for
the three of you.
    June and Dad get into the bed. You go into the bathroom and
throw up.
    There is screaming outside, sirens, loud voices and laughing,
cars going up and down the street. On the table is the peanut

butter and white bread Dad got for breakfast. The book Dad is reading, *The Empty Mirror,* is next to the white bread.

You don't put your nightgown on. You sit in the dark motel for a long time listening to first June then Dad start to snore. Finally with all your clothes on you get into the bed next to Dad.

Don't look away from me when I am talking to you, your mother says.

This is my dream house, you say, please leave me alone, I don't want you here now, you say.

I work very hard for you, your mother is saying.

All you can do is cry because of how guilty your mother is making you feel.

June and Dad are behind the door, in the bedroom, as if they were married.

It's this dream, your dream and you are aware that because this is your dream you should be able to escape if you want to but you can't.

There are families too, other families that are suffocating you, dictating to you what it is that you should be doing.

There is water to go in and you want to lay down in the water and have it close over your head.

In the middle of the night you wake up. The bed is shaking and June is laughing. Dad puts on his glasses and laughs too.

At Disneyland you and June go into the haunted house together. Dad waits by the fence in front of the lake where Tom Sawyer's Island is. Have fun, he says.

In line June doesn't stand next to you. In the car as it moves down a dark hallway, June says, everyone wants a fantasy. In the Haunted House in a mirror a ghost appears in the car between you and June.

. . .

JUNE lived alone with Dad.

She visits weekends, if she wants to.

Dad says, maybe soon he might come back home. Dad says

144

this but Mom is always at Big Herb's. Big Herb might be moving in, Mom says.

June shouldn't be here now. It hasn't stopped raining in Sleepy Hollow for four days. There is flooding. The wind is causing power lines and trees to go down. The house creaks and moans. The walls or the ceilings, the whole house could collapse at any moment.

Sleepy Hollow and the surrounding areas have been declared a disaster area. The National Guard was sent in to help evacuate people from the flooded areas.

People are supposed to stay inside. It is almost a river in the street out front. The rain is coming down so hard that out the window everything looks smeared.

June came by this morning. June came by to leave just like she always does. When June comes by she is always waiting for someone to come and pick her up to go somewhere else. She will call people, stand by the window, pace back and forth. You watch June.

In between looking out the window and standing by the phone June dumps the contents of her black bag on the floor.

The power is off. It has been off for three days.

The rain is coming down in sheets. The roof is leaking and all over the house Mom has placed bowls, pots, trays, anything to catch the water that is leaking through in every room. All over the house, on the tables, the bookshelves, the beds, there are the plastic garbage bags that Mom has cut up so that not everything will get ruined.

In June's old bedroom the ceiling has started to collapse.

There is really not anything that can be done.

On the news before the power went off, they show the Golden Gate Bridge swaying back and forth from the high winds. The Golden Gate Bridge is closed down now, you heard this on the radio. On the news they show the flooded streets and men in yellow slickers working on power lines, men in yellow slickers piling sandbags down by the marina and up in the hills at the reservoirs.

Manhole covers have dislodged in the streets and the muddiness of the water is making it difficult to retrieve them.

In front of June, on the floor among the contents of her bag, is her diary with the lock, a photo booth strip of pictures of her and her boyfriend Mick and one of June's scrapbooks that she brought up from the basement.

June started keeping scrapbooks when she was eleven. She said that someone needed to keep track of what was going on.

At first you never really thought about it, weren't interested. You didn't think there would be anything in the scrapbooks other than the usual things people put in scrapbooks: clippings out of magazines, pictures of friends, mementos like ticket stubs and matchbook covers.

One day you glanced over June's shoulder at the page she was working on. It was a very intricate collage. At the center of the page is a line drawing in pencil of a man and a woman naked. The two figures are each enclosed in a bubble. Two people, their eyes shut, their arms straight to their sides, palms facing forward, fingers spread. Out of magazines June cut pictures. There is a picture of a burning building, the flames coming out of the windows, a picture of the earth split open by an earthquake, and three newspaper pictures of teenagers that had disappeared in Northern California. You had seen lots of these pictures before, of children that just disappeared, were kidnapped, murdered or ran away. June had arranged these pictures around the pencil drawing of the man and woman. The burning building is between the man and the woman. The picture of the earthquake is under the balloons that surround and separate the man and woman. The missing children are at the top of the page. Sleepy Hollow, June had written on the opposite page in the scrapbook.

When June became aware of you looking over her shoulder she slammed the scrapbook shut. After that she bought a metal box and kept her finished scrapbooks in the locked box in the basement. June got two keys. One key June kept with her always on a chain around her neck. The other key June buried in the yard somewhere. June always had a scrapbook with her that she carried in her large purse with Scotch tape, scissors, glue and pens so she could add pages wherever she was. There were times when June lost her shoes, articles of clothing, sometimes she would lose her purse or it would get stolen.

Somewhere in the United States, besides the metal box Mom keeps that is locked, are June's other scrapbooks, the ones she lost.

You never know what to say to June. She is on the floor in front of you looking through one of her scrapbooks shielding parts of the pages with her hands. You are working on your English final, analyzing *The Adventures of Huckleberry Finn.*

A car honks out front. June shuffles everything into her purse. Do I look OK? June asks. You tell June that she looks very nice. June is wearing skin-tight jeans that she has drawn on with a black pen: a swastika above her left knee, initials of people she knows, rock groups, an upside-down heart with her and her boyfriend's initials, JAH + MZS. June has a white halter top on underneath her jean jacket. The jean jacket is too small and doesn't close at all. Her eyes are lined in heavy black. June looks Chicano really, like the prostitutes you saw on the streets outside the motel in Hollywood. When June was born your Dad hadn't been sure if June was the right baby or not. June was such a dark baby your Dad thought that maybe there had been a mix-up in the nursery. No, your Mom had said, this is the right baby. June has a body that makes people stare, men and women. She has a body that people want to possess, touch, control somehow. June is beautiful with her brown eyes that go black and her full mouth that is always painted blood-red. June always says she hates being beautiful. June says that being beautiful is a disease that makes the people around you stupid and blind about things that are important. June likes to make herself look shocking.

It used to be that June would hide her body. One time June

even cut all her hair off, cropped it close to her head like a boy. After June cut her hair she just wore jeans and a big plaid shirt of Dad's. When June cut her hair that's when it really started.

Dad said, just fine. Dad said, it's good to express yourself. Dad's hair is dark and wild. Mom didn't say anything. Mom had started to look at everyone like they were far away. You could be talking to Mom for a long time telling her something, and she would say, were you just saying something?

The horn honks again, a muffled sound with all the rain and wind.

You are afraid that the bay tree might come crashing down on the roof. Trees are blowing down everywhere. You wonder how June and her friend can be driving. June just does whatever she wants.

Dad said, June may be crazy but she is talented and needs more than other kids. Mom says, not under my roof she doesn't. It's really that everyone is afraid of June and no one really does know what she needs, not anyone. People just pretend they know what June needs. June is smarter than the people that tell her what she needs, but she is beautiful and this confuses everyone. June's eyes are brown and sometimes black.

After June is gone you go into her room. June's room smells like mildew. There is insulation on the floor in places. There is the hole in the ceiling next to the closet and puddles of water on the floor. There is a full-length mirror in there. You take off your clothes and look. Your body is not like June's. You think your body is ugly and fat. You don't eat, sometimes for days. You want to be able to see your ribs and your shoulder blades like how June's shoulder blades are, delicate and sharp. You make yourself throw up. You dream of food. Your breasts are so small and because you are so fat from different angles it looks like you have no breasts at all. Fat and ugly. Mom says you look like Auschwitz. You tell Mom that she just wants you to be fat when she tells you that you had better start eating. You just turn the shower on so that no one will hear you throw up dinner or whatever you ate that you shouldn't have. Mom says, she will take you to the hospital. What can doctors do? you tell her, you would like to know.

In June's room the beams of the ceiling look like the ribs of a giant sea creature.

On June's bed you lie down on the plastic garbage bags. There is a hole in the ceiling. You like to pretend. It's the fantasies that don't go away. You put your bra back on and fill it with socks. It looks better now, more appealing. With high heels your legs don't look so fat. With your underwear rolled and tucked a certain way, and through squinty eyes, you almost look like a Playboy girl. Delicious. Like the pictures in magazines or the advertisements on television is how you look now if you squint your eyes. This excites you. On June's bed you bunch up her pillow and rub it between your legs until the fantasy goes away. Then it's just you alone in June's room, alone in this house with a bra filled with socks and high heels sitting on a bed that used to have a white canopy on the top.

June's shade was not drawn all the way and you hope that no one happened to be walking up the street, happened to see you here on the bed.

You hate this body, this skin that tightens upon your bones that tortures your head with all its needs and functions.

You want to escape, leave your body. In dreams you can fly, take your body with you. It's slow how you fly in dreams, it's like swimming how you scull the air with your hands. Up and up you go or just skim across roads and mountains, your stomach three feet above the earth. This is how you can leave in your dreams. This is how you move with your body, flying.

Awake you want to do this, leave your body and go somewhere else. Leave your body and see it motionless, asleep, see what you really look like and not what you think you look like because of how alien your life has become.

As if anyone could see in with the fog on the inside of the window and the water crashing against the glass outside, the windows steamy as if you were in a shower. There is no one outside anyway. You think of what June told you once about the ghosts of the two girls screaming, Don't leave Mommy, no. You dress quickly. You pace around the house until you aren't afraid anymore.

You think of walking down the street, of going to visit someone. You would like to wade in the river that is forming over the street. Then you think of how you might fall into an open manhole.

There is nothing to eat. Not that you would eat. You can't. There is nothing at all. The floor is sticky in places. In the refrigerator there is a chicken carcass for soup, an empty milk carton and lots of condiments on the door shelf.

All the containers that have been catching water need to be emptied.

. . .

I think, June is saying, I think that I don't know who I am and then there are four people, four people coming in through the door at the same time. I knew then that that was how it always would be. This is what happened, Tracy, when she hypnotized me, when she gave me this drug.

In the kitchen eating breakfast you are listening to June. June just woke up.

June's back is to you because she is lighting a cigarette off of the stove.

There is razor stubble above June's nose between her eyebrows where she shaves the hair that grows there. There is black in the corners of June's eyes and mascara that is smeared above her cheeks. June hasn't washed yet and her hair is wild. You can smell her breath from across the table.

Do you feel anything? the doctor asked me and I couldn't answer her because words were in my head but my mouth didn't work right. I told her this story that I am telling you now. I don't remember telling her this, that is what the drug is supposed to do, make it so that I wouldn't remember telling this story to her when I woke up. But I remembered the whole story, just not telling it.

You don't say anything. You let June talk. June never talks to you, tells you things. There are long pauses. June gets up to rinse something in the sink or goes into the living room to get a bracelet or a shirt out of her big bag but she comes back, continues, will continue. You know that June will tell you if you just listen.

The doctor said, you won't remember this so it won't be painful. The doctor said it is important to go back. We will go back, she said. You see Tracy they want me to find something out, see what it was that makes me the way I am.

And so I suppose she was listening to me telling the story, the first one that comes to mind, a painful experience is what she wanted. I started. This is what I told her, Tracy, and I remembered the story for days and I wasn't supposed to remember it at all. I didn't tell the doctor I knew what I had just told her when I woke up. I asked her did she get the information she needed. I don't know why this is what the story was, I don't.

June lights another cigarette from the one she has been smoking and continues:

The four people press through the door to get a peek at the flower. These four people in answer to who I am. I know these four people are here to look at the flower so that they can tell someone about it, so that they can all say, I saw the flower in full bloom and it might never bloom again this one here, and if it does it won't be for a long time.

Two men and two women, but I can't tell they are men and women by the way they look I just know it to be so. They are two couples and they kiss and hug and press their bodies together and moan and look at the flower again. I am watching this all happen. I am in a bed and the bed is near the ceiling of whatever room I am in. The room keeps changing. In bed I am holding a big book, like an almanac or an atlas of the universe and as I turn the page, whatever is pictured in the book is where

I am in the bed. The bed stays by the ceiling but the scenery keeps changing down below and I am controlling this by turning the pages.

The pictures in the book are big and shiny and three-dimensional. I can almost touch what is in the pictures. When I look away from the picture and look down from the bed the picture has become life; a picture of Africa with giraffes and zebras running across a desert, or a picture of people in various sexual positions.

One page is a picture of Mom, a silhouette in profile but I know it is her and I look down from the bed but there is still just the four people looking at the flower.

June is talking to you as if you weren't there seated across from her at the kitchen table. June looks at you but it is as if her eyes were seeing a movie where your face is.

June continues:

The curtains are blue, different shades of blue sometimes light like the sky in the morning. My bed is in a small room. Mom, I say, I am sick, please help me. Mom just stands there like wax and then Mom changes into Dad. I am looking at Dad, not Mom but Dad and he is smiling and laughing. They must not see me in the bed because the room is so dark and the blue curtains are the color of blue just before it turns black.

I am sick, I say and I am hoping that if I close my eyes and open them that someone will be there by my bed to unwrinkle all the black and make the room light and airy.

I can't find the book anymore.

I am going now, Mom says and the room isn't dark anymore and Mom is still standing by the bed.

June's eyes are moving back and forth, still looking at you, her eyes moving back and forth across your face as if there was a cue card there.

I decide to draw on my sheets then, that maybe I can make a drawing that will change the room as the different pages in the book changed the room. I can't control what I draw on the white sheets of the bed and my fingers just make scribbles and lines. I want to make it so that Mom will go away for good and not keep coming back.

Mom's face by the bed looks too slippery to touch or too hard and cracked or too slippery. I remember your face, Mom says to me.

My fingertips are still trying to draw on the sheet to change the scene in the room. My fingertips go in between things: the pillow and the mattress, my legs, my lips, the space between the bottom of the bed and the floor, and then my fingertips just continue plotting out points on the sheets because I am trying to make a morning sky, trying to put white into blue, painting on the damp sheet. But I can't, from my fingertips just come lines and scribbles.

Don't say anything, there is nothing to say, and I am not sure if I say this or if it is Mom.

Mom has a glass of water. She is a statue holding water. Her mouth moves slow motion closing down around the lip of the glass.

I put my head to the floor because there might be sound. I know that the floors talk. There in the wood, there in the table, the wood of the table or the floor, things get absorbed there. If these walls could talk, if only they would. No one listens and the whispering is everywhere. Everything is porous and moving in and out of everything else, all sound, movement being stored. I put my head to the floor, to the wall next to my bed and listen.

I want the walls, the floors, the ceiling, to play back all that has been said, in this room everything held, everything contained in the containers that are everywhere, people too are containers. In the wood or in the glass, the window glass, or in the blue curtain, all this information, and finally all the withholding of knowledge, no, not withholding, it's just that no one wants to listen, is afraid, and the fear travels faster than anything else making it impossible to get into all the tapes that have been made. I put my head to the floor and there is whispering and garbled voices.

Mom didn't mean to say, don't talk, she meant to say, I just can't listen now.

June's face wavers in your dreams like a silhouette made by a flickering candle, features sharp and overpowering, then just shapeless shades of gray.

You listen best when you are dreaming. When awake you quickly unlearn the knowledge gained at night, clues slipping away like trying to hold sand in your palm.

What is awake?

You were standing behind Hanson's Funeral Parlor.

It is dark.

If you think about it what's there to be afraid of? June asks. June is standing in your laced hands pushing the window up. You had told her that you had already seen a dead body. June said she bet you hadn't really touched one. It smells like eucalyptus. There is rustling in the bushes. It is a cat. June is pushing up the window in the back of the funeral parlor. It's stuck, she says. There, got it, you just got to see this.

I don't think we should June, what if we get caught?

By who? Everyone is dead in here. June laughs. June's stomach is on the window ledge and she is kicking herself in. I swear the guy that works in here just sleeps all night. He is old and deaf as a doorknob. Come on Tracy I've been here lots of times. I'm going to open the door. Just go behind those bushes and there's a metal door. I'll be there in a minute.

The funeral parlor is four blocks from your house, right in between a laundromat and a dentist's office. The funeral parlor is in a beautiful old house with turret rooms. The shades in the windows in the front of the funeral parlor are always drawn halfway. Each window the same, half black. Funeral parlors are always in the nicest buildings.

June called earlier tonight. You were typing for school. June said there was something she wanted to show you.

Underneath the red carpet there must be plastic, then foam, because as you walk your shoes leave a print and then the print disappears slow making a crinkling sound. June walks fast. You are tiptoeing behind her trying to step on the carpet without making any noise.

Come on Tracy are you chicken? You are always chicken unless you have the upper hand. You should have seen last night man. June takes her hairbrush out of her back pocket and combs her bangs flipping them forward then back. June's face is swollen, the skin too oily in some places, peeling in others. June keeps sniffling, rubbing hard at her nose. Her eyes are open too wide. She takes a cigarette out of her sock and lights it. She is leaning against the wall next to a door, raising and lowering her eyebrows really fast. This is it, June says. She raps on the door. Last night me and this guy in here, ah never mind. Her eyes get fast all of a sudden and her whole face tightens, sharp.

You don't want to be here at all. Dennis, this is the last place that you saw Dennis. I don't think I want to really, you say, let's go.

June raises her eyebrows again. The door is open and on the other side of the room is a young man lying face up. The coffin is lined with puffy pale blue satin. See, not a care in the world, June says. She walks up to the dead man. She is smoking. She climbs into the coffin and straddles the dead man. She waves to you.

You don't go into the room. You are mad. June is never afraid of anything. You are telling yourself that all you have to do is walk across the room and touch the man. The room is miles long. There is a funny smell like candles and antiseptic. You can't go in there.

June I am leaving, you say.

June is straddled over a dead man and she is smoking.

Oh fuck you Tracy. You are always ruining everything.

Jade

ROB is standing just where the surf rushes up onto the dry part of the beach. His toes are just at the sea's edge. He has his hands in the back pockets of his green-and-white sweatpants. Looking down he backs up slowly step by step as the tide moves in. The sun setting behind him looks like a ripe peach splitting open.

In your hand there are small jade pebbles you have sifted out of the warm sand. Some of the small green stones are almost black, some are a deep red. They are small and smooth. There is no one else on the beach. Just think of it, Rob says turning around and running toward you. Just think of it. You throw the pebbles back into the sand. Think of what? you say into Rob's neck as he pushes you down.

You are in love.

It's about to be the first time. Out by the swimming pool the two of you are balanced, face to face on the lawn chair. The moon is on its side. Everything looks made of small newspaper dots. The sound of the pool sweep, an occasional car; lights sweeping fans of light around the corner over the fence, Rob's breath on your face, your heart pounding, these sounds mark the darkness.

Before when you told Rob that you wanted to make love he wasn't sure. He was at your house. He rode his bike home. I just don't know, he said. I love you, he said. I'll call you in the morning, he said. On your bedroom wall all the faces, small eyes looking down at you like hypodermic-needle points.

Rob's mother told him that it was up to him, that he was old enough to figure these things out for himself. Rob's father is dead. Rob's mother said that it was up to him.

You spend the night at Rob's. No one seems to mind this.

None of your friends are allowed to spend the night with people they love. You think that it is awful to sleep alone.

The pool sweep moves in a pattern around the pool. You don't understand this, how a little machine attached to a hose remembers to go around and around the pool in the same direction.

I want you Tracy, just let me, Rob is saying. I promise I won't ever hurt you, he is saying. He is supposed to be saying this. It's about to be the first time. You want him to.

And then Rob is inside of you. He pulls at your breasts like they were his own. Your legs are open wide. Your arms wrap around his sweat-covered back. He comes quickly. He grabs your face smothering your moans.

You feel empty. There is a stinging red fire ant plotting its way across the damp glossy edges of the brick patio, barely avoiding the brown mass that separates each stone. The mad zigzag of this ant mimics the plastic web of the lawn chair indenting your ass. No, you are thinking. Something else. There is semen on your belly button. It dries slowly on your skin leaving a mark like a removed decal.

Rob's mother had been in the kitchen the whole time. She is hammering designs into cans. The ting-ting, the insomniac voices of a radio talk show, you out on the patio not wanting to hear the sound of metal being punctured. You want to hear Rob's breath as your own. Not this.

Rob's Mom had shown you a finished piece after dinner. Lighting a small candle she had placed it inside the ornately patterned can. She centered the metal lantern on the dining-room table. Watch now, she said. She remembered to turn off the overhead light. The punctured can had cast a pattern around the room, many short rays of yellow light.

I am so sleepy, Rob says. You are so beautiful, he says.

You like to squeeze the pimples on Rob's back, the pressure of your fingers releasing fluids or hardened matter like bits of sand. Rob likes you to do this.

All night out by the pool you dream you are flying. Then you are trapped in a small room and can only see the outside through dirty windows. Rob is outside trying to figure out how to get to you trapped in the small dirty room. You can't escape. He can't help you.

You wake up coughing and Rob is there, eyes open wide, staring down at you like you were just born.

Your breath is as sweet as corn, he says.

Postcard

ONE day when you woke up your father was sitting in the kitchen.

June is gone, Dad says.

I am back, Dad says.

Dad's eyes, both of them, are bruised behind his glasses. The flesh on his arms is covered with deep scratches. You know that June beat him up.

What happens during the night.

It is cold here. Winter is just gray. Outside, a light snow is draped around the bottom of the bay tree. It's not supposed to snow here. There is frost on the olive trees, like the milky-white film that covers the eyes after a deep sleep. There are dark clouds in the sky tightening up like a fist.

.   .   .

JUNE ran away. She sent you a postcard from Denver. She sent you a postcard and not Mom or Dad.

Dear Tracy,
    This man wants me to dress up in a frilly costume so he can pretend I am his sister he always wanted to sleep with. I stole his

wallet while he showered. I slept in a graveyard. I slept in a motel room. All in one building hundreds of rooms that look the same.

June

The night before June ran away she was outside, in the backyard, not just June but other people talking, a man slurring his words, another man saying this window is open.

Mom isn't home. You are alone. You call the police, you have to do this. This is what you have to do. Call the police if your own sister comes around the house.

June beat up Dad before she left his house, before he came back here with all his things in boxes again.

Mom isn't home. You tell the police to come quick please that June is here.

Before the police arrive June comes into the house. June comes into the house because she breaks the window in the kitchen door.

You are in your bedroom with the door locked and you can hear June on the other side. In the kitchen June is going through the knife drawer. You can hear the men outside talking in whispers.

The police don't come quietly. The police drive with their lights and sirens on. June is gone before they arrive.

You know this time that June is gone.

Mom says, you don't have to go to school if you don't want to, mostly you don't. Dad plays his guitar and doesn't talk much. At night you can hear Mom and Dad arguing. You go away too, Mom says. Big Herb and I are going to get married. We are divorced now. Please leave. This is my house too, Dad says. Then you just don't hear their words anymore. You don't want to.

I'm sorry Rob says.

June's pupils would dilate wide open in bright daylight. She couldn't sleep at night. She was up for four days. She would come

159

over. She said, don't tell Dad that I can't sleep. You said, I won't. June said she was hearing voices, getting signals from somewhere. You didn't tell her that sometimes you hear voices. June said she could see the future. She didn't want to talk about it.

The police are looking for June in case she comes back. The police won't find June unless she wants them to. June is in Denver. You wish they would find her because you are afraid of what she might do.

June sends you another postcard from Denver that is a picture of a dinosaur.

Dear Tracy,
    I am going to hop a freight train from here, am heading East. It's thirty below zero and if I stay still I might freeze to death. I met this guy who can project his voice into things. Don't tell Anna Lea I wrote to you. Anna Lea is a whore.
                                                                            June

It is snowing outside. It's not supposed to snow here. Snow is swirling outside your bedroom window. Snow is swirling outside the bay tree. You feel like you are inside a water-filled Christmas decoration. The ones with the little Nativity scene inside. If you look closely you can see where the plastic figures were removed from their molds, a nose with an extra piece of flesh-colored plastic just flapping when you tip the whole scene, to watch the flakes of white snow glitter around and down over the whole assembly.

Before June ran away, before she was in the kitchen in the knife drawer, the night you didn't know that she had just beat up your father, before all this, June came over. She told you she had to talk to you please that something was happening and she was sure it wasn't the drugs, this is different she says. June tells you her eyes moving fast in her head, that there are signs given and that no one is listening.

First it was the line drawing of the jackal with the body of a woman that appeared in June's dream. The next day in the supermarket she saw the same drawing on the inside door of the bathroom stall.

In her dream, first the jackal with the body of the woman was in a cage. June said it was talking to her, pulling its hoofs against metal that was covered with beach sand and saying, let me out June. You have to let me out, it said. June said that the jackal drawing was being sketched by a priest and then it came to life. She woke up from the dream saying that she thought everyone in the world was lying about something because everyone's noses were long and pointed.

The graffiti jackal June saw in the bathroom was saying something else. A cartoon balloon from its laughing mouth said, when you finish wondering I'll be here. June told you this and now you can't remember if she said that, or if the words were, when you finish wandering I'll be there. Here or there, her words become a cicada drone.

It's not summer it's winter.

There's an aerial view of the universe, it could be a postcard. You are right in the middle of it. You and June and Mom and Dad, the whole family, not just an arrow pointing to something that has to be imagined.

June ran away.

You are running but your body is stationary. You are not dreaming.

· · ·

YOU heard your mother say, just see what's wrong, and hurry back please. I'm cold, she said from her bed.

It is night. Homer is barking wildly. The cats Dad brought when he came back home are screeching like brakes. Smoke is pouring down the hallway.

Water is at your feet. Mom is crying. The house is burning down. There are red lights and firemen running around frantically. It's too late. The house was old. It was a white house like Grandma's in Old Saybrook. Everything is burning. All the pictures on your wall, your clothes, Mom's paintings, the plants in the living room. My God, Dad says. Dad is crying and then he is just sitting on the curb in front of the olive trees with his head between his knees. Homer is nuzzled under Dad's bent legs. The neighbors are in the street. Smoke is coming out of everyone's mouths.

. . .

EVERYONE knew it was June but no one said so. They just say the house burnt down. Dad just starts building a new one on the same spot.

You are standing in front of the foundation of the house. There are temporary beams on the foundation marking out the shape of the new house.

Dad got his book out of the basement, but the love letters Mom and Dad wrote to each other, that Mom said you could read when she was dead, are gone, burned.

You are living at Rob's house. Mom and Dad are staying at Grandma Green's.

June is in a hospital in Seattle now. June's not there because she burned the house down she is there because she says she can see the future and because she let the cops find her on the Golden Gate Bridge.

June was walking on the freeway first. She was telling the cars that drove past, yelling at the cars, that she was a man and a woman at the same time. Then she was sitting on the railing of the bridge not threatening to jump but telling the fog that it might just as well get thicker.

June even said, I burned the house down. No, Dad said, it was an accident.

A small talc-covered insect whirs about your head. It's covered with white talc like the foam that comes out of a fire extinguisher, a talc-covered insect hovering about your head as you stand in front of the house's foundation. You have never seen one like this before.

THE house Dad built with the money Grandma and Grandpa sent from Old Saybrook (*A house for Dad's kids, Grandpa Hawkins said*) is a house like other houses; not an old house with character, not white like Grandma's in Old Saybrook, it is a house made from a kit. The new house is made out of wood that will season, darken with time. The new house is still two stories. The basement did not burn, it is the same. Sometimes you can still smell smoke. The ceilings in the new house are low and the walls are thin. The bay tree doesn't look right anymore in front of this house, and it is charred on one side.

You can't wait until you are in Equinox far away from this modern home. You are going to school in Equinox, a small town in Vermont. You are going to college to study photography. You don't ever want to come back here to Sleepy Hollow.

This new house would fit right in with the houses by the airport in San Francisco, the houses that all look the same block after block except for maybe the color or the direction the porch faces. You hope the bay tree just keeps getting bigger and the new house splits open, collapsing like the walls of a card house.

Mom and Big Herb got married. Mom is pregnant. Dad lives in a houseboat, in an apartment building that was built on a big barge. Dad went away, home to stay with his parents for a while, then he came back. Dad waits on tables and goes to school at night. Dad is taking classes, studying the lives of American Indians. Dad has taken to eating nothing but brown rice and he meditates and backpacks when he is not waiting on tables. Dad just built this new house and then Mom and Big Herb moved in. Dad visits June a lot. Dad has eyes that are wet. Big Herb's eyes are always red. Big Herb falls asleep on the toilet.

You want to make a movie someday because things might be easier to understand if they are put in something: a book, a painting, a movie. You want to make a real movie and not just someone else's fantasies over and over again. Maybe you will make a movie about killing your Mom and Big Herb.

You are going away, going to college but you don't feel older, aren't really sure how old you are at all, how could you know, why might it matter to know? The same things just happen over and over again, this is what is really important, that you want to make things stop.

It's starting out too fast again and you are not sure where you are.

You just wish you could send a postcard, that there was someone who would want to get this postcard. You want to send a postcard that would show the whole thing in one quick glance.

Yesterday I had blood drawn, June, you say into the phone.

The scuffed linoleum, the cool white hand of the nurse, the black rubber tourniquet on your arm, a needle going in. You told the doctor that you used to be afraid of swallowing your tongue. You laughed when you said this, a nervous laugh as you folded and unfolded your sweaty hands on your stomach. You told the doctor, when he had the speculum inside of you and was swabbing your cervix with a long Q-tip, you told the doctor that when you were growing up, there was a time when you were afraid that you might swallow your tongue. You tell the doctor that you are going away to college, far away and that you can't wait to go. The doctor says, just a few more seconds. You are hoping that he will hurry. You start to think about getting excited. What would this doctor do if you were getting all wet down there, would he notice the glistening? You think about how a doctor could ever get excited if he is seeing so many naked women every day, or that maybe he can't get excited with his own partner and he needs this much stimulation to please his wife. You are thinking about what might make this doctor excited, does he have to tie his lover up, or is it just really nice because he really knows how to love and not just always thinking about what he can't see? I am finished, the doctor says, you can get dressed now.

Then the nurse came in and took blood. She put the vial of your blood upright in a box with other vials of other people's blood.

June I am going to college next week. I don't know when I will see you again, you say.

There is a good wax museum on the wharf, June says. She phoned to say that. June says she is sure that while she was looking at the statue of Jack the Ripper, while she was looking, he moved.

June is in Washington. You want to see her. You want to tell her you are sorry. June will hang up before you have a chance. You are always sorry. June even said that. June said, what in the hell are you always feeling so guilty about? You have to tell her you are sorry. June's hair was so soft. June was soft. Her eyes asked you.

June are you still there? You don't have much to say, still you like holding her voice up to your ear, a voice and then the empty roar, like listening to a conch shell.

It was dark outside. One minute you are running through the woods behind the frame of the new house your father is having built. The next minute you can't hear. The outline of the tree branches had tickled against the morning clouds. Light was splattering everywhere like water on a hot griddle.

June said people weren't really seeing what was happening.

In the street watching the flames lick the house, then they were seeing.

There's a wax museum with thick red carpet in all the rooms, June is saying.

Out the window you can see the olive trees, not looking down like before. Now you can see their trunks, one side like cut-outs. It is better to be up high looking down at something than to see straight on and only one side.

There's a pause on the line, a longer pause than the ones in between June's breathy sentences. June tells you what she is doing in Seattle; that she shaved her head for cleanliness, that she is thinking about becoming a palm reader, that she is sleeping with her clinician Barbara, that sometimes the voices she hears speak to her in Chinese. After this long pause June says that she is glad she is in this place. Defined situations make things so much easier don't you think, Tracy?

You want to tell June that you went to the courthouse with Mom and Big Herb and that they got married in a room next to the County Jail. You want to tell June that Mom is pregnant. You know that June probably knows these things but the way June knows things, how she listens is different.

Tracy, June says, her voice crackling through thin wires that strap around the world.

I sent Dad a box of mice, June says. The phone is heavy in your hand. Your palms are sweating. The phone is too slippery to hold on to. I thought Dad should see how a family dies. It wasn't easy to package, you know. It had to be shipped just the way I found the mice family down in the basement here. I was thinking Dad would understand and that maybe he could use the mice to somehow finish his book. You know Tracy, Dad should keep writing. I want to tell him that. I had a difficult time packing the mice. I found the mice behind the washing machine. I'm going to be moving soon. The mice had tried to escape the rat-poison box. When I found the mice in their varying degrees of escape, some almost free, others grounded in the cereal substance, I had to know why the parents had allowed the small white babies to follow. Dad will see the delicate flesh, soft then rotting, falling away from tiny bones.

Sleeping out in the backyard before June had burnt the house down, blanketed up against the side of the house, the sun was bright in the morning like oil-marked pavement. The sun makes things smell. Your bones were like wax against the concrete patio. It was hot then cold. You were not hungry. You slept. You woke up. It was night. The sun was fickle to the trees. All along the street on the other side of town the trees, the elms became diseased and had to be chopped down.

I'm thinking about becoming a dental hygienist, June says.

June is in a lock-up ward. She will get out of it depending on her behavior. She is allowed to go out twice a week with her clinician, sometimes not at all.

Something excites me about cleaning teeth. When I have my hand on people's mouths I can see where their tongue is connected, June says.

Looking at your shadow calms you. Seeing a deep gray misshapen outline of yourself on the street or a wall or crinkled against the bark of a tree cools your anxiety.

The fingers of your right hand are five wills, June is saying. I want to subdue my pinky finger. Lately I have been tying my pinky down to my palm. The pinky stands for childishness. I have a friend here who told me that in the evolution of ourselves we won't need this finger anymore. It will just fall off. In generations to come people will have three fingers and a thumb only. When your hand is at rest the pinky finger suggests this. Bent backwards everyone's pinkies are threatening to fall off. June is laughing. Each finger stands for a will, Tracy. She laughs louder.

June's voice is buzzing. Your hand is shaky. Outside the sky is lead gray.

You were running.

What should be happening?

You are cold.

In college you want to make a film. The end will be of a person's lips blowing dandelion seeds. The small white heads will float breath force across shadows. June would prefer milkweed to dandelions.

You want the film to be like a postcard.

Nothing is happening. There is the phone. There are telephone wires. There is June's voice fading in and out in your ear, a hum that is loud then soft. Your hands feel slippery.

You are thinking how sometimes skin is like crepe paper. You recently read about babies that can't be exposed to light or their skin will burn and blister.

Did you know that during Hitler's reign in Germany a formula for telepathy was discovered? Tracy are you still there?

Wax

AFTER June burned the house down you went away for a long time.

PART II

Equinox

P.O. Box

DEAR Mom, you write. Dear Dad, you write. You can't write to June because June keeps moving. First she got away from the hospital and now there are just all the postcards she sends you from wherever she is living. You have a map of the United States. On this map you place a pin to mark each place that June sends you a postcard from. A piece of string traces the pins from point to point. The string makes a giant scribble on the map of the United States.

Dear Tracy,
　　If you blink you might miss something.

June

Geography

YOU start out. The blindfold is placed over your eyes and then darkness. Arms reach around you. Hands that are stronger and dryer than your own start to turn you. With your clumsy feet, you might drill a hole deep into the ground. This is a game. There are people whispering and laughing. The pressure in the air produced by the closeness of all these bodies excites you. You are breathing fast. The group disperses. You are alone. Marco, you say into the darkness. Polo, many voices yell back from different places on the lawn. The muddle of voices is too loud, too faint, then too loud again. You are getting dizzy. You press the heels of your hands into your eyes. Your lids become ribbed with orange light like the veins in marble. The backs of your eyes feel heavy as the night sky, a sky without stars, just black.

This game you are playing: you go through the motions, no one can take away from you what you think about. There is a blindfold around your head, a blindfold that divides your face, forehead from mouth.

The warm summer air prickles your skin. You can feel each blade of grass beneath your bare feet. You want to be in love.

Marco, you yell taking your hands away from your eyes. You want to open your eyes against the cloth that is tightly wrapped across your face.

The voices are so far away that Polo, Polo, sounds like below, below. The wind has picked up, melting their voices into a hum.

The Sculpture

THERE were dreams you had, romantic dreams, and you fell into his arms, mouth to mouth, passion tickling your body warm.

Let go of me you scream, because suddenly flesh is being torn away from your shoulder.

Dreams keep you going.

You are leaning over the back of a couch, a couch very much like the one in your apartment that folds out into a bed. Your stomach is to the back of the couch. Your father is in the room. The energy in the room is thick with desire. You and your father are nervous and laughing, saying silly things, then saying nothing at all. You can feel the corner of your mouth quiver. You are afraid of how your father is making you feel inside.

Your father is kissing the back of your neck, reaching for your hand, interlocking his fingers with yours.

You walk over to the windows to pull down the shades. It is dark. A man and a woman rush by outside. The woman is punching at the man, pulling his hair. The man is screaming.

James is from town, didn't finish college. You like his sculptures, but mostly you like his hands, and his eyes. It's the way he makes you feel, hungry, desperate, when he tells you that he will call you in the evening and then he does and it's not as if there is anything to say on the phone, it's just the fact that he called and the fact that you know something that he doesn't.

What you know is that your Grandmother Green was younger than you when she met your Grandfather Green, time flies. You are anxious. Your mother was only seventeen when she married your father. There are similarities. James is angry, has been hurt, needs someone that he can talk to. He had a brother that died in an automobile accident, a father that died of cancer. Solace is what you have to offer one another, solace and understanding that will make you both grow.

Stop staring at me, James says, his lips sucking at your eye from across the table. I don't want anybody to touch me now. The fish tank is bubbling. The floor slopes in the middle where the couch is, the couch that folds out to a bed.

You don't say anything. It's fast how hard he is, and you are wet the minute the space between you is crossed, his hand on the back of your head, then his teeth lightly on your chin, on your eyelid, on the bone of your wrist. No words. No kisses. Wet. Hard.

I don't want to hurt you he says, pushing deep inside, slipping in as if something like this belonged inside of you. You pull at his back, the flesh of his ass, your fingers splitting the cheeks of his ass as if it might split as you are being split into.

You are and aren't here. Your breath. James's breath. Nothing and everything.

It doesn't last, the urge to devour and be devoured.

In your head there are words first, then voices, then pictures.

James's hands push your hands away from his ass.

He is moaning and his eyes are closed.

Who is he doing this to?

You are thinking about how things get mounted: photographs, girls, dogs. Your eyes bolt around the moonlight-speckled patio. Your eyes move slow and heavy like fabric unwinding.

In your head: This is right. I want him. Then: I am an opening to be thrust into.

You can feel yourself not being in your body.

Mother. Father. The pictures start, this movie that doesn't go away. This is where it starts.

You will make it different. You hear your voice, moans and crying out because it does hurt, it does hurt to be pushed into this way. You think of being poisoned.

I can't breathe.
I think that from between my legs I will lose my mind, you said.

It is over, you keep wanting him. The desire comes back, the desire to be held and stroked, to cry and laugh at the same time.

James is going to make music, lots of it. In this world, he says, music is comparable to giving birth.

I'll have to think about that, you say.

I said, stop staring at me Tracy. I just don't want anyone to touch me, not now, not ever, James says this. Who else?

You don't ask about last night.

Love is unquestioning?

So you try to make him absent then.

You cut his shape out of the background, his figure becoming a blank space just set into the wall, the outline of a figure, surrounded by your own things, books, snapshots, the blue antique dress behind this figure. This figure.

James's hands are on his neck. He is reading the sports page. Daddy why are you always reading the sports page? There is dust on the books. With a dirty sock you start to dust the tops of the books. Then you go to the sink and wash the one cup that you just drank water from, wash it with soap and scalding water that burns the tops of your fingers. The newspaper is turning. It's not working. It might work.

You are hungry, can't eat, cleaning is something to do, something to put order on what can't really be ordered. You know this. Still you feel that you have to make things work, even what seems impossible, irreconcilable, the hatred that you felt move into you last night like poison.

Whose hatred?

Let's get one thing straight you want to say. I would like to know why it is that you couldn't really touch me last night, touch me and not just yourself, you want to say.

It's an all-over-green feeling, no, almost yellow, your hands pressing into the earth today, digging hard until beneath your fingernails were filled with heavy blackness, like the dull diamond press pattern inside a sunflower, your head, your hands. The sunflower's heavy head droops down.

You sit next to a hardening cow patty watching the sun that is as thick behind the clouds as your legs under this dress as you walked up the hill to this spot.

When you close your eyes you can feel the warmth of the sun on your face and when you open your eyes you can't feel anything at all, except this passion, this passion that turns into hatred because you can't have it, this passion that turns into a hatred that numbs.

You sit down.

James's hand is still on his neck. He rolls his head from side to side.

It is hard to concentrate, to make him be an outline for something.

This is the problem of seeing only what is in front of you, objects interacting with one another. Stones can't talk.

Concentrate. You won't register his eyes rolling around in his head like big green marbles, marbles that you can lick holding their shiny coolness to your lips. You aren't going to register his tongue sliding on pillow-soft lips. James's elbow marks a single triangle of the patterned curtain. You could concentrate on that.

This triangle surrounded by the white of his arm, an arm scooping a crescent around his face.

You know what his face looks like. You aren't going to look.

Seeing your own hatred in someone's face, your anger reflected in someone's eyes, this is the point where something has to happen.

Snap, he catches your eye, a feeling of dropping a great distance, the thought all of a sudden that your face is like the skin of an onion.

You can't breathe this way for long.

You think that one of you is shrinking from the confines of

the room. Eye to eye. Whose face viewed from the bottom of an unsettled pool? One of you is not equipped with gills and will slip, can't someone see this? One of you will slip like a clipped spider plant reaching aimlessly for the bottom, glass as an eye.

At the bottom the back of a head (whose?) peels away to contour the deceiving smoothness (head or glass?), colors kaleidoscope and mute. Even in the darkness the green eye sucks at another's tiny mouth, cotton filtering lumps of flesh for that second per second suspension (sex or air filter?). Stomachs prickle, rubbing murky heads, separating one's magnified weightlessness, from one's horizons of deflating angles.

As always it's for a moment, what you know and what you don't know, and then the waterline drops, collapsing flesh, evaporating moisture, escape just slivering away unnoticed through what could be a metal strainer, might be sadness, maybe fear.

Are you to sleep yet?

It's all about power isn't it?

You just want to be in someone else's head to look out and see the world through their eyes.

You always trying to see both sides at once, both sides of everything, unable to admit that without aid it is really impossible to see the back of your own head.

What is it that you want from me? James asks another time.

Come here little girl he says and it starts all over again.

There is always three, that's the pictures that you can't get out of your head, the movie that distances yourself from a situation. There is always three, your mother and your father and an ambiguous other. You? A man and a woman and then you. This is the picture. This is what can't be contained no matter how carefully you wipe the dust from the tops of your books, or how hot you can tolerate the water for dishes. You can't make these three go away. This triangle.

There can only be two.

In the dream there are a man and a woman lying face down next to each other on a wide couch. On top of the man and on top of the woman

*are two children. There is a boy on top of the man and there is a girl
on top of the woman. The man and the woman are asleep. From the
children, from their entire beings come deep guttural cries and gur-
glings. Let me in, let me in, the children are crying, flailing their open
hands against the backs of the adult bodies.*

Here on the porch waiting . . . The horizon really is slipping.
Two-dimensional mountain ranges deflecting their angles under
heavy skies.

Wait for me, James said. I'll probably be back around
five-thirty. So you wait.

Your eyes are open wide, transparent lids threatening to
disappear into the back of your head.

You are not going to believe that James wasn't seeing all that
you were seeing.

Two weeks? You had plans.

This time it won't be like nights pretending that you don't
have to sleep, nights when all you can think about is the
possibilities of the two of you together. The possibilities and
not you girdled in bones as sharp as the steel sculpture James has
in his mother's garage. The steel sculpture of a prehistoric sea
creature, its ribs suspended from the garage ceiling. Steel ribs
waiting to contain something, waiting to drop.

I might just kill someone if I didn't sculpt, James said.

*How many forms of murder are there? This is what you wanted to
know.*

*What you thought then, that the killing of some people's souls was
enforced over and over by works of art such as his, a steel structure. You
thought then that every work of art ever made had the potential to
instill again and again a vision of a world where no one could connect
and the only thing left to do was to frantically manipulate matter to
express what was inside. Denying the loneliness and dying and killing
over and over.*

What of talking? Touching? James? What of all the teenage
girls like my sister, lost?

If you have come over to preach. If you have come over to "talk," James said, then I am awfully busy.

You just wish that you never met.

There was three then too. There was a woman, James's friend that wanted you from the day you met the two of them on the porch of the college dormitory.

Just call me Missy, the tall woman with the cropped blond hair says to you laughing. Everyone calls me Missy. My real name is Lucinda, which is out of the question, as is Lucy, so I just started calling myself Missy when I was a kid, real individual-like. She shakes your hand that has already started to sweat because of the way her eyes are tracing you, the eyes of a man admiring an object. Missy, a woman and not a girl, not a girl to let someone take anything away from her, nothing taken away from her in the way she entitles herself to look at you.

Go away Missy, you say in your head. Go away Mother? June? Just two, just two, already ordering trying to contain the telltale sweat dripping from your palms.

Cold and clammy, she says. It's nice to meet you Tracy. Aren't you the girl that lives behind the old store across from the firehouse? I have seen you dancing in there before. You are pretty good, possessed really.

There is conversation, but you are not aware of what is being said, of what you yourself are saying about the prospects of summer: the lake, hikes to the Falls, the Indian burial ground, the carnival, and then the books, and the classes.

James is watching you. Missy is watching you. Three people on a porch. Three people to figure out what you are supposed to do with.

There is a shadow quivering across Missy's top lip as she leans against the porch pillar. The yellow evening light seems to be magnifying everyone's bodily functions: the sounds of lips moving, the sounds of breathing, the smell of James a perfume you want to devour, the touch of Missy's shoe against your calf as she shifts her long legs, a heavy ache mixing with James's sweat.

What is happening is that James whispers in your ear that Missy wants you. What is happening is that James pulls you next to him and Missy sits down next to you, too close. Your heart is pounding. Let me go, you say in your head.

I have a gun Missy says. I'd use it if I had to.

It is to see who is stronger, you and June tangled on the floor, all teeth and limbs and adrenaline.

On the porch through the yellow light and the swarming gnats you see this:

Two women and one man, their hands entwined like trusting children and they all laugh and laugh, faces like soft moons polished with perspiration.

You aren't laughing. Two there has to be only two.

Again Missy says, I have a gun, and now you see the pores on her nose, pores that are widening as you look at them, pores through which might ooze white tendrils, miniature noose ropes. Stop.

James is watching you as if you were in an experiment. His green eyes, glass marbles to put to your lips.

Stop staring at me, he said.

I have a gun, she said.

Where James is sitting, his back against a peeling white pillar is where you might be sitting too if Missy would just go away. James flexes and spreads his feet as if the porch were covered with sand.

The shadow moves into Missy's mouth.

Every day Missy comes by your apartment. You hide in the bathroom or just don't answer the door. James and Missy. Mom and Dad. Just go away then, all of you. Alone in the bathroom your face in the mirror.

How quickly you fell into James's spiraling green eyes, his gaze whirling your head, spinning you this way. Then there was her gaze outlining your shape, spinning you the other way.

You always trying so hard to make it work, so ready to give yourself.

You are standing on the porch.

Before summer began, how long before? Townspeople clad in flannel plaids, carrying buckets and drills and metal spouts, sapped trees. Where were you then, James?

It is important to want to work.

Next time you think you might try to find them there, there in the woods where the maples are swelling with juice. You are going to see if perhaps out of the small piece of bark removed from the tree to insert the nozzle that starts the flow of sugaring season, you want to see if perhaps out of that small piece of bark you can fashion for yourself a new pair of eyelids. These new eyelids delicately carved from this piece of wood and complete with tiny hinges would enable you to shut your eyes just as you pleased.

With your new eyelids you would step off this porch, leaves crunching underfoot, your bare blue feet crumbling the sun colors of the leaves. You wouldn't remember the calming of your nervous hands, after the white blister light of that one time, yes, only once grounded into a bliss.

You might cut into your back where the sharp lines of your shoulder blades protrude, quick incisions one on each side, opening up the flesh so that you might be able to breathe.

And whatever falls from your mouth in the autumn certainly you won't forget how long it took the townspeople to sweeten the bitter sap, gallons and gallons boiled down to almost nothing.

Sap as bitter and slow as the taste in your mouth after retching up your insides again all summer. Days spent alone in the bathroom looking down at the bowl of your muddy refusals. These things that really do come from your body, but not this way, not this way. Your wet red eyes examining smear-faced hatreds in the backward mirror. Your aspirations blurring, dissolving, dissipating into the confines of this tiny room.

You feel as though you were only glued inside this body, and vomiting dignifies this divided self.

You think of gray to gray. The possible solutions are gray to gray, how long it takes to leave and go back, leave and go back, and finally leave taking with you what has to be taken with you. It's the gray to gray of ordering and arranging all that you must carry because you can't give any of it away. Gray to gray like the paraffin patches that seal the bottom of the wooden sap buckets. Small gray wax patches, to prevent the sap from oozing out the bottom.

Ahead of you James is taking the corners fast. With the car window open you can smell the damp trees. There have been thunderstorms for three days, the humid air electric. Sky, trees, mountains. You feel glassed in. In a terrarium certain lizards can blend into their surroundings, become almost undetectable. The car moves through hot and cold spots on the mountain road that are like the varying temperatures in any deep body of water.

Orange tiger lilies line the roads, the red and orange blossoms pointing in all directions. This is not comforting.

The sun warms the dashboard. The landscape glows. The car seems to be floating.

James crosses over the double line. He is going too fast. Your speedometer says 75. You don't want to lose him.

There is a farmhouse that has Christmas decorations, a plastic Santa with a sleigh driving down an imitation-snow-splotched roof. The snow brown with summer dust. There is a green metallic bow on a front door. There are children on a porch, barelegged, dancing, one girl in high heels that don't fit, shoes that she won't want, will be forgotten, by the time they do fit.

You are going down a steep grade. The shadows from the trees that line the highway are hypnotic. In California roads like this smell of eucalyptus.

You had wanted to tell him that you were afraid and that you just wanted to be held, that you didn't want to be penetrated, because sometimes it made you feel dead.

While you were having sex you had tried so hard not to think of other things.

You got all dry and had to stop.

In a dream you are running along a ledge. It is dark on either side. The ledge you are on is a thin board. When you realize this, how thin the board is, you are unable to run. You must walk as if you were on a balance beam.

You can't see James anymore. It's there but not on the road. It's off the road, stuck on a tree. Not it's not James's car. But it is. Eucalyptus smells like flea powder. You aren't floating across straps of light anymore.

You get out of the car. There is no one around. James's windshield is shattered. James is in there. There is blood on his face and the flesh is peeled in places. His eyes are open and moving.

Oh my God. Oh my God. Drenched in sweat. Blood on an arm feels wet, water moving.

You can see all this, but it's not happening, didn't happen, not making love, not crashing, not James saying I'm sorry I hurt you. Not James saying I love you.

James doesn't look at you anymore. I love you, is what you said, and then he went away.

You can't sleep nights. The townspeople use steel buckets to catch the sap.

WISHBONE

YOU had started keeping lists.

One of the lists you are compiling is a list of all the things you want. First on this list is to open a detective agency in Equinox. It's hard to imagine all the things you could prove with a license to spy.

There is something dreadfully wrong in Equinox. You can't

see it in the eyes of the inbred or mentally retarded, you can't see it in the faces of the men, women and children that suffer from poverty and domestic violence. Where you really notice that something awful has happened is in the mirror, in the bank, at church; it's in the way people hold a given facial expression long after the emotion that triggered it has passed. You think that people talk to you at night. As soon as you fall asleep, just close your eyes, the voices start. When you wake up it is silent and uncomfortable.

You want to know why no one in Equinox recognizes how bad their symptoms have gotten. With your camera you want to show people what is wrong here. You want to know why it is that people's actions belie what they are really thinking. You want to know this but you don't really know where to begin because you don't want anyone to know about your lists.

Lists are a good thing to have. Lists help you to remember where you are and what you are supposed to be doing at any given moment in a day.

You are never exactly sure what you are supposed to be thinking in any given social situation, so the lists provide you with a guideline for appropriate behavior.

You are sure that you are being given clues, that with the right amount of clues you will be able to figure out once and for all what you are supposed to be doing.

Equinox is a small town, small enough to have boundaries, a city limit, streets that designate specific classes of people. Right here in Equinox you can see everything.

It's almost spring. It won't stop, the onslaught of new growth. The redwing blackbirds returned. The ice and snow melted, hints of color are starting to blend into the gray of winter. It won't stop. Sometimes you wish you could make it stop. Just go back, you say to the branches of the trees, to the swelling bumps beneath the silvery bark, don't come out you say pressing the palms of your hands along the braille bumps where soon leaves will be. Just not yet, you say, because sometimes it does seem like there is a better time for things to happen. Go back you say to all that is alive, all that is blanketed under the gray of winter.

At night the stars sparkle overhead, the eyes of the night, what you could be or are, as if many people were looking up all at once and the bright constellations embedded in blackness were the reverse image of so many dilated pupils.

You started making the want list about the same time you started working at the Mountain View Care Home. You met Miya then. Miya is twenty-three and the mother of two daughters. Miya's mother, Grace, is the manager of this care home for the elderly. But you really started keeping the lists when you felt yourself getting close to Father Stellehy.

Father's history interests you, a man who wanted to devote his life to silence and contemplation but who keeps coming back into the world because of illnesses that require special care.

Father Stellehy is a Cartusian monk, who has lived most of his life in the monastery just outside of Equinox. He has diabetes.

The first time Father got lost in the woods he was placed in Mountain View until he was well enough to return to the monastery. Back at the monastery the prior put Father Stellehy in charge of answering the mail. After he got lost the first time he was never able to function in any specific role.

What is the difference between running away and getting lost then?

The second time Father got lost hiking in the same woods the brothers at the monastery said he couldn't come back.

Father Stellehy tells you that he learned his sense of direction from his father. He tells you this when you ask him if he was afraid on the days when he was lost in the woods.

Father will tell you even when you don't ask, he will tell you that his real passion is for hiking.

One winter he led a hike with the brothers of the monastery and when they reached one snow-covered peak Father saw that the only way down was over the side of a slippery cliff. All the brothers came down the side of that peak in about five minutes, Father says wiping his eyes. Their underwear was all ripped and tattered.

Father has a twin brother in New Zealand, a twin brother who is not a monk.

You have always wanted a twin. For as long as long as you can remember you have been envious of the fact that two people can be born at the same birth, of the same single egg.

This, a disease? Wanting to escape the lie of individuality, to recognize a real sameness, see yourself incarnate in another body? You try so hard to be different. You are not. You try so hard to be different that you crave what you have to deny to really be different, a commonality between yourself and another person that you think you could really see if you were a twin.

When Father Stellehy was a little boy he and his twin brother would go out into the woods with their father who sometimes worked as a prospector for the major insurance company he owned. Father tells you that if you are ever lost in the woods, if you have a compass there is really nothing to be afraid of. Father didn't have a compass.

You want to know why Father looks at you the way he does, like he knows something about you that you don't know about yourself. You want to know why you have this recurring fantasy of making love to him on the pullout sofa in your efficiency apartment. You want to know why around Father and around Miya you always feel as if this had all happened before, so many times.

At night when you are making your rounds you have heard Father say in his sleep things like: Here, if you want me, or, My soul is bleeding.

Does the truth come out when people talk in their sleep? You are glad that you live alone because you are afraid of what you might say when you are asleep. You are not sure why you are afraid, you just are.

Father watches you. You just need to know what way he likes you. There are so many ways to like a person.

You want to know why Father Stellehy keeps coming back into the world. You want to know why some nights when you come into Father's room he is crouched over his roommate Henry's bed. Father will quickly pull up Henry's covers. He is breathing fast and his hands are shaking.

You think that Father is beautiful. You imagine how he might hold you. You imagine this while you rub lotion on his vein-exploded legs before he goes to bed at night. You imagine that his eyes are closed and that he is moaning and drenched in sweat pressing you against him. Father is blind in his left eye. As you pull back the lower lid to apply the lubricating ointment to his cloudy green eye you are afraid he might ask you why your palms are so sweaty, or why your pulse is racing. He holds your hand sometimes.

Miya is a small woman. Her clothed figure looks boyish. She wants to be an artist maybe: draw or paint. She tells you that there are things inside of her that she needs to get out. She is not sure what she is supposed to do. She has her two kids, and her husband Skip. She is sure that there has to be something else. Her face is pale and she always wears an expression of boredom.

Miya's handwriting is beautiful. You look forward to reading her shift reports. Miya's handwriting changes from day to day, large or small depending not on the contents of her reports. Nor do the contents of the reports reveal why sometimes Miya presses the cursive words so heavily onto the paper. When you turn over these pages and brush your fingertips over the back the space on the paper between the lines that shape the words is puffy in places like the flesh around wrinkles. Miya works very hard. You would like to take Miya away from here, go somewhere and talk. You don't think she belongs in this place. One of the things on your list is to save people; help them.

Miya tells you that she dreams of you at night. When she says this she is always doing something else, doesn't look you in the eyes. She says, don't forget to bring the milk up from the basement, I dreamt of you last night. You don't tell Miya that you have dreamt of her. A good detective listens.

Father Stellehy says that he is sure that he dreams during the day, when he is wide awake, because often he will be engaged in an activity and when asked about what he is doing, he will have to think for a moment. Grace says it's amnesia. Father is sure that when he is not aware of the motions that he is performing, he is dreaming.

Miya thinks that the reason Father keeps coming back into the world, is unable to stay in the monastery, is because he is just a horny old man. Miya is sure that he has probably been that way for his whole life. Miya says that Father's desires just got the best of him and that is why he is sick. People get sick from denying, Miya says. You want to know why no one in Equinox sees this.

Most of the residents here are in a constant state of mourning, Grace says. You ask Grace why it is that sometimes Father's roommate Henry will for no apparent reason look like he is being strangled. The pills help, Grace says, making sure they get outdoors helps, she says. Hypnotic pills, they give old people hypnotic pills. Symptoms of mourning, you must learn all of them.

There is a disease that marks the afflicted with an increasing loss of memory. The disease occurs mostly in old people.

You must keep remembering.

You want to know why Miya's family is the way it is. You want to know why they keep doing what they are doing. You are sure that they are not happy. Miya's father deserted Grace when Miya was seven. Miya's stepfather, the cook at the Mountain View, Don, drinks vodka like water from the moment he wakes up. Don used to race sailboats. Grace doesn't listen to his long stories about the ocean. He tells them anyway. Don has the biggest hands you have ever seen, they must be twice the size of your head. Miya's sister Justine wears combat boots and likes girls. Most of the residents are afraid of Justine and like to be out of their rooms when she comes to clean. Justine wants to open a restaurant. First Justine wants to locate her father. She says she might kill him. Lately Justine has been working in the yard, planting things, pulling up weeds. You can't understand why Justine stays here. You can't understand why you don't like her, you just don't.

Don reminds you of your stepfather Big Herb. Don is cooking. He could easily pass as Grace's twin brother. They both have short curly black hair, large stomachs and massive thighs. They both have nervous hands. Honey do you want me to save this? Don asks, taking a drink from the vodka that he keeps in a tall coffee thermos. Grace is not listening. Don is holding a wishbone. There are still strands of meat on it. Grace is out of sight where she is standing in the breakroom. Don repeats the question. Grace doesn't look up. Whatever you want, she says. He places the wishbone on the windowsill above the sink next to the six other wishbones.

For dinner there is lasagna, a big salad, and garlic bread. It's dry now, your Mom says after everyone has almost finished eating. She goes to the sink. You aren't sure what your Mom is talking about. Above the sink are her violet plants, a tarnished silver spoon that was given to her father when he was born, coupons, popsicle sticks and whatever it is that Mom is getting. Here it is, Mom says, ready to be split. Your father and I did the last one and I think that you and I did the one before that Tracy, so I guess it is either Tracy and June or June and Dad. I'll get this one so let me do it with Tracy, June says finishing her fourth piece of garlic bread. Oh but I want to do it, Dad says.

June stands up and you each hold an end of the wishbone. There are still pieces of dried chicken on the bone. June doesn't pull and the end you break off is smaller than hers meaning that you don't get your wish and June does.

You are not to think of June.

After a while your mother told Big Herb to go away. Your mother never really liked Big Herb. You know this. How could she have? But Grace reminds you of your mother and this is what is really important. Grace reminds you of your mother because her eyes look past Don.

It's because most things seem to happen to you now as if you were in a movie. You have started seeing your life as if it were a movie, but this awareness hasn't made the movie stop, the signs have only become more confusing. What you do every day: go to school or to work, these frames of events you have peopled with the only characters you know. The only characters you feel comfortable with, feel safe with, the ones that don't go away, the ones you manifest in everyone because this is how you see now.

These are three characters that you give to the people that come into your life. These characters are of course your mother and father and then there is June, your sister June. Sometimes someone will remind you of your Dad, sometimes of your Mom, and sometimes a mix of both or maybe all three. How you know these three people, this is how you know others.

And then there are your parents' parents and people that you have never even met (these voices, actions you find yourself doing, the things that happen to you, that happen again and again, what has happened before, *déjà-vu*).

You see your life as a movie on a speed so fast that you must keep your eyes wide open to catch what you are sure you are supposed to see if you just look close enough. You keep your eyes open so that you can catch the signs, the subliminal cues that whiz past, the cues that will show you where to go. You take pictures.

You take pictures, photograph things so that you can hold on to what is slipping away. No, you take pictures of other people, small likenesses of people that you don't understand or are afraid of, people that you want to see without being seen by. You take pictures because you want to hold something.

Sometimes it seems like you have to fight to make things not happen because most things seem to happen in a pattern. It seems as though you were given so many warnings of what was to come.

You started it.

The people you have met and meet and the places that you have been and go to now, everything seems to point to a future already made, a future where there will be very specific things that you will have to do.

How things happen, get arranged in space, not randomly but orchestrated. It's just that sometimes people make the wrong decisions, and other people might not be paying attention.

You are running but your body is stationary. You are not dreaming.

First there is a woman standing in the street holding a big white pillow to her chest. She is pacing back and forth in front of a group of people. They are huddled beneath a willow tree. There was an accident. There are tire tracks that swerve off the road. There is a car crushed into a tree. Your heart is pounding. You are running. You didn't want to see the lady there on the blanket, her right leg, knee up, delicately bent like she was sunbathing. Should you stop? There is a light snow falling, the sky is lead gray.

Miss, Miss . . . the man next to the pacing lady with the pillow yells to a woman driving past in a cream-colored Toyota. She stops, her face is attentive to the urgent arms waving directions. Her expression stays the same as she drives up the hill.

The lady's face is white. She is laying on a blanket on the snow-wet grass. There's blood on her forehead as thick as Halloween makeup. Her car is crushed into the willow tree, there are tire tracks. The trees cast a shadow across the lawn like grabbing fingers. You are running, trying to figure out who you are going to tell this to. You look over your shoulder. A small black boy is standing next to a fence. He is watching you. The lady might be dead. No, you think. The urgency of the word no, like standing in the icy river behind your house. What should be happening? This is all like playing Hide-and-go-seek. You are cold.

Does it ever really matter where a person is?

This an accident? What can be stopped?

There is a man who lost everything, has nothing at all.

How it struck you reading the obituary of a young man who was killed when his motorcycle crashed into a retaining wall, hard, then ironic, then not at all. As does everything tragic that has lost its meaning because no one can hear the same things over and over without going numb.

But it did strike you, because there is something to be said about this man who died, something to be said about this man who had lost his family in a fire the previous year, something to be said about the fact that you are still alive.

Is this what you must hold most sacred then? Your luck thus far?

You wish to be handicapped, physically unable to perform the tasks at hand. You wish for this reason to explain away your helplessness.

In your dreams it is hard to distinguish one person from another. In your dreams people's faces switch from body to body. Bodies might evaporate into settings. A person might disappear into the surf and reappear on the dunes with a different face.

In your dreams you might be making love to a man only to find out that it is really a woman.

You wish to be handicapped because awake you don't know how to generalize this information.

With crutches you wouldn't be expected to walk straight and confident. You could think anything you wanted and wouldn't have to be afraid you might act upon your thoughts, passionate or otherwise. This would be a definition. With crutches or a wheelchair you wouldn't have to explain that you are more interested in the way someone's gaze locks into your spine creating an eerie feeling of helplessness you don't want to explain. You are more interested in this feeling, in understanding this feeling than in pretending self-confidence. With crutches or a wheelchair you would be helpless.

There are games to play that you wouldn't be expected to participate in wholly.

You can do anything you want, your mother said.

But why should you do anything you want when there are people that really are handicapped?

You just don't like these games at all. You are having a hard enough time contending with the game at hand, deciphering the coded messages people share with one another. You are trying to understand these games, what it is that people really want. What is it that you really want? You are trying to understand.

You are supposed to be perfecting your behavior to achieve the desired results. You are to be so many different things all at once. Someday you are to be a mother, and at the same time you are to have a successful career.

You are immobilized in this story.

Is this all you can do, absorb other people's grief as if you were a sponge? This fear, this pain beneath everyone's actions is all you see. When people smile they are lying. You know this because when you smile inside is something else.

To absorb grief seems to be the only way you know how to survive because it seems as if you have never had any other choice. This is how you can relate to this world at all is to seek out your pain in other people's lives.

If you were handicapped, had a cause to identify your grief with, it would be something to hold on to because there would be no other choice.

You think about the Donner party, people eating people because this is what they had to do to physically survive.

Hungry people.

When events actually occur they are neither romantic nor sensational.

It is only you who possesses the sickening power to think of another's life in the terms that you want, to place judgment on others' lives and choices, what they must do to survive.

There will always be the bones of a hand that once held another, blood and flesh then bones.

To put judgment on another, what it seems you must learn to do in order to play the game that you are somehow special and important, distinct from others is something that you are unable to do. This survival?

In your dream house faces change from one person to the next.

You are supposed to have learned this, how to put words into another's mouth, how to see yourself as worthy of taking from others

what is not rightfully yours (making a fiction out of another's life?).
You must do this if you are to believe in the order of things.

    Sometimes it seems as if you don't belong here in this world.
Sometimes it seems as though you are seeing everything for the first
time and sometimes it seems like you have seen too much, are tired, just
want to go to sleep and never wake up.

    Sometimes it seems that to live in this world at all you are required
to be asleep.

SCIENCE

It is dark outside. Beneath the trees the shadows on the
snow-covered lawn look like giant spiders. Anna is supposed to
be somewhere but she is not sure where. The girls are not
allowed outside, especially when it's dark. Behind Anna the
Equinox School for Girls sits, but she is walking down the icy
gravel path toward the stone pillars at the entrance of the drive.
She is safe so far.

Anna has to get out, has to leave because she doesn't want to
be in the house anymore.

It is dark outside, dark and cold.

As soon as the night assistant in the resident home finds out
that Anna's bed is empty, she will call the police, but Anna's
absence is not realized for a good two hours and by that time
Anna has hitched a ride and is in a car heading toward North
Equinox. Anna wants to go somewhere but she is not sure
where.

"This is where I go," Anna tells the driver of the car. Anna
is left off in front of the North Equinox fire station.

Anna walks up the street away from the fire station. Anna
walks to the lot behind the Lawn and Garden Equipment Warehouse. Behind the lot is a small lake that runs into a waterfall
where the old mill used to be. There is steam rising up from the
lake. There is a pile of coal next to the fuel truck and in front of
a row of tractors. Anna walks through the coal on the ground in

front of the snow-splotched mountain of coal. The coal is sharp beneath her bedroom slippers. Anna crawls under the fuel truck. There is no snow there. Anna lays down on her stomach. The ground smells like oil and is frozen hard. Anna turns on her side and pulls her knees to her chest. She can see Christmas lights that are blinking off and on across the street. Anna tries to warm up a little, tries to think of where she will go.

Tracy is in her apartment. She is alone in her apartment. The apartment is one room except for the bathroom that is in the room where the closet would be if there was a closet.

The room has everything: a stove, a refrigerator, a sink, a bed, a small table, a desk, shelves for books, a rug. There is even a square of linoleum on the floor in front of the stove and refrigerator and sink and small table, a square of linoleum that marks out the kitchen area in this one room, linoleum that is white with gold specks and splashes, glittery.

Tracy keeps Christmas lights around the windows and has set the two strings of lights each with the special bulb that makes the lights blink off and on. Each strand blinks off and on at different times, first the left string lights up around the window and then the right. Up close to the lights there is a faint clicking sound as the lights blink on, then off, a pulse.

When there is a good song on the radio Tracy will turn up the volume.

Tracy is nervous, anxious really, can't figure out what to do. It's almost Christmas and she is not sure where she will be this Christmas. Tracy is drinking cheap wine and smoking too much. Dancing is good, spinning and turning, pretending someone is watching. Tracy goes into the bathroom a lot to look at herself in the mirror. Tracy sees herself in the mirror, a body with eyes that keep looking into eyes that keep looking back. This is something to do.

The streets of North Equinox are empty. Tracy looks out the window and sees what is always there: the tractors, the warehouse barn, the firehouse, the fuel truck, everything dark and dotty and still except for the steam rising up from the lake and the waterfall. It is too cold outside. Pipes have frozen in nearby towns, and there have been lots of fires. On the news, before the weather report about the bizarre subzero temperatures and heavy snowfalls expected, there was an apartment complex in flames. Faulty wiring. Dead children. A newscaster saying that a fund has been started for the homeless families that lived in the apartment building that is shown still burning on the news report even though the fire must have been out for some time. These records that distort time. A place to call to donate money. Poor people burn and freeze. Spring? Telephone numbers.

From beneath the coal truck Anna has been watching the blinking Christmas lights.

Anna has remembered where she wanted to go. She wanted to go to Miss Wassick's. Miss Wassick is Anna's favorite staff at the Equinox School.

Miss Wassick lives past the firehouse. But Miss Wassick will make Anna go back to the school. No she can't go to Miss Wassick's because Anna is not going to go back to the school. The Christmas lights are all colors and blink off and on. Anna wants lights like that someday for her own place. The coal pile smells like big tires. The ground is hard and no matter how tightly Anna pulls her legs to her chest she can't get warm. Her lips are turning blue. It's past midnight. Through the curtains of the small apartment where the Christmas lights are Anna can see the shadow of someone dancing, moving fast.

Anna thinks to go knock on the door of the apartment with the Christmas lights, that maybe whoever is in there can tell her what to do next, help her to remember where it is that she is going. It's too cold and Anna's hands and feet feel like they are burning. Anna uncurls her body, climbs out from beneath the truck and goes to the coal pile. From the coal pile Anna scrapes off some of the snow that is not ice and rubs this on her hands, but that burns worse.

Tracy is staring at the curtains. She is seated at her desk now and staring at the curtains, the ones that came with the apartment just like the stove and the sofa bed and the square of white linoleum with the streaks of gold glitter.

The curtains are a flowered pattern in ugly colors: neon green and orange and brown, a big pattern that reminds Tracy of beach clothes.

There is about to be a knock on the door.

Anna is walking across the street heel to toe like she was walking a balance beam. Anna has decided that if her left foot is the one to touch the concrete porch in front of the apartment first, that she will knock on the door.

Within the flowered pattern on the curtain there are lines, short lines like the pattern made by a seamstress's transfer wheel, stitches. The lines aren't part of the petals or the stems of the leaves. A person designed the ugly pattern on these curtains. A fabric to make things with, fabric that makes shirts and dresses and curtains. The radiator is hissing.

Anna is halfway across the street. It is a game now, and that is what she is thinking about.

Tracy keeps looking at the pattern in the curtains and in the pattern she has begun to see things, a grimacing face, a house hidden in trees, small faces with open mouths or squinted eyes.

There is a blank piece of paper in front of Tracy, and she starts to draw on the paper. Under the desk her feet move. She could walk a mile for all their movement under the desk. Ticking.

Tracy is making scribbles with her pen, moving the pen across the paper, she is trying to draw nothing consciously, like how the patterns in the curtains become something other than what was intended by the designer. Tracy is trying to make her pen draw something by itself, is trying to allow her hand to be guided from somewhere inside herself, someplace she is not aware of. From the scribbles Tracy is making on the paper she hopes that something will appear, something recognizable.

Tracy is making scribbles on the paper, sometimes fast and sometimes with her eyes closed or by turning and moving the paper beneath the pen. Tracy is remembering the phone conversation she had with her mother last week.

"This is the operator, collect call from Tracy."

"I can't accept the charges," Viola says.

Tracy holds the receiver, listens for the dial tone, clicks the receiver, then dials direct.

"Mom, I just had to talk to you. Something is wrong. What is it? Did something happen? Is everyone there all right? I had this feeling today that June was dead. Have you heard from her?"

"I haven't heard from her, no. If something had happened, if June was dead Tracy I would know about it, I would feel it inside. Mothers know these things about their children."

"Mom I really . . ."

"Tracy this is a bad time. I am really burned out, can't talk now, was there something important?"

"Mom are you all right? I worry about you. I have been thinking a lot lately . . . it's this idea I have that I have been trying to show in my photographs of the people of Equinox. It's that . . ."

Inside it feels like I am dying, Tracy wanted to say to her mother on the phone right then but instead she continues with her idea.

"I think Mom that people make their lives stressful, want the world to be constantly pressing in on them from all sides because then they don't have to contend with what is on the inside trying to get out."

On the other end Viola's tone of voice has changed. "I didn't mean to snap, Tracy, it's that I'm so tired. It's strange but lately . . . I have been working on this with my therapist, telling her about this . . . lately I feel as if I were finally getting in touch with the little girl inside of me. It's part of myself that has been lost for so long, Tracy, the anger that forced the girl deep inside, buried her with my father, but she is coming back into my life now."

Tracy wanted to scream then but instead listening to her mother's voice, a soft voice that catches in Tracy's throat, instead Tracy fidgets with the cord of the phone, the spiral of rubber that stretches out a distance then coils back.

The scribble beneath Tracy's hand is a heavy, pressed knot, a squiggle of concentric circles that is dark in the middle where the pen has almost pierced through the paper.

The toe of Anna's left slipper touches the cement of the porch.

It seems to Tracy that her mother always voices first what Tracy herself has been thinking about as if there were nothing for Tracy to discover.

Tracy wants to go home.

In the apartment Tracy is standing more or less in the middle of the room. She is standing next to the fold-out sofa that divides the kitchen from the rest of the room. She is trying to figure out an interesting self-portrait.

There is a loud knock on the door. Tracy moves her camera from in front of the door. Someone knocks again. Tracy opens the door. The cold air fills the room. "Let me in lady, you gotta let me in."

The blinking lights frame the dirty face of a young girl with short cropped hair. The girl is holding a shopping bag. She is wearing a parka that is too small over a nightgown. Her lips are blue. On her feet are bedroom slippers.

"Help me. Help me. You gotta let me in lady. Hurry they're after me." Anna's head bolts from side to side looking up and down the street. "Please can I come in? You won't call them? Just let me in."

Behind the girl's head the trees are motionless. The trees that line the streets look like eyelashes. Shadows and trees. This girl's eyes are wild. The sky is heavy and gray. It is supposed to snow tonight.

A girl in a nightgown with a dirty face, someone running. Tracy is afraid. The girl's lips are blue and her teeth are chattering. The girl's eyes blink innocent then sinister then innocent again.

"You gotta let me in lady."

"I'll let you in but only for a minute. Who are you?"

The girl comes into the apartment and Tracy shuts the door. The girl moves about the room. She goes to the radiator and leans her back against it, turns and rubs her hands together over it then turns back again.

"My name is Anna Murray and I'm running away."

"Where are you going? Here you can sit down for a minute. Where are you from? It's kind of late to be outside. You must be freezing."

"This is a cool place. Are you a punk or something? I've been watching this place for a while. You like to dance."

Anna walks into the bathroom. There is dried menstrual blood on the back of her blue print flannel nightgown. Anna looks at herself in the white frame oval mirror and then she sits on the toilet seat and looks at the snapshots plastered on the wall above the bathroom sink.

"Who are all these people? Are you sure you aren't going to tell on me, 'cause I'll leave right now."

"No I'm not going to tell on you. Are you running away from home? Your parents must be very worried."

"I was taken away from my parents, lady. Give me a cigarette." Anna reaches the pack away from Tracy and lights a cigarette.

"Are you sure your name is Anna Murray? Where are you running from?"

"You don't believe me. That's OK lady. My name is Anna Murray and I'm eleven and I live at the Equinox girls' school and I left there because I hate it, and I always leave and they find me and I go back. See these?"

Anna pulls up the sleeve of her nightgown. On the inside of her right arm in a line like Orion's belt are three cigarette burns that have almost healed, purplish welts the size of Anna's dilated pupils.

"That's from playing chicken the last time I ran away. My Mom just got out of jail. I hate the Equinox School. I always leave and then I go back. And I fight it when they bring me back and they put me in a room in the basement. This is a cool place you have lady. Give me another smoke."

Anna didn't finish the first cigarette. She set it on the edge of the sink and it is slowly burning itself out. There is a gray ash lengthening on the white sink.

"Are you sure you aren't a punk?"

"What's a punk?"

"You know someone who does whatever they want and wears wild clothes and stuff. How come you have these lights up? It's great. Where are your parents?"

Anna walks around the room looking at things like she was in a store. "Cool," Anna says going to the fish tank. "Blub, blub," Anna says moving her finger up the side of the tank as fast as the air bubbles from the filter.

Anna isn't aware of the cigarette in her hand. Tracy thinks she might burn something or just drop it. Anna stops in front of the snapshot on the refrigerator. The snapshot is of a young girl in heavy black eyeliner wearing a T-shirt with a butterfly on it. The girl in the snapshot is staring hypnotically. The girl has her hands folded on her lap. The snapshot is ripped on one corner and has many thumbtack holes from hanging in different places.

"This girl looks crazy. Who is it?"

"It's my sister. She ran away from home when she was eleven."

"Cool."

Tracy looks in the refrigerator. "I'll make you a sandwich."

Anna isn't interested in the sandwich and chips and seated across from Tracy at the table Anna is watching Tracy watch her.

"Aren't you hungry?"

"Yeah I'm real hungry." Anna's eyes jerk around the room and she can't keep her hands still. She doesn't touch the food.

"I hallucinate." Anna is moving the chips around the plate, encircling the sandwich with the chips by carefully lining the chips up around the edge of the plate. "I see things. This scares me. There are people all in black and they follow me around in the day. Sometimes they tell me what to do, to hit someone or throw things or to run away. They lock me up at that school lady."

Tracy is going to call the school. She is afraid of Anna. Tracy thinks of knives, thinks of her sister June. Tracy doesn't want Anna here anymore and then she feels guilty knows she should try to help this girl, that maybe the place Anna is in, the Equinox School, is a horrible place.

Tracy feels dizzy because she knows that this girl is supposed to be in her house now, that this girl is here for a reason, sitting here in the kitchen telling her these things. Tracy knows that this is what is supposed to be happening.

"Listen Anna, I am going to call your school. Please stay here." Tracy is afraid that Anna will hit her all of a sudden or that Anna will try to run while Tracy calls the school. The phone isn't in Tracy's apartment. The phone is in another part of this house that Tracy's apartment is in. Tracy can't let Anna get away.

"Yeah all right lady, tell them I'm tired. Tell them to get the locked room ready."

"Anna please stay here."

Tracy doesn't know what to say when the person on the other end answers the phone and says, "Equinox School." Tracy doesn't know what to say about the business at hand, because what she wants to know is how come her house? How come out of all the houses in Equinox Anna is in hers?

The woman at the school is friendly, says she hopes Anna isn't being too much of a problem, tells Tracy that the best thing to do would be to get Anna to Paula Wassick's mother's that is right around the corner and that she will send Paula who is at this moment out looking for Anna.

"I'm not going back there lady," Anna says as soon as Tracy sits down at the table. "There was this girl Jamie who graduated from the school, you know. Last week she shot herself right in the head in her Mom's kitchen. At the school they tried to keep this from us. It's a school for crazy girls." Anna says this and laughs. "I was going to see Paula. She lives around here somewhere. But I got scared. Paula she'll tell me what I am supposed to be doing. Did you ever do the finger game?"

"What's that?"

"Lookit. Take your index fingers like this." Anna brings her hands up close to her face and points her index fingers toward each other. "You gotta get them just so and then you can see an extra finger with a fingernail on each side floating right in between. It's a third finger."

Tracy tries it.

"See what I mean?" Anna laughs and then her face hardens. She drums her hands on the table.

"Why don't you show me where Miss Wassick lives now?"

"Why? I can go there myself."

"No, let me take you there."

"Yeah, but when I show you the house and you see that I'm there then I want you to leave, OK?"

The room and the lights, the camera, everything in the room has shifted slightly. Tracy thinks of June and how one time she almost killed the man who owned the liquor store with her bare hands. That snapshot on the refrigerator of June is what Tracy sees when she closes her eyes. When Tracy opens her eyes there is a girl named Anna seated at her kitchen table. In front of Anna is a plate of an uneaten sandwich encircled by potato chips. Stage props.

Tracy gives Anna a coat, a big green coat that she took out of the box of clothes she was planning to get rid of.

Outside Anna and Tracy are walking up the street toward where Anna says Miss Wassick's Mom's house is. Anna's figure in the olive-green coat is hunched. Tracy is next to Anna, moving closer to Anna while Anna keeps moving away. A light snow has started.

In front of a white house that is dark inside Anna says, "You can go now. Please go now. This is the house."

Inside the house a light goes on then off. A shadow moves

past the window in the front room. Anna doesn't see this because she is facing Tracy. "Please go now," Anna says.

"Knock on the door first."

"OK but you stay here." Anna goes to the front door then comes back to where Tracy is standing in the street in front of the white house where Paula Wassick's mother lives. "I guess no one is home."

"I won't leave until you knock on the door."

"Forget it then." Anna starts to walk up the street. "I'm going. I have to go somewhere."

In the house the lights go on. A car comes around the corner and stops in the middle of the street in front of Anna. The car door slams. Anna starts running back down the street toward Tracy's apartment. She jumps out of her slippers. Tracy picks them up. The person from the car runs after her.

"Help me. Help me."

"Anna, stop," the person chasing her yells.

"I hate you Paula. You leave me alone." Paula catches up to Anna and grabs her. Anna shakes loose and runs. Tracy feels as if she were running, as if Anna were Tracy running. They are both running but Tracy is watching. Anna runs past the grocery store, past the newspaper stand. She runs across the bridge by the fire station and then runs back to the empty lot where the coal pile is and the fuel truck. Paula Wassick is close behind.

Anna picks up pieces of coal and starts flinging them at Paula and Tracy. Tracy is not sure what she is supposed to be doing. There is a light snow. Sprinkles of snow are in Anna's and Tracy's and Paula's hair. Anna is barefoot now. Tracy is still holding Anna's slippers. Anna is backing away, throwing rocks and coal, picking up more and throwing them at Paula and at Tracy. "Get away. Please leave me alone." Anna's face is wet and her voice cracks in the icy darkness.

There is a snapshot, a self-portrait. It's a picture that didn't require a photographer because cameras can be set on automatic. It is a picture of eyes looking out. What a strange thing, that someone took a picture of their own self. The act: eyes looking into a camera and no one really taking the picture.

What is in front and what is behind the lens?

What does it matter to think like this when someone is dying and no one screams that this is true?

The lie of the self is the truth of the photograph.

You have a hard time sleeping but you know that you are no longer awake.

And you are looking for signs, signs to tell you what is right. There are people you meet that remind you of your parents, remind you of June. This is how you look for people to love.

So what is happening here? What are these people; this family doing in this home, preparing people to die?

There was a girl that was running away. Some people just want to be in other places.

It started off at church, where else?

You are thinking about the place where your wisdom tooth used to be and your head is pounding.

Every Sunday you take Father Stellehy to church. You like to be alone with him. You like the way he pays attention to you. Father says you would make a good nun. He says if you win the lottery you could go to Europe.

The preacher's robe is pale blue and shimmers when he stands between the altar candles. The robe is much too dignified for this man with a wet hysterical mouth.

If your foot is your undoing, cut if off, the preacher is shouting. Better for you to enter life a cripple than to be thrown into Gehenna with both feet. If your eye is your downfall tear it out. Better for you to enter the kingdom of God with one eye than to be thrown into Gehenna where the worm dies not and the fire is never extinguished, the preacher is yelling.

Father's hands are folded around his cane that is upright in front of his knees. Your face is throbbing. Your pulse is racing because the skin on the back of Father's neck looks so soft.

The throbbing is everywhere. If someone touched you between your legs you are sure that the ache would go away.

Don't forget what I told you, your Mom said. Never talk to strangers.

Father Stellehy is shifting in the pew next to you, his long beige robe tucked tight between his legs. His knuckles are white. He grips the cane tighter. You want to put your head in his lap.

After church Father Stellehy will conduct a small mass in the living room at Mountain View. When Father blows out the altar candles that he set up in front of the large screen TV next to the card table he uses as a pulpit, the fire alarm goes off and you have to evacuate everyone. It is almost a half hour before everyone is escorted out of the house, buckling and unbuckling wheelchair straps, finding robes. It takes so long that you can't turn off the fire alarm and it keeps blaring.

Something is happening to you. There are the notes from home. You tell people about these things, what upsets you, makes you angry or sad. You say these things and it is your voice but it doesn't sound right, words that aren't connected to you telling people these things. I'm sorry, people say, but no one really has time to be sorry, people are just glad when grief doesn't belong to them. You get up, there is school and then work. This skin is yours. You hold on to your lists always.

The hardest thing about this job is changing Flora's colostomy bag, Grace is saying. She pulls hard on her cigarette. You just have to breathe through your mouth, Grace says. Grace's pupils are direct as thumbtacks. The fluorescent light in the breakroom makes you feel sleepy. There are crumbs on the red-and-green spillproof tablecloth, crumbs and cigarette ashes. Grace makes you nervous when she looks at you. She talks over what you are saying. Just words anyway. There is something you both know and words are just clutter over what is really going on here.

You just have to remember that what we are doing here is preparing people to die, Grace says. Don't forget that and your job is much easier.

You ask Grace if anyone has ever died here before. Grace has black hairs on her chin and massive hands that never know what to do with themselves. She is heavy. Her face always looks like it is about to close up into itself, small features disappearing into the flesh. Every day her eyes sink deeper into their sockets.

You are afraid that Flora will die on your shift. Yesterday you heard Grace tell Miya that it was only a matter of days, that Flora wasn't long for this world. If she dies on your shift you don't know what you will do.

Has anyone ever died here, Grace? you ask again. Grace stands up and tugs at her panty hose. Her fingers are clumsy pulling at the slippery tan nylons. Grace takes a maroon ledger from the metal file cabinet under the window at one end of the break-room.

Outside the window Justine is leaning against a maple tree. Her hands are in her pockets. Justine is watching you and her mother. There is a pile of weeds at her feet. Behind her there is a row of daffodils. Justine winks at you and starts raising her eyebrows up and down really fast. The branches of the trees that line the driveway show the progression of spring; small slender green shoots of new growth peak off the wintered branches.

Dear Tracy,
  I can see the future. What people think they really want is to all be like newscasters, that is the goal they want to have, costumed men and women performing their roles like zombies. The man and woman inside us all is at a self-destructing war. The city is poison. Because of the war men and women secretly hate each other. I am still the trickster.

June

WHAT of the letters that you wrote? What of all that you keep? There are all the letters that you wrote to June, most of these letters never sent. And then there are the letters that you wrote to June that were returned unopened. There is this letter that you wrote to June when you were in college dated ——. What was June doing then? Why these outbursts of sharing with someone that you really didn't even know? June only wrote to you to tell you what she wanted to tell you. June didn't want to listen. You don't listen very well, do you?

Dear June,

I am studying the classics now. Interesting books, biographies of men that did whatever they wanted to. I get a laugh now and then because human beings don't change, just their behavior, the things that they do, whatever is fashionable at any given point in history.

What definitely has not changed and this may still be behavior (behavior meaning what someone does and that even though they are doing something they might really be wishing that they were doing something else). What I think has not changed, what I get from all this reading and comparing it to now is that men and women have confused biology: the need to be together, to procreate, and made this, or forced this to be a lifetime destiny, with men and women not whole people but each handicapped when they are together because they act according to these roles that they keep supposing their sex dictates. Men and women are handicapped and mostly don't even know it, except in how violent they are because they keep confusing their biological beings with their selves. Men and women don't like each other when they confuse their biology with a supposed destiny. People can do anything and if they do it long enough they will start to believe that it is true. Men and women are stifling each other in that they are constantly looking to each other for what they really possess within themselves, that there is a man and women inside all of us. It's complicated. The other half of this is that men and women get sick of being with a handicapped person (thinking that they are not) and opt to spend their time with the same sex. It doesn't really matter, what matters is that most people are handicapped and opting to just be with the same sex just makes the problem hide for a while. Men and women need to figure out a way to be alive and to be whole at the same time. You said this before June, on the bridge, do you remember? Is this what you meant? That men and women needed to be whole within themselves first before they could really get along with one another and not just pass on their diseases to their children.

What has really changed is that whereas people, men and women used to think and act at the same time, I mean do things as it occurred to them, now people think and act separately, have gotten their ideas away from their bodies so that the bodies hardly matter anymore.

People no longer think of a common good because our society is based on individualism. Everyone is supposed to be conquering something, conquering and at the same time belonging. A common good supposes a sameness in all human beings, and we are all trying so hard to be different, unique.

This compulsion to control and be powerful, these overwhelming souls that constitute a force of evil, that is never conquered, these souls that have no match and keep coming back, might be met finally if people would be human again and follow their hearts and challenge once and for all the evil in themselves and not always following the leader, seeking an outside source to contain what can't be contained.

Hitler will come back again because everything comes back when unchallenged. The only thing is that each time these evil souls come back they are harder and harder to locate, evil dispersing, maybe finally evaporating, but it must be recognized fully first.

Back to the classics. Mostly, and definitely in the books that I have read, which were all written by men anyway and you wonder where all the women were at all, mostly men and women just didn't spend that much time together, at least that is what is reported by the men who wrote all these books.

Oh shit, it's so easy to say, for the men that wrote these books, that they bought and sold women or that women were waiting for them on islands in castles somewhere, and for people that read these books to believe that women were weak and miserable and slaves, but most people say nasty things about the people with the most power anyway. You know what I think? I think that all the women were so busy doing other things, better things and couldn't be bothered with what the men were doing. That's what I think.

Women didn't need to write all these books because as far as they could see the world, their world was just fine, and they probably were living this grand life of luxury that excluded men and so you have all these frustrated men running around making war. Just like now because most women get so fed up with men just wish that they would go away and men don't seem to be able to change and just get more and more violent all the time.

Most men have a substantial-sized hook on their foreheads, for any woman to latch on to and drag these men around. It's because women, more than men, are whole, and beautiful. It's men, more than women, that imitate the opposite sex or try to play women against each other, it's because men fear the truth about how powerful women really are, just as most women now don't want their power because of the state that the world is in.

Men are horrified by the power that women have over them.

Once a woman lets a man inside of her, and once a man lets go and allows himself to be taken which really happens instantaneously and is just something that men try to deny from the outset, once a man allows his body and soul to succumb to the power that he is of, he is lost, afraid, because he is back where he started from in the beginning. Men are from women. They have tried to pretend otherwise for so long. God just laughs.

So anyway what happened is that before, I mean when the classics were written, women had locked men out. It's the ones that are compelled to do things like write and record that are the ones that see that something is wrong. These men were trying to compensate for the fact that they had been rejected.

Still from the perspective of these men, what I do read, what is the most interesting is that these men recorded actions that were done as the actions occurred to them.

This is important. What is also important is that men and women were not living together, really. Are men and women really living together now?

I am not just here to procreate. I am here for a reason and so are you.

I have three dreams now that keep coming back, three dreams that are almost one because of what they mean.

There's this house in one dream that is all screens, a whole house of screens and I move through this house like liquid, my body slicing through the screens of the house as I move from room to room.

The other dream is of being a fetus stuck in different parts of a body, in a jaw or an arm and I scream to get out. I don't see that I am a fetus in the dream, I know it to be true because my hands are webbed together and I can see my heart beating through my transparent skin.

I am a man in the third dream. I am on the *Titanic* and drowning in the icy sea. I am the only one alive and there is a voice screaming that I need to go now and get ready to notify my daughter as to where I am so that she won't be afraid, so that she will know that I am safe and know that where I am about to go is to another aspect of life. Hurry, it's important, the voice says.

In all these dreams I am almost to the point where I am saying to myself in the dream that I won't wake up when I fall asleep.

That's the point I have to reach, to stay in the part where I am drowning or in the jaw of another person or where my skin is separated into a million pieces in the screen walls of the house. Because if I stay in these places, I am sure that I will be able to wake up, wake up into this reality and be whole.

I know this.

I read that dolphins are smarter than humans maybe and that they are so smart they just live in their heads and swim. Everything they could ever need is right there in their heads. Possibly they communicate with one another this way too.

And this is where this unmailed letter ends. This letter started as a letter to June but who does this letter really talk to? This letter written to your sister who would eventually kill two people, a man and a woman. Finally kill all that you are trying to understand within yourself. Outside of yourself? It is so hard to see when you are so caught inside.

And what of these thoughts of yours, what you try not to think about?

The change in the weather is becoming more and more apparent in the staff reports. These comments on the conditions and complaints of each of the fourteen residents have changed from: OK ate some dinner but little dessert, or, nature call at I A.M. to: She says the new plants make the place look like a funeral parlor, and, She cried all afternoon because she had a dream about this couple she used to know and she wants to write to them but she doesn't have their address.

Grace is scanning a page in the ledger with her puffy right index finger. The names and dates of a person's arrival are on one side of the page. The date of their discharge is on the other side of the page. These columns are divided by a faint pink ink line drawn by a nervous hand down the middle of the page.

Well one person, Grace says. Her finger stops midway down a page. One person died in the living room of a heart attack.

On the wall in the living room there are fourteen yarn God's Eyes in a variety of colors that the residents made in the winter.

You think of Father's mass or how you can't always tell if the residents are breathing when they are asleep. When you are not sure you put your ear to their mouths and listen.

The menu says that supper tonight is split-pea soup and bologna-spread sandwiches. You go to the sink and fill the teakettle and the coffeepot. Above the sink on the window ledge between the yellow and orange Dixie cups and the food scale there is a drying wishbone from the noon meal of turkey and stuffing. A black carpenter ant rushes across the counter. You crush the ant with a paper towel.

Oh God, Oh God, Flora is saying from her bed.

Scotch-taped to the front of the yellow Rubbermaid file are two notes. You read them each though you know what they say. One is a list of emergency numbers: Grace, Rescue Squad, Hospital, Electrician, Plumber. The other note is the dress code for nurse's aides: white pants or uniform, no clogs or sneakers, no painter's pants or sundresses, and in capital letters, NO BARE FEET. Grace says, have a good night and call if you need anything, and then she leaves.

After dinner, after all the residents are asleep except Father Stellehy, who stays awake most of the night, you sit in the breakroom and try to read a textbook: *Values and Power in Society*. At 9 P.M. you will go upstairs because Father asked you if you would like to watch *The Sinking of the Titanic*.

. . .

YOU are standing over Flora's bed. She is not going to make it through the night. You called Grace and she said to call Flora's doctor.

There is a woman and she is dying.

In your dreams there is a woman and she is dying but you can't find her. There is nothing you can do.

In your dream house there are two women: twins.

We are twins but not by blood, they say in unison.

There is an angry dog jumping and pushing and barking at the closed door at the end of the hall. The dog's teeth tear through the wood as it slams its body into the door trying to get to where you are.

We are twins but not by blood, the women in your dream house say.

You are waiting for the doctor. You look at Flora and think of why old people get left as if there was something so important their children had to be doing. Urgent.

How are you tonight? Dr. Donovan asks.

Fine thank you, how are you?

Dr. Donovan is an oncologist, a tumor doctor. He is young and good-looking, with a rugged gait. Dr. Donovan is wearing bell-bottoms. You notice this as you bend over to pick up a hairpin under Flora's bed.

Stick out your tongue Flora. Flora's moaning continues, the same tone as it has been all day. It is a low sound coming from somewhere in the middle of her head.

She hasn't eaten anything solid for ten days, you say. The moaning stops as Dr. Donovan holds down the end of Flora's tongue. He pulls Flora's blankets down around her ankles. Her skin is crimson in places. Over her buttocks and the back of her thighs her flesh is streaked with black-and-blue marks. Her skin is just draped over her bones.

Did she fall? he asks.

Not that I know of, you say thinking of how easy it would be to abuse someone so helpless. You think of Frank Pierce the night aide and how he frightens you. The doctor checks Flora's pulse. He takes her blood pressure. He says he is going to call the paramedics. He says they will be here shortly. He leaves.

The skin on Flora's arms is rough and cold. The hair on her head feels like wires. Her eyes keep disappearing into the back of her head. When people sleep they go somewhere else. She is leaving. Her hands feel empty, unreal. Flora turns on her side, moving her own dead weight. Her colostomy bag has come undone. The smell of rotting attaches itself to the air in the room. Box. Flora grabs the bedpost by the window. A crack of darkness slips under the curtain and draws a heavy line toward Flora's body.

Twenty minutes later the paramedics arrive. The backs of three men in red windbreakers are walking down the hall the wrong way.

No, she is in here, you say.

What's the matter? a man with a flat metal notebook asks walking toward you.

She has to go to the hospital you say.

OK Flora, we will move you over a little at a time. The moaning sounds hollow. The men take a long time lifting her, she is heavy. There is nothing for you to do. You watch. Flora's eyes move about in their sockets, just eyes moving, not with Flora in there, empty.

A letter on Flora's bureau from her son in Florida says:

Fishing season has just started for me but I can't get out much because of the rain. So this weekend I put a new floor in mine and Eileen's upstairs bathroom. I only yelled half the time, so basically it went pretty smooth.

Women left alone. Mothers. The secret wish, that one's parents just die for making them be born in the first place.

Once Flora is on the stretcher the moaning stops.

. . .

OH hello, Father Stellehy says. He is sitting on his bed. He still has his robe on. He likes you to help him take it off. Sometimes you pretend to forget this and leave the room, say goodnight, before he starts taking it off.

You tell Father that Flora went to the hospital, that she won't be coming back. You want to hold Father. You can't. He can't ever stroke your head. Boundaries. You are afraid. Father is beautiful. You want him. It can't ever happen. There are lists.

On Father's desk is his Zip-Loc bag of butterscotch to take when he feels an attack coming on, and a stack of books: The Cartusian Hymnal, the Bible, the Holy Eucharist. On top of this stack, leaning into the typewriter, is his latest interest, a book written by children from Equinox Elementary about being the kids of single parents. In this book Father has underlined certain passages. Next to these passages he has written in names: Toomy, Father Rains, Frederick. These names in the margins because what these kids are saying reminds Father of his brothers at the monastery.

On the TV screen the *Titanic* is sinking into the icy sea.

Women and children first, the captain is saying. People are fighting their way into the life boats.

I have to do the drops now, you say.

You what?

Your eyedrops.

Oh yes, yes, yes. Your hands shake as you apply the ointment to Father's blind left eye.

When Father went into a diabetic coma last month and was rushed to the hospital he remembers coming to in the ambulance. He thought he was dreaming.

You say goodnight to Father. You pick up the blue plastic medicine tray with the thirteen empty med cups. You turn out Father's overhead light leaving him in his robe on his bed watching the conclusion of *The Titanic*. You go into his bathroom to pick up his urine specimen. You put the toilet-seat lid down. In the mirror above the sink is your reflection; it sticks out its tongue.

. . .

Dear Tracy,

   Do you remember being a fetus? Five times the whir of the vacuum. It's like water floating through. Can I keep it? I asked the lady. Growing inside of me, any man's baby.

June

. . .

THERE is a dream. You are alone in a house. It is a house that wasn't built to last. There is a tar-paper roof covering the plywood structure. In place of doors and windows there are screens.

   Outside there is a young woman whose facial features and build closely resemble your own: big bones, brown hair, a round face, unremarkable physical characteristics.

   The woman comes first to the front screen door (there are two, front and back). I'm coming in now, she says.

No, you can't, not yet, you tell her and rush to bolt the other screen door and secure the screen windows.

As you move inside the house, the woman outside is following you from window to window.

I will always be here, she says. If the illusion that you are keeping me out makes you feel safe, then for now so it shall be.

It is raining outside. Lightning and thunder. The house is not sturdy, it will leak or collapse. Each bolt of lightning illuminates the woman's face, her eyes are trancelike, eyes that are so calm and seductive that you can feel your heart beating faster, fear that you might let this woman in. You want to touch this woman and you are afraid.

Look, she says, no longer outside in the dark but right next to you on the plywood floor that smells of sawdust. Look, she says, I am in here, and, she says, pointing to the dark outside, there you are.

Outside is your face pressing against the screens of the windows, eyes and hair and clothes, wet, then gone.

You dream of Miya? You wake up sweating. You were running through a forest together and the ground was wet and smelled of rain.

Dear Tracy,
    I am finally coming into my own now. I am becoming a whole person. Of course my life-style change has been hard on everyone but being honest with oneself is so hard to do in this society. You would like my new lover, she is very good to me and the kids. Big Herb never sees the kids. He is still drinking himself to death. I haven't heard from June. Your father says she is still on the streets somewhere in New York . . .

Love
Mom

Your mother's father died of alcoholism and lung cancer. A slow death. He had been dying since you could remember. After he is dead your mother tells that when she was growing up he forced her to have sex with him over and over and over. . . .

• • •

Y ou go to pick up your paycheck. Miya is there. She doesn't look at you and asks you how you are, her head down, busy. Miya's ears look as red as your own ears feel. Her ears are red, the ears of being in love or being afraid or telling a lie. You say you would like to do something tonight, and would she like to come. You hear your voice say this. Your hands are sweating.

• • •

Dear Tracy,
  Think of this, America disappearing into the ocean probably just blowing itself up, a failed experiment. On the back of your eyelids there are the answers. Men and women don't like each other. This is a game.

June

Miya hesitates. She says her husband doesn't like her to go out. She says she is tired. You say, come on, we'll get drunk, go dancing, talk.

You think you know what other people need.

You have your lists.

Miya says yes, yes she will go out. She still doesn't look at you. You think of June. The breakroom is walls that push in. You can't breathe.

It is dark. You are both drunk. Everything looks soft like you could put your hands through objects, soft and movielike.

Miya says, Can I spend the night here? In Equinox everyone is sleeping. The stars overhead dangle precariously from the black sky like spittle at the corner of someone's mouth.

I guess so, you say. Your heart is racing.

Miya says, do you ever dream about bees? You dream about bees a lot, bees swarming around your body. Your mother told you that bees are a symbol for reincarnation. Miya is rubbing the base of the bedside lamp. The air is heavy in your room. You think of Father Stellehy. You feel like one of you is slipping from the confines of the room. Miya is so nervous and keeps saying the same thing over and over again. No, you are so nervous and keep saying the same thing over and over again. You are afraid to look into Miya's eyes because your own eyes are so watery. Swallowing, like the sound of the air rising out of your fish tank in bubbles, you tell Miya you dream of insects but nothing specific.

Has anyone ever died here? you asked Miya's mother. She had said, yes, and Justine had been watching you.

June says everything you need to know is on the back of your eyelids.

You tell Miya how when you were a little girl you were afraid you would swallow your tongue. Miya tells you that sometimes, even now, she is afraid to fall asleep at night because she is afraid she will never wake up. Miya says that some nights her mother will come over and stay with Miya in the living room until Miya can fall asleep.

Miya is small. Just people, alone and afraid. You think of the way the world looks looking up through the water from the bottom of a pool. You think of the way a face looks under water. Tammy wanted to be invisible so she could swim.

I want you to love me, Miya says. You just don't know. Her face is wet and she is crying.

· · ·

You told a friend that everywhere you go you see people naked, can only think of everyone fucking and ugly. You can't think any other way, you say. Everything is hidden, enticing. I think I am going mad, you say. You are afraid to touch, because any touch is fraught with possibility and danger. Your friend says, when you find God that will all stop. She says, when I found Jesus he made all the ugliness go away. She says this. You are looking in each other's eyes. She looks away quick. She swallows hard.

. . .

MIYA takes off her shoes. Miya tells the catfish in your fish tank to get out of the corner. What a strange creature you are, she says. Then she dips her fingers into the tank to show you how catfish will nibble at whatever is on the surface. You didn't know this.

You sit in silence, then tired of staring at the plants on the ledge below the window, and tired of tracing over and over again the sharp spines of the cactus plants, and counting and recounting the nine leaves of the aloe plant, you open your mouth.

It was so depressing to watch Flora die, you say.

It was more depressing to watch her suffer, Miya says.

You tell Miya that her eyes look like the eyes of a fawn.

No, she says, just eyes.

Let me give you a back rub, Miya says.

No, I don't think that would be a very good idea, you say.

Can I be your daughter now? Just for a while let me be your daughter. So often it seems the other way around, who is whose daughter. So often it doesn't seem any way at all, just people. Your mother is massaging your back on the living-room floor. It feels too good. You are my mother. Your stomach is getting sick because of how good her hands make you feel.

What is happening? There are boundaries between people. What is love, to touch someone? Your whole body is tingling. No. Please to make this go away.

I'll just rub your neck, Miya says and starts to do this.

Your mother's hands. Miya's hands. Hands.

There are labels for people that do this sort of thing. How could you and this woman be friends, how? You are breathing faster and Miya's hands are on your shoulder on your back on your breasts.

You gasp.

You let this happen.

In the dark, lying on top of each other, the crickets sluggish outside, the sheets tangled, your hands slip over each other's bodies like you were both blind.

You are moaning in the darkness, drunk against everything you are supposed to be doing. The tape player, you don't remember turning it on, on the tape player The Velvet Underground sings, Margarita passion, they had to get her fixed, she wasn't well she was getting sick and then *these songs really were playing* what costume shall the poor girl wear to all tomorrow's parties? A hand-me-down dress from who knows where?

The night before you had applied for the job at the Mountain View you had a nightmare.

In the dream you are being attacked by two bearded women. They are pinning you to the ground at the bottom of rickety stairs. There is dust everywhere. You have to work here they say.

You are screaming to your friends that are crowded around watching these two women attack you as if this were a bullfight, you are screaming to your friends, help me.

No one had moved. All the onlookers were mute.

Before you fall asleep you think about a world unclothed, nothing hidden, would it matter?

You think about how sometimes, when you are lying next to someone, maybe watching them sleep, you wonder how it is that behind their closed eyes, above their half-open mouth, beneath their hair that is soft when you touch it, you wonder how it is that two people can ever really love. Lying next to someone, watching them sleep, their eyes moving fast behind closed lids, you wonder about where that person really is, you wonder if maybe they are standing on a platform somewhere, just about to step through the open door of a train.

As if another might make a difference, as if someone could. If you take an inventory of the things you need, an other constitutes the whole list or there isn't any room.

What might anyone say that would override an eon of your actions? Your heartfelt yearnings, a tangle of hatred and passion that is not at home in this body.

What you really want is lost, seems irretrievable. Your body is this one. There is a voice calling from somewhere inside your veins, voices like those heard in an etherized stupor. You don't want to hear these voices. They don't stop. You want meaning, safety.

You aren't fitting in your skin.

You think of two children sitting in the middle of a big room. Each child is surrounded with the toys it likes, with the objects each child calls mine.

These two children that sit in the middle of a big room are sitting on a wooden floor. Each child has its own toys but likes the toys the other child has, mightn't care less about its own toys at all. Perhaps one child offers all its toys for one object of the others. The child says, here you can have my dolls, my rocks, my special shiny ribbon, you can have all this if I can just have that there.

This the wanting to possess another's goods that gets confused with the yearning to be alive?

You wish to demolish what is here around you, what is solid, all the structures you create, help to create, that don't, can't make a difference.

What is it that you would put in the place of what you wish to demolish?

When you were a little girl you believed that God was when two people dreamed of each other at the same time. Now you don't know what to believe.

Miya had big plans. Miya had her own lists, her own movies whirring in her head.

Miya wants you to love her again. Father Stellehy thinks you would make a good nun. You just want to know what you are supposed to be doing.

You want to know what kind of love Miya means. You don't know what love is.

You want to scream at Father, What kind of Father are you? You don't know what Fathers are for.

Miya is sitting at the breakroom table. She runs her fingers through her hair and blows out a breath that vibrates her lips. I guess this is my little world here, she says. I just have a hard time understanding how anything so tender and nice could be so wrong. You are folding and unfolding your list in your lap under the table. A good detective listens.

Well I guess I'll go and let you get back to your work, she says.

From your backpack you pull out a lavender paperback and place it in her lap. Miya's face looks puzzled and sad. For an instant you want to hold her again, hold her against everything that has hurt her, but there are no guidelines all of a sudden. There is a ringing in your ears and your skin feels itchy and dry. Flora's skin.

Since that night it is becoming more and more difficult to follow your schedule. You told Grace you are leaving. You don't want to be in this house, preparing people to die. There is nothing to hold on to anymore. You are sure that people know what you are thinking. You are struggling to rework your lists.

Perhaps you could read this to your daughters at bedtime, you say. The book is *Alice's Adventures Underground*.

Well I guess it was just something that happened like everything else. Miya gets up and walks to the door.

There are so many boundaries between people. This bridge you are suspended on, holding the rotting rope sides, inside you are swaying to cross.

You are softer than you imagine. You feel for the bones that mark this deceit.

There is a little girl that you must find, a little girl that is inside and outside at the same. There are people that are dying and it is hard to tell which is really dying, a body disintegrating, preparing a soul to go away, or people that are dying because they are so afraid of what is really in their hearts.

You look at the big picture window at the end of the breakroom. Until morning the window is a mirror. Behind your head is a whole kitchen reflected backwards. On one side is a coffee maker, and hanging from the ceiling above it, next to the cabinets of food and medicine, are twelve cooking pots and pans of different sizes. On the other side of the kitchen, below the window that looks down the hill to Equinox, is a double sink. To the left of the sink is the refrigerator and to the right is the stove. Two women are in that mirror; one is walking out the door.

Go away, you said to Miya. You said this by not returning to work. Go away, you said by where you took your body.

You must hate?

No one can change what has happened.

Except you.

The living-room clock strikes eleven. Frank Pierce, the night aide, is always punctual. He walks into the kitchen. Frank smells of English Leather. His eyes are magnified through his thick glasses. Frank has a scar on his face, a gash mark like a heavy seam of drying glue that starts over his right eyebrow, crosses his jaw and disappears down his neck beneath his shirt. He wears an identification tag on his starched white uniform. You want to get out the door before he has a chance to tell you fifty violent stories of all the aggressive things he has done in his life. That pin is all you can see: Frank Pierce, aide. Your eyebrows are crunching into your nose.

Yes, Flora is gone, he says.

The doctor asked me if she fell, you say. Her butt was all purple and bruised. I didn't know, did she fall? you say. What causes the purpleness?

I have seen that twice, Frank says. It usually starts in the fingernails, turns all purple at the cuticles, and works its way up. When I was in Nam, I saw this guy, he had the gray death glow about him and the purple stains were creeping up his arms. I knew he was going to die and two days later he did. She was suffering for so long, you say. How come they couldn't give her anything? You want to get out the door. Frank has scars on his left hand; scars that look like his fingers were sewed back on once. His hands are big.

What did you want? Frank says. His eyes look lidless behind his glasses, like the stare of a fish. Did you want them to give her a needle and put her out of her misery like a possum? Did you want them to make her all stoned?

In the yellow light of the breakroom, behind Frank's head the gray pots and pans are just hanging there.

You know, Frank says, lighting a cigarette, I could take a wet washrag and smother you with it, and when they did an autopsy they'd never find out about it, how you died, the water would evaporate.

Why are you telling me this? you say.

You got to have money, he continues. You could wind up in a corner of a room somewhere when you are old. I took out a policy yesterday. For a hundred bucks a year, I got a million dollars' worth of coverage. So if anything happens to me I got pension from the Marines, Blue Cross from here, and inheritance.

You have made it to the sink. It's maybe five minutes to the door. He continues. When someone is dying, you know, you can't ever say to them, God you look awful today, or God you look tired. You got to tell them they look good. Once you let a person know they are dying it's all over.

You are out the door. You start to run. Father's light is on upstairs. The street is dark. Only a few rectangles of light seem to hang from the fronts of houses. There are no streetlights. The trees that line the road and the trees in the yards of the dark houses look scissor cut like pictures from a magazine or two dimensional props for a play. You run faster down the hill.

Past the old mill waterfall you stop in front of the fire station to catch your breath.

The water in the creek babbles under the bridge where you stand. The water moving under the bridge sounds like the whisper of a crowd growing silent before the start of a performance. In your backpack is a pamphlet Father gave you that describes life in the monastery. It says:

The desert is barren of comforts, naturally poor; and it is in such a setting that God lets his own riches become known and experienced.

The night air is warm and comfortable. You remember something your own father said to you. Deserts are freezing cold at night and inferno hot in the day. If we are lucky we will hit the desert at night. The family hit the desert on their way to California in the middle of the day and the heat was unbearable.

Hovering

YOU are in a play. Holiness, Queen of Heaven, you say. Holiness on Golden Wing who hover over earth. You are perched on top of a stage platform. There is a spotlight on your face. Your face makeup won't smear. It is stage makeup. You are playing a part in the chorus of the Bacchae. Father Stellehy is in the audience.

You forget what your next line is. You are focusing on Father's face. You wonder if he can see you. You look down from the platform and quickly say the lines that are at the end of your speech. You skip the whole middle part. The chorus alters their movements.

You wish you could disappear. The play continues.

Surveillance III

THE same year that your mother was born, 1945, Marcie Holland, an eighteen-year-old sophomore at Equinox College told her roommate that she was going out for a hike in the woods. Marcie was never seen or heard from again.

Marcie's story, the one she wrote, the one that was written for her? This story is one of the most famous missing persons cases of all time.

There were no clues, are no clues, usable ones anyway. The kind of clues that are understood, the ones that hope to turn up the remnants of a body violated. These clues are no good sometimes. Because sometimes people just don't want to be found.

Marcie Holland liked to hike. She liked to hike alone. She wasn't afraid of the dark.

Marcie didn't get along well with her family.

There was a lover, a man that it was speculated she might have run away with.

Not everyone wants to do things the same way.

Marcie was a student of botany. She was very familiar with the trail that she was last seen at the foot of, the trail that stretches from the Appalachian Mountains, all the way through Canada.

Sometimes people know what they are doing.

For nearly a month, day and night, hundreds of people covered the forested mountain area looking for clues. They would walk in a straight line, hundreds of people, an arm's length from each other forming a human rake. They even dropped confetti on the ground to mark the area searched. This lasted until the first snow came.

Go away, people say when they want to be left alone.

There are so many ways for a person to feel trapped.

Eventually her parents, the people of Equinox, students from the college, friends and interested persons, private detectives, state authorities, the National Guard, clairvoyants, had to give up, admit that Marcie Holland had disappeared.

Everyone is right about the same thing, that she is either dead or alive. What might have happened to her, if she ran away, got lost, was abducted, or killed, these possibilities make up the mystery, the story people hold on to. If Marcie Holland lost control or took control is the real issue, and there seems to be no way for anyone to come to an agreement about this.

For the longest time you thought that you would be able to figure out what had happened to Marcie Holland. People don't just vanish without a trace. The world is just not that big. There had to be clues, some way to figure out what had really happened.

Leave me alone now, people say, not with words but by where they take their body.

What you didn't figure into your search for answers then was that Marcie Holland if she were alive would be fifty-six, and not a beautiful young woman.

The agelessness of her picture, eyes that can be interpreted in as many ways as you can think of. Her picture in the newspaper, blond hair, soft features. The fantasy over and over again. You just didn't think about how old she would be if she were alive.

In the woods, in the mountains outside of Equinox in late November the hills are the colors of fire. Some of the leaves on the trees are blood-red. The sky above you a blue as sharp as a paper edge.

Winter

PEOPLE'S eyes pant, but this is obvious: the quick inhale of an averted gaze, or the slow exhale of drowning in someone's stare. But what you are really interested in is the passion that people can't quite contain in their hands.

Mr. Lorian's eyes were panting when he hired you to take care of his ninety-five-year-old mother. His eyes watch you and then his hands tangle together in his lap. Mr. Lorian's eyes become like nettles and you are unable to look into them as he is explaining what will be expected of you. Listening to the sound of his voice, you don't really hear what you are being told. You are thinking about sleepwalking. It is difficult to tell a sleepwalker from a normal person because a lot of people sleep with their eyes open.

Listen, Mr. Lorian says.

I am listening, you say.

His voice: Walk her once a day . . . an hour . . . her lunch tray . . . very particular . . . hairnet . . .

You hear these things.

It will basically be touch and go, Mr. Lorian is saying. On the wall behind Mr. Lorian's head there is a glass case in which are arranged, American Indian arrowheads, rocks and dried plants. But the room is a jungle: children's artwork, plants, and family photographs are suffocating the white walls.

Mr. Lorian is showing you the house. You walk, move through these rooms; this body that does these things.

Sometimes you see yourself doing things: developing pictures in the darkroom, or telling someone how you are angry about the state of the world, a voice saying words, yours? Sometimes things just get done; a bed is made, or in your hand there are five finished photographs. You don't remember actually doing these things, because always you are thinking about what is

229

going to happen next. The photographs in your hand. Dear Mom . . . Dear Dad . . . sealed in envelopes, dropping into the out-of-town slot. Where are you when these things are getting done? Floating.

The flash of remembering or the bliss of forgetting. It's in the recall of the moment, this is now, this is now. Your face in a mirror. It's the recall of the moment, what is beneath trying to exact things, this isn't holding.

There are lots of hallways in the Lorians' house. Mr. Lorian walks with his back bent as if he might fold up any minute.

Sometimes you just want to get out, you want to push away from this body. Other people too, there they are, doing things, saying this, saying that, and sometimes eyes get so wet, look like drops of water on leaves, a microscope to that drop of water, eyes that look far away beyond the confines of a setting, and it's there, that other people want to escape too.

Down the hallway to your room Mr. Lorian is taking you. You already know about this room. Mr. Lorian never tells you: Yes, this is the room where Mark killed himself, Mark my only son. Mr. Lorian doesn't say: In this room my son shot himself in the head one hot day in July. Other people told you this, friends from college who say: Why don't you get out of Equinox? Why don't you go other places where things are happening? Don't stay here.

People are running when they move from place to place, always hoping to mend what is broken inside by going somewhere else. There is no better place to be than right where you are. Believe this, believe this, a small voice cries from inside.

Where is there to go? You want to leave, go other places, but you stay in Equinox because everything that happens to you, each job you get, every person that you meet, you are sure this is all part of a bigger plan, one that you yourself have no control over.

You are taking toll of where there is to go. There is a point that has been reached now, a point into which finally everyone is thrust as if by

*the power that can be seen in a baby's eyes. This point this place is
where you have been all along?*

Mr. Lorian says, this will be your room. Mr. Lorian doesn't
even say anything about all his son's things: bookcases of red
leather-bound journals, a shelf with rocks arranged in patterns,
dust-covered.

The house is dirty. There is a smell that you will have to clean
away or get used to, urine and filth.

Why am I here?

Why am I here?

There is no place else to go.

You will clean this house, make it livable.

You want Mr. Lorian to go away so you can be alone here in
this small room. There is a smell in here beneath the smell of
urine and rotting like Christmas candles. The gaps in the
floorboards where the dust has collected for who knows how
long, the bookcases with Mark's journals, photo albums, pieces
of this house that you want to know as your own. It's a
compulsion really, to gather up information about other people's lives, order, fit it all together.

Mr. Lorian's voice: I expect . . . I will be gone weekends . . .
my wife gone during the week . . . a lot of work . . . qualified.
Mr. Lorian doesn't say: you will be preparing my mother
to die.

Why again, another job like the one you had to leave? It's
because you think that there are no choices. You equate choices
with trying to run away, trying to escape? You must take care
of what has to be taken care of and you are not sure what this
might be.

I think you might see a doctor sometime, your mother says
on the phone. You could come home for a few weeks. We can
work through our grief together.

Have you heard from June? Have you?

June may never come back, your mother says. I have to
go now.

You take pictures.

Mr. Lorian's voice: This house was built in the late 1700s for the family of the town judge. The maid lived in these quarters.

Not his son, Mr. Lorian doesn't say this is where my only son lived. Denying the evidence: the journals, the family photographs in the living room, this bed and how the blanket, the quilt is frayed. Blankets don't get frayed by themselves Mr. Lorian. You don't say this.

This room is just beneath the widow's walk hidden in the attic. Everything in this bedroom, bathroom, small sitting room is half normal size. When you stand up in the room your head brushes the ceiling. The bathroom, which was built much later, Mr. Lorian says, used to be a prayer closet. Carved into one of the splintery wood beams is an ornate crucifix of Jesus in relief.

You watch Mr. Lorian's back. He is looking out the window. The snow-covered lawn is rising up around Mr. Lorian's bent body. People are like sponges, except there is a will beneath what people absorb. You want to show this will in your photographs, this will that fights to know God, the God beneath words. God, like the eyes in photographs, all the photographs in the world, millions of eyes looking out, this surging beneath the skin, not where blood is. How to convey this? Words just trample people. You wish to be mute then.

Mr. Lorian's voice: get adjusted . . . fruit on the kitchen counter . . . I'll be in my study . . . I'll take care of my mother tonight . . . tomorrow at 5 A.M. we will start.

In one of the books next to Mark's bed, the bed that you will call yours, there is an article about avalanches. You turned to this page randomly and you take this to mean something. The mechanics of an avalanche are simple to understand. Mark underlined this. Scientists can read the secrets of a threatening snowpack like a brief history of each winter's snowfall. This is underlined too.

The drawing in the book shows a giant wavelike construction curling across the page in blues and ochers, with dots and streaks of gray. Superimposed on this delicate painting of a snowpack is a technical diagram showing how any one of the seven layers can be equally responsible for the possibility of disaster.

Where are you? What are you to look at?

The voice that you hear now is the distinct voice of a woman. Mrs. Lorian downstairs? Your mother in your head?

Below you can hear the sticky vinyl sounds of children crunching around in the snowdrifts close to the house. The bedroom window drips with warmth.

The will in Grandma Green's letter, and there were no pictures, just words. Let me out, the spaces between her words say. Someone let me out. Where is my mother? Where is my father? the spaces between the words in Grandma's letter say. Your mother's mother. You have the letter in your pocket. One letter resting sideways in your post-office box this morning. One letter from Sleepy Hollow arriving way after the fact of Grandpa's death, your mother's father's death.

Dear Tracy,

Things have certainly changed. But since I've lived this life, I find I can accept most things and love people more for being themselves. Just because your sister does the things that she does we can't love her less. Your mother's change, too, won't make her love you any less. I met her lover and she is nice. The twins are doing fine. Your Mom is working on a painting of them. I don't have a fish tank anymore. I sometimes miss my fish, but I'm glad I don't have to feed them and clean the tank. I do have a cookie jar (the same old one) and sometimes homemade cookies.

Gramps had a lovely funeral, a long hard death, he didn't want to go, but said all his Marine buddies were waiting for him. I asked if he saw his Mom and Dad and he said no. The family kept a death watch two days and two nights. He gave up eating one week, but I gave him milk shakes with protein and juices.

I had to call Hospice because I couldn't clean him alone he was bleeding so much. When the bleeding stopped I called the doctor. The doctor said that was to be expected (but I forgot). Grandpa was in the hospital for two weeks before he passed on. But when he did I forgot, things really happening.

The flowers in my yard are beautiful this year. Except that when I pulled up the weeds I cried so much. I sit on the hill and wonder what the people across the way think of this older woman sitting in the weeds blowing her nose.

I love you,
Gram

This letter that you get so long after Grandpa's death, of course things like this never really get lost, don't go away.

It is springtime. Daphne is there, standing on the porch, her arms covered with gooseflesh. Daphne is clutching her chest. She is looking north off the same porch her daughter will look off of when her daughter is born. This is Daphne's mother's house and Daphne is a young woman, a girl really. Daphne is wondering, wondering about what will happen, about what the world has to offer her, because this is what people do when they look off of porches, wonder and dream. From the porch, arms to her chest, arms that have gooseflesh on them Daphne can see down, see the garden and the street. Below the garden is the tunnel where trains rush through, day and night on a schedule that is always the same; 6 A.M., 12 P.M., 3 P.M., 6 P.M., 12 A.M., clockwork, train whistles at night, a rattling beneath the garden.

It is springtime and Daphne can't remember the dulling of winter. She is anticipating the summer. Summer, Daphne will be in Hollywood. Daphne is anxious. Daphne can sing, act. Daphne is a soprano. She has won lots of contests for her voice. Daphne wants to be in movies.

Daphne hears laughter; the laughter of the neighbor children running through the train tunnel beneath the house. Their laughter peals through the hills, spring-green hills, echoes beneath the house and across the street, laughter close then far away.

In the train tunnel broken glass glistens on the tracks between the railroad ties like a haphazard mosaic. What lives down there in the tunnel? The children know and they conjure up the ghosts they have come to fear. They are learning how to be afraid.

There is a desire beneath Daphne's sweater that makes her pinch her toes together tightly in her shoes.

The children in the tunnel yell that a train is coming, the staccato of footsteps crunching through the damp tunnel, running from the light at the other end of the tunnel, a light like a lid to a jar. The children run fast, fast so that their throats burn.

Daphne is standing on the porch of her mother's house. Her mother is inside baking bread or knitting or quilting or mending, the things that mothers do to make people comfortable. Daphne's father has been dead for a long time. Daphne is standing on the porch of her mother's house, the house that she will live in, raise her children in, but she doesn't know this yet. Daphne is filled with passion now, a passion that she is not sure what to do with. Daphne can sing.

. . .

It is much later now and of course everything is different. All the children are grown, Daphne's children, and she is standing on the porch again, and it is spring and she is looking down at her garden. Daphne is remembering because that is how she lives now mostly, gardening and remembering.

There were certain things Daphne remembered about their meeting. The most important thing is the place: Sunset Boulevard, that's the street where they met. Daphne saw him across the bar, she saw his uniform and the way his shiny black left shoe rested on the middle rung of the empty bar stool he was leaning away from.

Daphne remembers feeling her ears get warm and her hands sweat inside her white gloves. She hoped that her lipstick wasn't smudged, tried to remember when was the last time she put her lipstick on. It was after the casting call, yes that's when it was, and she had blotted her lips carefully, her lip print red stamped on an envelope she had in her purse, the envelope that her mother had sent money in.

It was murky in the Acappella Lounge and crowded for early

afternoon. People were moving about slowly and Daphne had thought of three things. First she wanted to meet the man at the bar, the man with the distinguished nose, a nose that reminded her faintly of her own father's nose but only for an instant, the resemblance. She wanted to meet this man who was twirling his drink in his hands like it was a child's head. Second she had thought about her lipstick. Thirdly she had wondered whether or not she got the part she had auditioned for. It was a bit part, she would sing too. If she got the part.

This setting on Sunset Boulevard, the bar, the way her hands felt wet in her gloves, the day Thursday and her horoscope: Today is the day Bulls get what they want by taking matters of the heart with a head-on attitude, all pointing to something magical for this moment.

Daphne thinks she is gifted with second sight. She tells people this. Right now it seems as if she has been here before, in this moment, and that this moment is a decisive one. Daphne walks through the slowly moving people toward the empty bar stool in the Acappella Lounge.

At first Daphne doesn't look at the man contemplating the drink between his palms. She places her bag on the bar and waits for the bartender to notice her. Daphne can feel the uniformed man's gaze, he is looking at her ears, her chin, her hair. His gaze tightens on her profile like plaster.

Daphne knew she would fall in love. She knew this initial moment, this meeting as if she had done this all before. Her spine tingles.

Could this meeting have been for another reason?

"You are an actress," he says to her as she takes the first sip of her drink. "I can tell. You are so sure of yourself," he says. "I like that in a person."

He said person. She will always remember that, he said person and not lady or woman.

Daphne looks at the man and notices how dark his eyes are, almost black. This man is serious, preoccupied, important, angry, maybe angry and lonely, but handsome.

The noise in the lounge is like a silence all of a sudden, like the roar late at night when everyone is asleep. People are talking in the lounge but Daphne can't hear the words.

Daphne finishes her drink fast and gets the bartender's attention. "Two of whatever she is having," the man in the uniform says.

Daphne says thank you but that she will buy her own drink, that she doesn't accept things from strangers.

What was that feeling of connectedness Daphne felt toward this man at that initial moment, seeing him there at the bar for the first time? Did she make a mistake? A man next to an empty bar stool, Sunset Boulevard, his tightening gaze that made her feel dizzy, feel silly, desirable. The attraction of energy. But mightn't the overwhelming feeling have been something other than what she made it out to be, pity or repulsion? Fear is so often confused with longing. The desire to disappear in that overpowering energy of another's gaze, as if pressing against one another brings relief. A child always presses the spot where a tooth is coming in though it hurts to do so.

What was Daphne really thinking then?

Now standing on the porch, just as her mother stood on this porch, just as her daughters and granddaughters had stood on this porch, now what she is thinking about is certainly not what it was she was really thinking about then. Daphne remembers things, but in the only way she can, the romance, the good parts, what Daphne will tell people about that first meeting, how she will change that first meeting, give it many meanings over and over.

There are seeds to be planted, buried in the just-tilled soil beneath the porch where she stands: tomatoes and marigolds and petunias.

After that moment, the initial meeting, she never would be a movie actress. There would be a war to travel, too, and children to have. Her yearning so great then.

How do you know about this meeting? How do you know how your mother's mother, Daphne, felt when she first met your Grandfather Green? What do you know about your Grandfather Green?

You know about this meeting because it seems to be implanted in your being like the genetic code that shaped your features.

This is what you are afraid of. Because sometimes it does seem that the only thing that there is do with your desires, no, your passions, and energies is to give it all away. This, control, to give yourself away before you are taken?

Daphne will wait for spring to come again. She will remember the meeting or any memory at all in the only way she can, in a way that will enable her to move through the days.

And when the spring comes again and soon when all the flowers are ready to be picked Daphne will pick the flowers from her own garden, the purple petunias, the apple blossoms from the trees, the yellow marigolds, and she will pick these flowers because finally it has to be enough to gather an armful of blossoms.

Daphne will arrange these flowers in ways that please her. Her daughters, her children don't visit much anymore. She will place the bouquets next to the window that frames the beginning and the end of each day. These days that gather her up, no not like a plucked first flower or anything as romantic as a uniform, as mystery, as a man who takes control.

These flowers she will pick with guilt, with anger, with a moroseness never equal to, but just as yielding as, the pain that she has to live with as if lives were dealt like wildflowers waiting to be plucked and not waiting to be left alone.

Daphne will gather these blossoms and the act will leave her breathless. She will wonder might it not have been ordered different these years. And then she will remember in the only way that she can.

It is winter now, not spring.
Grandma's grief over her husband.
They beat each other.
Love.
You think about all the plants in Grandma Green's house. Deep-green tropical plants that climb the walls, thriving in the dark environment of that house. Grandma Green never talked to her plants. They say that is what makes plants healthy. Those

plants on like tape recorders anyway, plants threatening to engulf all the rooms, muting private histories in their monoecious simplicity.

Out on the snow-covered lawn there are three black crows. Mark, yes Mark, Mr. Lorian's son who shot himself in the head in this room that is to be yours, a room like a box. What is yours? You are going numb. You fight to stay awake.

Dad's father is dead too. Deader than what? In Equinox people are sleepwalking. You have to stay awake.

Let me out, the spaces between the floorboards scream, spaces that are lines between the floorboards, parallel lines that collect dust.

It is important to want to work. You have to work whether you want to or not. This is part of the list, one of the rules. You know this fact to be true by how guilty you feel when you don't want to work, the same guilt that doesn't fit on your list and is the guilt that admits you really can't control your emotions, your feelings toward other people, the desire to touch that overwhelms then sickens because the more you try to suppress your urges the worse they become.

Sometimes it is hard to know when you are lying and when you are telling the truth.

It is important to want to work even if you didn't have to because hard work strengthens the soul.

Who taught you this?

Where is it on earth that people feel comfortable in their bodies?

The will to live murmurs.

What is it to be alive and not be afraid?

Life murmurs, doesn't whoop or holler like the sounds from the playground, the sounds of children already contained by the hurricane fences that surround nearly every park.

The voice inside murmurs, says don't be afraid, do what you want. It is a lie to be so afraid, a lie that keeps you searching for someone or something to protect you. This voice gets louder, sometimes overwhelms you, overwhelms your surroundings.

People do exude certain energies. Another's hatred can fill up a room.

You break things.

There are no easy answers the ominous voice of learning says.

Helplessness works from the inside the ominous voice would have you believe. You can do anything you want, the voice outside says.

Why is it that you have spent such a long time identifying your feelings of helplessness with a cause? The voice of a victim. It is something to hold on to and not proceed.

You look for someone to identify with, and all that you can find are models of death. Is killing yourself the only way to have control in this life? You are afraid. You sit in Mark's room and wonder who you are. You read certain books and are certain that you lived before.

Has that soul come through here yet? You think this trying to bridge the gap between lives, imagining yourself to be the soul that existed in others before, will exist again. Other women, women long dead, their bodies gone, these women you liken yourself to, the ones that couldn't find a home in their lifetimes, the ones that took their own lives so that no one else could.

Sometimes you think that soul is in your body now, maybe the soul of the woman who took photographs of people, the kind of people that most are glad that they are not, and in these pictures of midgets and giants, transvestites and white trash America there is something magical happening: anger and passion seethe through these "freaks'" pores, something that says, just bodies, let me out, love me. These things these pictures say. The woman that took all these pictures took her own life the day the first men landed on the moon. You are sure some days that part of her is inside of you right now and it is your job to make things different this time.

It is evil that you can't escape, your will to be great, to make your mark somewhere, this frightens you, makes you want to never go outside at all, or just work harder, work at jobs that no one wants, the jobs that have to be done, taking care of the people that no one wants to take care of.

Sometimes you think you know who someone really is: Hitler or Freud or Shakespeare (What about the souls in female bodies then?). The great men. You think that you know who they are, the ones with power, the ones to influence and change things. (What about the souls that gave their power away? What is it then to give power away? Is this love?)

These souls, these men, the great ones, they keep coming back, the ones with mothers and lovers, these men that crowned themselves then? These men that do great things or terrible things and what is the difference if nothing really changes? Who's to know where these great men have gone? Sometimes you think that you know who they are. In the midst of innocent conversation, it's a fury that makes you tongue-tied, wish to all of a sudden not be here at all.

The first night in Mark's bedroom and you are unable to sleep.

In this room which is really the attic, the third floor, you get down on your hands and knees and put your ear to the wood. In Mrs. Lorian's room there are voices. You want to know what it is that is being said below where you are. What is it that Mrs. Lorian is saying to her son? What is it that Mr. Lorian is saying to his mother? A mother and her son alone. Mr. Lorian's son killed himself. Mr. Lorian's wife left. What is it that keeps happening?

The shadows in this small room look like people sitting in chairs, people watching you. Every time you close your eyes Mark's voice begins. You turn on the light, you think about being in love, how you wish you would have known Mark then because it would have been different, you know this. When you first heard about Mark, your heart raced and you got dizzy. This happened before. Mark shot himself in the head. The newspapers said it was a hunting accident. But Mark never hunted. It was a lie. People pretending. Grandma Green pretending her husband didn't do that to your mom.

People pretending that so many young people aren't filled with grief, don't kill themselves. The house is creaking. Shadows move through this house like smoke pouring down the hallway.

Mark's journals are waiting to be read. You will read all of them.

Grandma's lost letter.

Your grandfather was a prison guard. Your grandfather made sure that all the people that no one knew what to do with didn't get away.

This compulsion, make it stop, make it stop, this imprisoning and guarding in others what you wish you could control, could make disappear in yourself.

You told Miya that her eyes looked like the eyes of a fawn.

No, she said, just eyes.

In Equinox most people are sleeping. People's dreams rising up to the stars? What people are, really, rising up from sleeping bodies, people's dreams mixing, energies intertwining, separating. Or maybe people's dreams only rise as high as the ceiling, dreams pressing against walls. A whole nighttime of dreams, and the other half of the world is not in darkness now.

What is it you want?

What is beneath what you say, what anyone says, this is what is important, what is underneath language or photographs or a sleeping face. What is beneath all this is what you want to know. Because something has to make a difference now.

There are so many records already, and documents and histories of what has happened.

These records, films or photographs, or books, all about bodies doing things. These records, proofs of bodies and their lives, their physical being. Bodies that looked this way, bodies that did these things, bodies that were with these people. And what of it, these records, all these documents? When the people are no longer here what does anything mean? Where do they go? Where?

The record of dreams, the record of what was beneath all of

this is what you really want. You really don't want this film footage or these photo albums but what is inside.

If you shut your eyes, Mark's voice begins; just a voice, a livingness, not words. The flesh is porous. Emotion, the livingness won't, can't stay inside when you try to keep it there. The wind presses against the sides of the house. There is the sound of footsteps on the widow's walk. Trees.

You wake up and you are in a house, a container through which generations have moved. I am breathing. This you say to yourself opening your eyes and quickly closing them, not wanting to go back to sleep. This you say to yourself. This. But it won't last, this momentary non-identity. The contents of the room, light and wood and fabric and all Mark's journals and books neatly ordered on shelves; all this starting to close in around you.

In the dream your hands were of ice.

In the dream you have enrolled in a camp that is a very exclusive place where people can go for euthanasia. At first the camp is a place where people can go about their daily routine without being bothered, without anyone bothering them about the choices they have made to take their own life. There are classrooms, and boutiques and spas and beauty salons and green lawns that stretch over rolling hills. Everything is at this camp, everything luxurious. Then you realize that at this camp you may be here because you have chosen to take your own life in a peaceful way except that the people that run the camp, people that you had not been aware of, thought before that no one actually ran the camp, these people perform the euthanasia by lottery. You don't want to be here anymore because you don't have the choice to die when you want to. It is already too late because you signed a contract. There is no way out in the dream.

Awake you must do things; you must find yourself. Now you are in a house but mostly you don't feel contained at all. You have lost your boundaries if ever you had any and only see yourself in others.

So many times during the day you feel that you are dreaming and that you will soon wake up.

Mark's journals . . .

You look through other people's belongings to find what you have lost. As if you somehow had a right to snoop through other people's things, other people's lives.

The Mobile

TODAY I walked in the park. After I took my mobile to the craft store I walked to the park and sat on the swings. The three crows were watching me as always, ready to bring things to the fore as usual. No secrets here on the swings today Mark, the damn crows say.

The crows started talking about it as soon as I sat down. The three black crows that must be older than me, must be twenty-five at least, so black their feathers look blue. The crows had seen it happen, remembered that day in the park when I was eight. The crows were huddled together talking about me like children whispering in church.

One crow said, yes I remember Mark when he was a boy. I saw what he did. That's quite a burden to carry around with him. The other crow, the biggest one, looked at me, its beady eyes yellow like cold nipples. The swing was tight under me. I was sitting in the swing with the mobile on my lap and the crows were talking about me, old crows. The thing is, one crow says, he won't forgive himself, I have watched Mark for so long and he just won't.

I yelled from the swing that it was an accident. I was yelling it was an accident, it was an accident. Mrs. Mattison was walking up the street and she just looked at me, looked away

fast and kept walking up the street. Old Mrs. Mattison walking
up the street, her mangy dog at her heels, her bony fingers
pushing her shopping cart filled with costumes and batons for
the tap-dancing class that she teaches at the church. She pushed
the cart fast and stumbled away. I yelled at her, Good morning
Mrs. Mattison, but she didn't turn around.

The crows moved up on the top of the hill after I yelled and
I couldn't hear what they were saying anymore, just whispers.
I got up and threw the mobile in the big green garbage
dumpster by the merry-go-round. I could hear the echo of the
metal and the shattering of the glass pieces long after I dropped
it in there.

This is nice, the lady in the craft shop said, it's very
conceptual. I like the square-inside-the-circle motif.

No, that's not it, I told her. Can't you see how the whole
mobile is a microcosm for social injustice? Don't you see the
tension here? I yelled at her.

The idea for this mobile is based on the fact that the four winds
meet here in Equinox. I was getting very angry at the lady.
Inertia, I said, nothing ever changing, the four winds pressing in
on an object from all sides, people can't move. Don't you see
that? I knew that my face was bright red. This mobile is designed
so that it won't move in the wind; rather it will produce specific
tones made by the different wind directions. I told her I could
show her the blueprints. She was laughing at me. She was lying
with her words and inside she was laughing.

That's very nice, she said. Come back when you have more
than just this one, and maybe I will consider putting your work
on consignment. The crows were cackling up on the hill after I
threw the mobile in the dumpster.

When it happened, when I was eight, I don't remember
seeing the crows.

Is this your only one? the lady asked me looking at me over
her glasses then looking at her watch. Inside her head she was
saying: this guy is crazy, I wish he would leave. Bring back
more, she said, lying over what was really in her head. In her

head she was saying: Doesn't this boy bathe? She just didn't understand.

It happened in the park when I was eight. I killed Susan Vocelli by accident.

We were all in the park. All the kids except me were playing Hide-and-go-seek in the snow. I had a snowball, a special one that I had made by packing the snow hard, and smoothing it so it was ice, hard as a pool ball. I kept it in the freezer.

I brought this ice ball to the park. I was going to use it, really trick Tom in a snowball fight. I had it in my pocket and I was waiting for just the right moment.

That day there weren't any snowball fights. Tom was playing Hide-and-go-seek with Mary and Steve for a long time. This was making me mad. Tom hadn't asked me to play. He hadn't come to my house that morning like he usually did.

Tom was it and he was counting on the picnic table. From where I was standing on the hill I got ready. Tom was on 54 and he was counting slow and steady. Mary and Steve were right behind Tom on the merry-go-round between the five big snowmen we had all made the day before. Susan Vocelli came up behind them just as I threw the snowball.

I was going to scare them, that was all. I was going to get Tom on the back. I was going to make them all wonder where the snowball had come from. If it missed Tom's back it would hit the merry-go-round. The ice on the merry-go-round would make a very loud noise. I had planned the whole thing. I aimed carefully and threw it. The shiny ball glistened and sailed in an arc against the gray sky.

I could hear the crack as it hit the top of Susan's head. I saw her fall and then I ran.

For a long time I would wake up at night and see her lying there face down in the snow like she was going to make a snow angel. When I would wake up there was no one to talk to. I never told anyone and no one ever knew. The crows knew.

THESE secrets people keep. The walls of Mark's room get smaller and smaller. People can't breathe.

Telescope

TONIGHT it is thirty below zero. You are going to see Halley's comet. The last time the comet made its appearance your grandfather on your father's side of the family was getting ready to be born. There was a soft snow outside and Grandfather's mother, who loved violets, was panting deep into the night. Each breath opening her body as if by exhaling she might bolt down the wavering confines of the room. Her eyes connecting patterns on the wallpaper. Green petals stretch to faint blue lines. Red triangles pulling toward lavender dots. The burlap texture of the wallpaper bumps delicately across the wood of the walls. She won't scream even though she is burning from the inside. The crown of Grandfather's head glistens. His mother's auburn hair is matted to the outline of her face. Great-Grandfather's surgical equipment on her nightstand reflects her face small and warped. Her face, Great-Grandfather's dark figure. The fire gluttonizing in the wood stove. When she moves her head the silver instruments still reflect light, sharp needles piercing into the dim room. Grandfather forces himself out from between her legs. Wallpaper. Silver scalpel. White-hot flames. Doctor Great-Grandfather.

Behind the gray blanket of the winter sky a comet moves.

On the roof of the observatory you are trying to keep warm. You are waiting for your turn to view the comet. The bitter cold has silenced you. Standing beneath the gigantic telescope you huddle in your muffler.

Through the high-powered lens of the telescope the comet appears just after sunset. It is nothing more than a thick piece of dust against the purple sky but you feel a sudden sense of strength looking through the lens. Your throat tightens. Your vision goes blurry.

The comet looks like a piece of lint. This piece of lint, on a photographic negative, would leave a small white mark, marring the image of eyes looking out into the future from a piece of paper.

When your great-grandmother died, your father's grandmother, you got her locket. In it is a piece of hair and a picture of your great-grandparents. Their eyes burn out of the scissor-cut frame like nettles.

If you blink you might miss something, June wrote.

The China Tattoo

THERE are three china tattoos, it says in faint pencil across the bottom of the tapestry drawing your mother gave you for Christmas. I can't believe you are giving me this, you say. It's beautiful.

You watch the blue veins in your mother's hands; veins that stand out in places then disappear abruptly, veins like the long awkward stitches made by someone sewing for the first time.

It is Christmas Eve and your mother is finishing up the gift wrapping. You are in the dining room watching her. All the lights are off in the rest of the house, except for the tree lights that are blinking off and on in the living room. Pearl and Paul are asleep. Twins, your mother had twins.

It's been three years since you have seen your mother, three years of wishing that things were different, of trying to disappear into a calm of soft sleep and not this. You lean on the rickety dining-room table and watch her.

I'm coming home for Christmas. For Christmas. For Christmas.

I think we have a bad connection.

Here, hold there, your mother says, and the green string on the gift for her mother tightens around your finger.

Your father is in his new house with his new wife. June is in New York. Before you came home you had been in New York.

June is somewhere in New York. You came here to stay with a friend because really you are always looking for June and at the same time hoping that you won't find her.

What you are doing now is sitting, sitting in a chair. Girdered up fifteen stories, you sit in a chair against a white wall. New York. You are watching the sunlight move across the room, getting closer like an incoming tide, as it sets somewhere past California.

Out the window there are clouds, a brown wooden water tank on another roof, the outline of skyscrapers and the air. The sunlight is moving closer to your chair. You think of the air that is filled with atoms, matter pulsating and zooming through the city unnoticed. It is possible that right now or before, matter, atoms, passed through June, through the water tower, through you. Why not? Pulsating energy fields, this. Containers, houses or bodies or buildings or air.

Small things look lovely down below, people the size of your thumb rushing home to houses with doors that have too many locks to make a difference if they needed to get inside quickly.

You think of atoms. You think of June, two things about June: trees and then drawings, these images that stick.

On the way there was one thing, on the way to wherever it was that Dad was driving because he just drove and you and June would be playing in the backseat.

On the way back it was the game again.

Above the silhouettes of trees that lined the highway like upturned rakes, the sun pulsating orange through the thick gray clouds (all these words for a feeling remembered?).

Dad says no, we can't get ice cream. Dad says this. It's after the circus or on the way back from the store or on the way back from school or Grandma's and Dad says this because he likes for you and June to hope that he will change his mind. You are caught under his will. You cross your fingers tightly and hope Dad doesn't drive past the Dairy Queen or Baskin Robbins. Dad heads the car up the hill toward home. The trees that line the road open up like a zipper.

The trees are always likened to something. Trees stay where they are.

Dad drives all the way to your house and slows down. Then he turns the car around and heads back toward ice cream, heads back past the trees that June says make her dizzy to watch them go by out the window.

The sunlight in the room has reached your feet. Sweat is on your forehead. The shadow you are sitting in from the wall to the edge of the sunlight is not even a foot and a half in length. The afternoon is almost over.

June is kneeling in the window seat drawing stick-figure people in the corner of a large piece of newsprint. She holds the oversized forest-green crayon in her left fist. The crayon could be a shovel the way June is kneeling over the page and pushing the crayon, sometimes pressing the crayon off the page and leaving short green wax lines on the saffron window seat.

"This is Mom," she says, finishing off the figure.

The corner of the paper rips as she says this quietly again to herself for the second time, "This is Mom," trying to bring the crayon back onto the page without lifting it.

June fills in the round O mouth of Mom that is in profile at the edge of the page. The figure is heavy in the stomach. The belly button is too high, is up where a heart might be. The belly button is a squiggle of concentric circles. A beltline across the middle of the figure looks like the opening of a kangaroo pouch.

You are watching June. It is the middle of summer and outside the bay window small beads of hail are bouncing off the picnic table.

Children's drawings are more realistic than photographs.

The city smells like urine and exhaust and there are tunnels, vaults, and empty spaces beneath all the buildings. Trains run beneath apartments, beneath park benches, the park benches that are next to fenced-in trees. Trains run beneath hospitals, beneath Bellevue where you know June has been because she called Dad to tell him this, Bellevue the mental hospital.

You think about Bellevue a lot when you are in the city. You want to know how anyone can decide who is sane and who is not. Why aren't you there? It is you who can no longer decipher reality. The privilege of forgetting. You think about that phrase and try to remember where you heard it.

June disappeared. She burned the house down. She was many different people and no one at all, just like you. Now June is somewhere in this city.

You tell people that June is here. A person might look at you with a listening face, not really hearing you, your need to talk about June as if the talking might change what you don't understand, don't believe.

What is important is June, and it's hard for you to see anything else, respect anyone's words then?

You go to the store.

"It's the little things," the checker says knowing what to say. Appropriate words for appropriate situations. And all of a sudden you want to yell in this store that New York is a fucking graveyard, and that your sister June is in it.

"It's the little things you can't possibly remember," the checker is saying as she rings up the purchases of the lady in front of you: a can of water-packed tuna, seedless grapes in a red

plastic net, a large beef bone, a giant knuckle in plastic wrap
with purple ink stains on the red-and-white bone, and a small
jar of cinnamon. Little things, you think, what is important at
all. Words, language, and you wish the checkout lady hadn't
talked to this woman about her purchases, wasting time.

Sometimes people say that June might be dead, and you say
deader than what?

At 5 P.M. in front of the store ready to start work young girls
with pale faces are walking up and down the street.

There is a construction site, a gaping hole next to the
sidewalk where there is a crane and a trailer. There is a walkway
with an awning you walk under. The plywood wall is plastered
with posters: the same beautiful woman, a singer, her face
duplicated many times, one poster next to another next to
another, this one woman's face.

Under the awning you pass two girls. You clutch tightly at
your purse. The eyes of these girls are hungry and move about
fast in their pale makeup-plastered faces. Plastered faces. Posters
of faces. Their jeans are too tight around their heavy white
bodies, their haircuts are cheap, ugly, wrong. They have
pimples. They are girls. Other girls aren't here. These girls
won't look much prettier when it is dark. They won't need to
look much prettier.

In New York when it rains all of a sudden everyone has an
umbrella. When it is windy garbage flies around the streets and
the eyes tear and get dirt in them.

In Equinox the wind in the leaves sounds like rain.

．　．　．

I LOOKED for June in New York, you tell your Mom.

Not far from where you grew up in Northern California
there is a strange old house that a woman built after her
husband died. There are doors that go nowhere, stairways that
lead up to brick walls and rooms that can only be viewed
through windows that don't open. No one can enter these

rooms. The house is a mansion, your mother used to tell you. Someday I will take you and June there, she said. My father took me there quite a few times, your mother said. There are guided tours.

When she told you about the house you would try to picture Grandpa walking up the stairs to a brick wall. You would imagine him scaring your mother with eerie tales about the ghost of the woman wandering through her house at night. You could hear his voice tell how sometimes people got lost on the guided tours and never came out. The woman who built the house was very young when her husband died and when a fortuneteller told her that if she ever stopped building she would die. It is called the Winchester House of Mystery. When the woman was in her late fifties there was a builders' strike and she died.

Please don't lean on this table. I am trying to address this card. Your eyes meet across the table, the dining-room table that your mother ate at as a little girl, that you ate at as a little girl, something concrete.

We will go to the Winchester House while I am home.

No, they closed it down.

The dining room is reflected in the window. Your mother's hand moves across the creamy paper of the card she is writing on. The scratching of the pen against the paper sends a shiver up your spine. Your right shoulder twitches.

The dining-room table is a mess of scratches; initials are etched into the sticky varnished wood with forks. It was a beautiful table once. The table legs are carved. Two of the four legs still have brass feet. The table doesn't belong in this flimsy house that your father made from a kit. This table belongs back in Grandma Green's dark house on the hill.

Don't talk with your mouth full, hold your eating utensils this way or excuse yourself from the table, don't speak unless you are spoken to, Grandpa Green said. Where your hand is, fuck you is scratched into the table.

Please don't do it Grandpa Green, you are thinking, wishing

you could have been there before, because there is no mystery. You just want the aching to stop.

At night Sarah and I would put our dresser against the door, your mother told you. Bill's room was down the hall and he never knew. My father walks slowly down the hall and snaps the broken lock on the door. The dresser is pushed away from the door. Sarah and I never told our mother anything, she is so filled with denial, your Mom said. Mother, she must have whispered into the darkness.

Your grandma worked the night shift at the army base hospital. When Grandpa Green got off duty from San Quentin he got drunk. Your mother had to touch him in the darkness. Mother, her lips must have formed as Grandpa Green presses into her. China, it says in red ink right beneath his belly button.

Your Mom is still writing on the creamy white card. You imagine then. Your mother's eyes opening into the dark of her bedroom, humming a song that she doesn't quite know the words to. Her sister in the other bed, awake, watching maybe, helpless.

Fathers and daughters.

I am dreaming, you say, I can wake up if I want to.

Sitting at the dining-room table with your mother. Her eyes look shut because she is looking down where she is writing.

What happens to people.

Will you wrap these? your mother asks. Her eyes look tired now. This is for Bill and this is for Sarah. Two small cardboard cubes for Mother's brother and sister. Inside the boxes are crystals nestled in scraps of deep green velvet. It's Christmas Eve and you are home.

Where you are is in front of the TV. There's the blue light from the TV washing over the room like food coloring mixing into dough, more like how the romantic lighting in a black-and-white movie seems blue, seems blue.

Mother's cigarette is out, but the smell of the ashtray is thick in the air. There's that smell and then there's the smell of the carpet: a mix of spilled drinks, spilled a long time ago or minutes ago, muddled, and there's the smell of cat piss that has been covered with Pinesol and different cleansers, and there is the smell of your father, sweat and alcohol and something else, yeast.

Mother is asleep on the couch, exhausted from work at the veterans hospital. She snores on the couch over where you and your father are on the floor. Mother's face is toward the back of the sofa, a half-sleeping face, because you can only see half of her face the way she is lying. Please wake up now. You know that your mother is not dreaming. You know that she won't wake up.

Your father is next to you on the floor.

There is no one else in the house.

Your father is rubbing your back, first on your sweater and then under it. You get tingly and warm and want him to touch your breasts and your father's legs are bony and his robe is open, a brown robe that is the same material as a bath towel. Chicken skin and hair. Your father's hands are rough and his mouth is wide open and his breath smells like gin and he is touching your breasts.

Your mother is snoring.

The blue of the TV and the room is snapping on and off.

You think about other things now. You think about the new girl in school and how she looked in her white ankle socks before she yelled at you, asked you what you were always staring at please. The new girl won't be back at school on Monday. You won't be back at school Monday. Times before, up, breakfast, the walk to school and no one's there, there's no school, you forgot, your mother forgot, the empty blacktop, hoping no one sees you.

This time you know there is no school Monday.

Your father's hands are everywhere.

The new girl goes to Catechism Sundays. You are never at Catechism but you would like to be, to go there and see candles and shiny silver crosses and clean books and the new girl. No one asked you if you wanted to go to Catechism, no one made you go. You want to be made to go to Catechism like other kids.

Your father's hands are at your nipples rough then tickling and his breath is fast and raspy. He coughs. There is school but not Monday.

The new girl called you a dirty girl with dirty clothes. That was Wednesday. By Friday you forgave her and she wore a new sweater and you could have sworn you could smell the red vinyl of her father's new car on her sweater, the new car you can see her get out of when you wait in the schoolyard in the morning by the tetherballs and the rings. You get to school early so you can see her come, get out of her father's new car, kiss him goodbye, the same every day.

The new girl wears white socks and her legs aren't fat like yours. Her ankles are thin. She always has two hair clips above her ears and her hair is shiny and curly from being set overnight in curlers.

Your father's fingers are inside of you and you can feel how wet you are there because it feels good. You just lay there.

Not tonight it won't happen because your mother is home. She won't wake up.

Your father grabs your hand and puts it under his robe, holds your hand wrapping his hardness. You know this part and then the room is silent, snaps off and on, the blue light, and your father makes a sound like going to the bathroom, the squirting, warm on your father's stomach and your hand, and then he lays on his back, closes his robe and tells you to get up and change the channel.

The new girl is not your friend but you wish that she was.

This is not your father.
This is your mother, not you.
This is not your picture.

. . .

YOUR Grandfather Green is buried at the army base graveyard where thousands of other war veterans lie squeezed together under the ground, box to box. This image frightens you. It takes a while to find his headstone. His name chiseled into the white marble of one stone. His name the only difference from the thousands of other white stones that ripple over the hills that are green in the spring and brown mostly. Stone ghosts.

You are afraid. You are afraid to stop moving. You are afraid to really listen because then it is like nighttime.

People are layers of grief, Mark wrote. People are afraid to really grieve when they hurt because they are afraid as the grief comes away, layer by layer, they are afraid they might lose themselves, the selves they are trying to become. Mark.

Mother, you have whispered so many times in the dark from your bed in Equinox, I am afraid.

. . .

You didn't tell your mother about Miya or Mark.

You don't tell your mother you want to disappear. You tell your mother that in Equinox you are taking care of a dying woman and then you tell your mother's lover to get out of the house, that she is grotesque and that the twins should be taken away from her. Your mother tells Diane to go away for a while. Your mother listens to you yell like this and when you are finished she says, you know children only know something is wrong when they are hurt or when someone tells them something is wrong. Your mother says, people are afraid of too many things. The only fears people are born with, your mother says, are the fear of falling and the fear of noise. You are yelling. You feel like you are falling away from your own body.

Mark wrote:

It's too bad we are trapped in these aging bodies. And children don't want to procreate and of course they can't and don't think about it. Children are filled with desire for desire's sake, desire to touch, to feel, to know the world in every way, experience the world, everything sensual. Children are so curious and blindly forgiving of the world's injustices. Are codes of injustice somehow inside of children waiting to be discovered, waiting to get out? Are there genetic codes for destruction that have not revealed themselves but are there nonetheless?

. . .

THE park is muddy. A man in a hat and long gray overcoat stands next to a stone fountain. It is your Grandfather Green and this is your dream. You have a pail and a small plastic shovel. What are you doing now? he asks. I am going to dig to China, you say. He opens up his coat and you laugh hysterically. You wake up. It is Christmas morning.

You were in that park before. Awake, you remember there was a man in the park then too. There are swings suspended from cold iron bars over brown puddles. The man is your father. He lifts you on to the swing so that you don't get your shoes wet in the puddle. You say, thank you.

Was there something else you wanted to say?

Women remind you of your mother. Men remind you of the gap between people. A gap, and not the space between two tightly held hands. You are afraid of this space. Your mother says she knows about this space that separates people. June is the space between people. It is the eye of a cat; a dark center that fluctuates. People don't get lost really, your mother says. What about June then? you say. What about June? People don't get lost, your mother says. You are sure people do.

There is a sound that you hear that is louder than screaming and thicker than night. It jolts you out of feeling. It gets the loudest when you become conscious that you are really listening, that you are really hearing what is happening, what is really being said beneath what people say. Looking into people's eyes is when the sound gets the loudest. Your hands start to sweat. It is impossible to hold onto anything. Please, you want to say when this is happening. Please don't make me look into your eyes, I am afraid I will fall in. This feeling becomes muddier than the puddle you stepped into when the swing stopped that day in the park and you turned around to see your father. You will have to understand this sound or you will have to make it stop.

There is a rush in your ears. A loud ringing. Sperm makes that sound, sperm makes that sound, a roar that can be recorded by microphones. Your mother's eyes make your ears ring when she looks at you. Other women too, when they look at you, when you look at them, cause this roaring to start, the women that remind you of your mother and make you look down.

Your mother makes you look away, other women, women as powerful as your mother, women whose eyes search yours for answers, make you look away, then down, down to where there is no reality, just ground, a floor, the corner of a chair, down at your own hands.

What you see in your mother's eyes, in other women's eyes (how you used to say you would die if your mother died, couldn't, wouldn't live without her), what you look away from, don't want to see is the impossibility of denying what is true, that you are the same and afraid.

You are afraid of being a woman of having between your legs the space for letting life in and out of, of having so much power and not wanting it finally. This truth, that you wish someone else to take responsibility for this power. Eyes that make you look down.

You don't want to be the carrier of life, of nurturing within your body what you yourself see as hopeless.

There are patterns, some of which have to be broken. You are not sure where to begin.

And it's too much, to look into another woman's eyes and see this commonality, to admit in a glance this power you possess, this power to give and nurture life, to admit in a glance that you are so ready to give this power away, to admit that you are dying.

In these eyes, blue eyes, or the ones that are moist with kindness, eyes that make you look down, down to where you don't really want to be. Forgetting.

★   ★   ★

Your father is standing there, his nearsighted blue eyes gazing into the pine trees, his neck muscles tight, his hair wild. Lips are like lids. The noise gets louder. The sound of the swing seat hitting your stomach occurs over and over and over again. Coat to zipper to rubber and your father looks down at you. The look in his eyes is the same as the time he zipped your stomach by accident trying to help you into your snowsuit. It's hard to look into his eyes.

Before you were born there was no way of knowing that there would be habits to learn, or wisdoms to undo. These wisdoms that become as useless as trying to do over and over again what you never really knew how to do in the first place.

.   .   .

YOUR father was writing a book. It was called *The Alley of Eden*. It was about how people were being smothered but knew how to love despite this. He never finished it.

.   .   .

IT'S Christmas night. You are sitting on the toilet watching your mother bathe. Do you mind if I stay here? Your voice sounds like Mother's movement in the tub: water lapping against porcelain, Mother's hands soaping her belly. Beneath her belly button her pubic hair glistens. Your mother's body is strong and beautiful as a carefully designed contour map, but not as deceptive. Her pubic hair beneath the water, the stretch marks on her stomach, her hips, her small breasts that have nursed four babies. Her body is just what it is and it is strong and beautiful.

The day before my father died, your mother says to you, I was standing in his room. Not kneeling by his bed but looking at his photographs on the wall opposite where he lay. Snapshots:

myself, Bill and Sarah when we were kids, birthday parties, at weddings. My mother was in the living room, her knitting needles clicking fiercely. I could tell that her lips were pursed tight between pulls of her cigarettes, or occasional mumblings to one of five Siamese cats. I could feel my Mom's eyes squinting with alcohol, focusing the dullness of dust and dark smoky colors. Mom in the living room smoking cigarette after cigarette, and my father in bed wheezing for breath. His lungs a condensation of the whole house.

One of the pictures was of myself as a chubby adolescent, my eyes looking sideways to something outside of the frame, my legs squeezed tightly together beneath the olive-colored bath towel, hair wet to my face. I had just gotten out of the shower and my father caught me with his camera.

Your mother is soaping under her arms now, the hair there filled with suds. She cups the bathwater in her palms and splashes away the white foam. My father asked me while I was standing in his dark bedroom listening to the slow rattle of his breath, looking at pictures on his wall, my father asked me if I would try to resuscitate him if I came into the room and he was dead. I kept looking at the snapshot of myself as a chubby adolescent. Me before they sent me to Catholic school because I couldn't tell anyone that anything was wrong except through not doing what I was supposed to be doing. Me before I started the endless visits to psychiatrists who never addressed the real issues. People always letting men off the hook, Mom says.

. . .

THE park is muddy. Yesterday the mud was hard and cracked and the sky was tinged pink from morning until night. Today the mud beneath the swings is soft and you felt like you were being watched so you took off your shoes and stood in it. You are five and there is a place on your stomach that burns because yesterday your Dad accidentally zipped your stomach up helping you into your red snowsuit.

Dad's hands on your belly then, Mom's hands soaping hers.

The veins beneath your father's hands are hardly visible, and branch under the flesh like delicately drawn blue crayon lines. Your father likes to tie flies for fishing. You like to watch him do this. He can spend hours carefully winding colored threads around feathers.

On one of those afternoons I spent in his room, he told me about being back in prison, your Mom says. I had this dream, he tells me. He was up on the wall doing his regular surveillance and he hears three screams coming from different directions somewhere in the prison. He said the searchlight stopped where he was standing on the wall and he could see his face and his eyes and he was frightened. A fourth scream came even louder than the others and then a fifth scream. And with each scream the searchlight would light up my father's face where he was standing on the wall. He said the screaming was so loud that it felt as if his forehead was peeling back across his skull.

Could you hand me that towel? As your mother stands up the water rushes down her legs. Her flesh is right in front of you, flesh like your own, flesh that you struggle with when you are three thousand miles away. You have to remind yourself that she is right here. The space between things, that overwhelming silence that becomes a bloodcurdling scream.

It's the possibility of touch. You must unlearn your shame you are thinking. Can your mother read your mind? Your mother. You want to hold your mother whose flesh is your own. You are afraid of eyes. As soon as you think that the voices start up, a hum. Whose voice is yours?

For Christmas your mother gave you a tapestry she made. At the bottom is faintly penciled in her whispering handwriting: *There are three china tattoos.* The tapestry is a collage of embroidery, photo snapshots, clippings from magazines, pencil drawings, and watercolors. June. Has there already been three or just two, china tattoos, what repeats? June.

All I can say is I hope that June is not dead, your mother said.

You think that it is remarkable how your mother pieced together so many things to make a whole. She is an amazing seamstress, you think, fingering the silk threads that outline the magazine image of a child. It is a delicate piece and the pencil writing could easily be erased. You want to roll it up, protect it so it doesn't get touched too much and smudged with fingerprints. Your mother doesn't mind if people touch her work. She likes the idea of non-precious art.

There are three china tattoos it says beneath the drawing of a woman in a bridal gown holding a bouquet of wilted roses in her left hand, and a baby to her chest. Behind the woman three figures walk across a horizon of black embroidery thread that winds beneath the figures' feet like the stitches holding a wound together.

The Opera

THIS part, what you can't remember, what exactly it was that your Grandfather Green said to you, your mother's father. There was an interview, a formal one. It was a project you did for a history class in your junior year in high school.

Rob was with you. Grandpa liked Rob, approved of him, said he hoped the two of you would get married someday because he could tell that you would take good care of one another. But that's not important. What's important is that you can't remember exactly what your grandfather said to you that day.

You had a tape of the interview you conducted with your

grandfather. You brought a tape recorder because even then you must have known how memory and recall get distorted.

The questions you asked concerned Nazi Germany.

Your project, the interview, was to be an essay, personal views concerning the Holocaust, not your personal views, your grandfather's.

Everything is muddled now. The tape isn't lost. It is blank. The questions you asked and the answers your grandfather gave have disappeared. Not dates, not who was lost then, killed, not how Grandpa Green's name was shortened, just one thing you remember; Grandpa Green saying that he is almost certain that his brother died in the gas chamber, this brother Grandpa hardly knew, because this brother was the oldest, didn't come with the family to America from wherever it was in Europe that your grandfather's family came.

(Specifics, sometimes you starve for specifics, want to know facts and not so much uncertainty, not so many individuals struggling with a guilt you can only feel but aren't exactly sure from where it comes. When people are struggling to live they can't be bothered with the details sometimes. What is there to hold on to then? This is what you would like to know.)

What does it mean that a Jewish man would be in America, a Marine in World War II, a Jewish man who must have known what was happening in Europe, in Germany then? These places that you read about in books or see so many movies about, movies that want people to see to remember these atrocities, these Holocausts so that they won't happen again. It's just that people are numb to seeing anything over and over again. How to make it stop?

What you remember, seated next to Rob on the couch across from your grandfather seated in his green chair is that his brother was on the Isle of Man first.

Grandpa's voice keeps in the back of your head. Sometimes you aren't sure in what way.

Grandpa's brother was on the Isle of Man and it was from

here that he kept writing letters to a woman that he loved. But the woman was lost, never received these letters. This is what your grandfather said.

This is what you remember, a missed connection between a man and a woman.

What you think of now is someone's worth measured by their love sent in letters never received. What you think of now is how Grandpa's brother would never see the pictures of men and women like himself, pictures of people bald and melted down to bones or just eyes, starved people reduced to unopened letters.

What you want to know even while you are thinking about how you might solve this problem of order, of containing, putting things in their place is finally what becomes of letters anyway.

There are letters that are returned unopened, canceled with the postal mark of the place to which they were sent. There is so much time spent writing letters, time spent carefully articulating thoughts, sharing with someone what seems so crucial and important, so urgent. Not just any letters, but love letters, the letters that scream off the page. What becomes of all these?

Some letters are only read once, boxed away. Maybe some day these letters are briefly looked at. But who has the time to reread letters?

There are some people who carry letters with them and read them over and over again for a long time. A good portion of their lives might be spent going over the words written to them a long time ago.

You wonder about the documentary film footage of Nazi Germany, film in which people's death, a person's death is shown. You can see a face just before it breaks up like a puzzle. You wonder if there are children, people who are shown certain pieces of these films and told, there look that was your grandfather.

In the dream you are brought into a room by a group of men. It is dark. You are in your body and aware of this.

You are being shown a black plastic bag that is box-shaped and lined with white plastic.

The bag is open on top like the corner of an envelope.

Touch it, one of the men says. You can't see which one. You can't see any of these men.

Inside the bag are ashes, black ashes that are wet as something just born or something that is dying, disintegrating moist into the earth. They are human ashes. You know this just as you know that you are really in your body this time.

You filter the ashes through your hands while the men whose faces you can't see and whose presence you no longer feel watch.

June is gone.

Grandpa said that he and Grandma will pick you up at 4:30, early so that there will be time, time for dinner, time to talk, time to show you the opera house.

Grandpa invited you to the opera after the interview you never did write up, receiving an F and a warning that you were failing history. Grandpa invited you and then he played opera records, as if he were proud, happy to have shared with you what you can't remember, couldn't remember as you were being told. The feeling of falling. Grandpa Green sitting in his chair with the handle on the side to tilt the chair back for comfort, Rob sitting quietly next to you his hand on your knee. Grandpa Green telling you about the Isle of Man, his face hard or far away. The whole time he is talking you are nervous, anxious and you nod your head and hear the words but you can't remember what he is saying.

You are thinking about the Isle of Man. You are sure that it is a concrete place. This is how you picture it, like Treasure Island, the army base that divides the Bay Bridge. Treasure Island where a World's Fair was held once. Land in the middle of water. Land that can only be reached by boat or plane or by the bridge that runs through it. The Island, a halfway point between San Francisco and Richmond. Separating. Dividing. Connecting.

The Isle of Man must have been cold. This is how you picture it, a cold concrete place where everyone is frightened and trapped.

You are thinking about the cancel marks on stamps, ink patterned in waves like the ocean surrounding islands, ink that branches out like veins if you look closely at the cancel mark.

At 3 P.M. you are ready. Not dressed as nice as you would like, and unsure as to what you would wear to the opera if you actually had a choice of nice clothes, not just Mom's dresses.

Mom says you look nice. You decided to wear a dress of Mom's. It is an old dress, forties style with shoulder pads. Mom said that you look like Billie Holiday. You are sure that she said that not because you pulled your hair back into a bun but because of how round and fat your face looks. You tried putting a flower in your hair above your ear but you burned the red petals with a cigarette. You have already had four since you have been dressed. You don't think that Grandpa knows that you smoke. Grandpa had to quit because he has emphysema. Grandma still smokes about three packs a day.

Mom says that Grandma is getting back at Grandpa by refusing to quit. You aren't sure what Grandma is getting back at Grandpa for. Mom says there are some things about Grandma that won't ever change, that once Grandma decides to do or not do something nothing will ever change her mind.

When Mom told you that you looked nice she said not to get your hopes up, that there was still a chance that Grandma and Grandpa wouldn't come. With my parents you never know. If Grandma decides that she doesn't want to go, then I am sure that Grandpa will call and say he is sorry, and Grandpa is sick, don't forget that he is dying, Mom said.

But you know that they are coming. Just before you were almost dressed Grandpa called.

You were trying on Mom's shoes, standing in front of the closet in June's room with one black pump on your right foot, and a blue lace-up shoe with sequins on the toe on your left. The blue shoes, just a few shades darker than the dress, matched better than the pumps, but the leather shoes fit better. The other ones, the blue cloth, are too big.

The phone rings. The closet, this closet with the messed-up mural that Mom painted for you and June when you first moved here is where Mom keeps her clothes now. This closet that smells like cat spray, a smell that never goes away. This closet smells like cat spray and mildew.

Grandpa asks you how you are doing. He tells you that he is very excited. Listening to his voice you all of a sudden remember the plastic musical instruments that Grandpa gave you and June for Christmas one year, the first Christmas in California.

There were so many times before that Grandma would tell you and June that she was going to take you places, the zoo, the Winchester House of Mystery, Disneyland someday, lots of places. At the last minute almost every time Grandma would call. You and June would be all ready to go. June would be looking out the window. You are unable to sit still in the chair, your favorite chair, the orange rattan chair that has a heavy wooden base and spins around and around fast. The chair that your Dad took when he moved into his own apartment. The apartment where Dad and June lived together.

I am sorry but something came up, or, I am sorry but I just don't feel well today. Grandma sitting in her dark house, nursing her pounding head, the curtains drawn, smoke moving slow near the ceiling.

If it was something good, something you had been counting on for a long time, a place that Grandma had been talking about for a long time, the Exploratorium, or to the Presidio where you can eat as much as you want at the buffet, then you and June would usually end up fighting, because first June would start crying and Mom would say I told you so. Shut up June you would say because you had started to cry too.

The opera is *Rigoletto*. The story is about a father and a daughter, a daughter who unknowingly sacrifices her life so that her father will be saved.

This is what you get from the opera, this is what you read. How do you read things, you the one who failed history?

The opera, it is sounds, hypnotic voices or anguished tones, a dull screaming that sends Grandma into the lobby where she smokes cigarette after cigarette until the opera is over.

Her eyes are tight and mean when you and Grandpa find her in the crowd.

Back at Grandma's there is a green satin dress in plastic, and a pair of black satin pumps with many-colored rhinestones on the toe that Grandma shows you. I wore this dress to the first opera your grandfather ever took me to, she says, not remembering how many other times she had shown you this dress.

The things you can't carry with you: the rock collection your mother's father's father arranged on sheets of paper, paper as thin now as tissue, the ink disappearing beneath each small piece of solid matter.

There are rocks in this collection from Pompeii, your grandfather said, holding the lid of the crumbling shoe box like a teacher would hold a blackboard pointer. Lava rocks too, he said, and bits of matter that fell from the sky. There are rocks in here from Pompeii. *Pompeii, where is Pompeii?* I have kept these for a long time and I want you to have them Tracy. My father collected these rocks.

This is history. This is how you move from one point to the next, holding on to what you can't carry with you.

I want you to have these, give them to your children, your grandfather said, still in his uniform. The suit of a prison guard: creased cloth the color of mud that has its own history, the slippery mud that is exposed at low tide by San Quentin prison, chemical mud, not just wet soil.

The rubber plants, their leaves smooth as dinner plates, collect dust. You wet your finger on your tongue and wipe the dust away along the seam of a large leaf. Now there is no dust along the seam of the leaf that divides the two sides.

Thank you Grandpa, you said.

Observing from a distance already, making a memory of

the moment while in the moment as if all that occurred in the muddle of shame and hatred and guilt had already become the gibberish of the voices heard right before sleep, voices to decipher or to leave alone.

All the things you can't carry with you: the voices of grandfathers that become the voice of your father, that become the voices of what hurts you the most, what it is that you can't take with you, can't do anything with, the ink fading beneath rocks, small pieces of solid matter glued onto thinning paper, a legacy of fact.

The Night-blooming Cereus

THE hothouse was not made of glass.

Mr. Lorian ordered it through a catalogue. It is a heavy plastic like the semi-opaque material that body bags are made of. He set it up on the sun porch the summer that Mark shot himself in the head. The hothouse contains a variety of cactuses and tropical plants. Mr. Lorian's prize possession is a rare breed of night-blooming cereus. It blooms once every year in the middle of July.

Who do you think you are? I have no time for your monkey business. I have important things to do today, Mrs. Lorian yells from her wheelchair. She is hunched there. A moth-eaten black sweater that is about to crumble is wrapped around her shoulders. Her shoulder blades look like wings. She is wearing only her underwear. It is 5 A.M. and Mrs. Lorian is ready to be dressed.

Listen here little lady, why don't you keep your hands to

yourself? Why don't you just go away? Mrs. Lorian says, I don't think we understand each other very well. Mrs. Lorian slaps at your hands as you try to help her dress. This routine every day. Sweat is already beading on your cheeks. The night brought no relief. People are dying from the heat in different parts of the country. In Equinox the purple hue of the mountains is quietly swallowing up the slow-motion play that has been going on all summer. There is something wrong in this town.

After breakfast Mrs. Lorian must do her laps. Thirty times you walk her around the ten-by-twelve-foot balcony at the top of the stairs. You hold on to her shoulders from behind as she lifts her metal walker, places it in front of her and steps toward it. Laps take over an hour.

Soon the people of Equinox won't remember Mark. Do people really ever die to save others? Mark took his own life, or did he? The people of Equinox, even those that have lived here for a lifetime, can't really say for sure what tribe of Indians lived here. The four winds meet here, Mark wrote over and over in his journal. Pages and pages of this one fact in small tight print.

Three of Mark's leatherbound journals are filled with a detailed description of what it was like to look out his bedroom window for twenty-four hours, without even getting up to go to the bathroom. This after his first lover said it was over.

.   .   .   .

SHE just said, "It's over," one day. "This is a joke," she said, "how you are going to do all these things, make these mobiles to illustrate these grandiose ideas, what about real oppression Mark? Why don't you get a real job, work with the handicapped, do things, not just all this thinking and megalomania crap, get out of yourself," she said. "All you really do is just sit in this room all day looking out this goddamn window. I just can't take it anymore."

She was right. I couldn't let her know this. "Please don't go,"

I said to her. "Please, let's just try." But I knew she would leave. After she left I just sat here in this chair where she left me looking out this window, counting my breath, holding my breath for as long as I could. Control. I just don't know what I am supposed to be doing, whether to stop and see what is here in this instant or to keep moving as does everything. If you stop moving you stop seeing, no, if you move you stop seeing. What is important is to stop moving and to recognize the movement in stillness. There is the motion that ticks behind closed eyes, like time-lapse photography, showing in seconds a full life cycle of a plant, everything behind my eyes until I am thirsty and dry as sand. My organs functioning in total darkness. Darkness. People are closing in on themselves. I don't mean they are closing in on themselves like they are discovering something, narrowing in, I mean entirely the opposite. I mean people are disappearing. There are bodies going through motions but for the most part something is missing.

The dream, yes the dream. First my father was rocking in a rocking chair and filing documents in a metal file cabinet that looked like morgue drawers. As my father opened each drawer I noticed that there were children in these drawers. Each child was engulfed in a plastic bag. I say engulfed because they were still alive and the precipitation of their breathing, their movement inside of the bags was causing the plastic to adhere to each child, but only around the eyes and mouth. I could see the children's, each child's tiny rosebud lips sucking in and out against the plastic. I was crawling through a space like a voice that can travel across continents as if we were talking in the same room, except my father couldn't hear me when I was trying to tell him what was happening to these children, that they were still alive and trying to get out. I had screamed, was shaking my father, and he wouldn't even look at me, or couldn't see me at all. My father was staring blankly into the blackness outside. The file cabinets opening and slamming shut in rhythm with the children's breathing. This dream. Doesn't anyone understand this, can't someone see what is wrong? We have blindfolded ourselves to what is important. What this all comes to, the beauty of the moment and the possibility of all that exists right now. Pen to paper and up above a satellite is tracking the movement of ships, tracking everything external, trying to bring the world, reduce all possibilities to one answer, one formula that fits on the head of a pin. There are suited men of power, telling people to photograph everything, fit it all into one book, photographing the changes in the weather as if being able to accurately predict the weather was the real goal. What is it that we are trying to do, everyone in this together, this life? We are trying to clean up all the problems of the world, order, manage and control everything so that finally the only thing left to discover will be how we might come back to life again. We are missing our potential. I am sure that if people ever tap into their true power they will be able to fly and walk through walls.

At first I didn't want to go inside of her, to hurt her at all. It must hurt. I didn't want to hurt Lisa. She says put it in, hurry up, do it. She was looking at me as if I would know exactly what to do. What was it that made me think that this was something violent to do?

I was inside of her, her face looked up into my eyes like she was seeing down a long tunnel. I was inside her and she closed her eyes when I told her she was beautiful, so beautiful I couldn't stand it, how good she felt all over, like silk melting. She grabbed my head wrapping her arms around my head so tight that I was lost. She came and sighed. So quick she said, "Get off of me, get off of me." Lisa.

I am sad now. It hurts because she said it was over, couldn't be in this life. I am grieving.

There is a chronology for grief, how we must all grieve. There are four stages, maybe more, layers of grief that are accumulated over a lifetime. I do know that the final stage is denial, the second stage is acceptance and finally mourning, and full mourning that enables people to move on. This full mourning can manifest itself in physical ways, disease, everything cyclical. Lisa?

The problem is that the fourth stage (we have to have stages because people want to order their lives, have stages to recognize, a safety) isn't acknowledged by people in their own life, people don't see that they possess the power to rejuvenate their own existence by peeling away the layers of pain. What happens is that people bestow their grief upon their offspring, their grief and all that they have denied themselves in their lifetimes. First they think that in the act of giving life they are starting over, giving their own self a chance. They think this is enough, giving life and the possibility of this new life making things better somehow. But they bestow their own grief in their children and the cycle continues. The pain doesn't go away, this new life carrying in its genes' histories, eons of denial or hurt or sadness, or anger, this new life handicapped from birth unless it can free itself, free like the parents. People have children for all the wrong reasons. Deep inside of everyone, God is saying, I can't breathe, let me out.

It's like a grain of sand. In a grain of sand the whole history of the place from which it was taken can be read. A grain of sand is like a map. A newborn baby is like a grain of sand and it brings with it in its genetic coding all the grief that was denied by its parents, all the feeling as well. Everything returns.

What will happen in the world when people stop denying their feelings, let God out and stop just bringing more people into an already overcrowded world, a world that is suffocating in its own fear? People are mourning their own death as if that were a way to live, so afraid they might lose their self, that they don't know how to love. I don't know what to do anymore. It's too hot everywhere. Pen to paper night and day. I can't sleep. I want to help people get better. People think I am crazy, won't listen.

Lisa said, "Get off of me."

.   .   .

MRS. Lorian says, just leave me alone you little know-it-all. Get your lousy camera out of here. You want to like Mrs.

Lorian because she is dying, but you don't. Mrs. Lorian is mean and nasty. Her husband died when she was very young. She raised her son and has lived in this house for her whole life, gripping Mr. Lorian, bending him. You think of pushing Mrs. Lorian down the stairs, of calling Doctor Donovan when she pinches your arms when you are trying to help her dress. Then you think of Mark. You think of your mother. Mark's journals. You could have written these words. Everyone thinks about the same things, Mark said, everyone. It's just that there are bodies that get in the way, male and female. You read this page.

Then of course there were the pictures of Lisa and myself. The pictures we took setting the camera's timer. The proof sheets we had showing our embrace over and over, variations of our physical love.

Two people touching, wrapping bodies as if we could merge, trying to melt into one.

Lisa said, It's your mother. I can't be like her. I won't take care of you like that. Don't you see that she has crippled you?

My mother, I think. My first and only term at college, the longest period of time that I was ever away from home, my mother sent me a grafting kit. It was a set of special tools, delicate equipment with which I could graft different species of plants together. I never used the tools.

I think of those grafting tools and I think of the space between people, how obviously separate the two people in the proof sheet are: arms touching arms, legs around shoulders, the physical boundaries of the flesh.

My mother said try the grafting set. You can come up with so many interesting species, she said. For some reason I could never bring myself to use the tools. I probably just didn't want to admit that I was interested in what my mother was interested in.

My mother who is never home now. My mother reading or writing critical papers about critical issues.

Lisa's face that of a little girl, no, not my mother's face that is worn and distant.

The seriousness in Lisa's voice a passion to understand. You think too much, I said to her. You think too much she said to me.

Sometimes it is right.

Tell me a story. Tell me about something that you think had an impression on you, Lisa said. Did you ever hear your parents having sex?

Under the bed maybe five, probably younger. The room was dark and I was afraid and I went there to sleep between Mom and Dad like I did when I was afraid. It's too dark and there is something going on in the bed. I crawl under the bed, stay there till it stops until it is quiet and then I sneak back into my room and wait for the sky to get light outside. How I remember this, in the third person, remembering a little boy remembering.

When I tell Lisa this story she cries, asks why, and then she asks me to explain about mothers again. Her eyes are like potato peelers sometimes.

It just doesn't seem fair, it's the nurturance that is missing. I think that is it, Lisa said.

I think about all the times I rub Lisa's back or head, how she can fall into such a deep sleep when I do this.

You get a facsimile Mark. Come on you can be engulfed. It is you inside of me. I don't get to go inside, she said. What about my mother? she said. How do I find her, how?

Lisa said that maybe she is swallowing me up then just like a mother might. Isn't this murder? she said.

It is violent on both ends I guess. Lisa is trying to simplify. We both are.

I think of how sometimes I leave my body when we make love, a swimming, rushing, surging and not a calm. And then I think about my mother and if we really are trying to get back then why is it with this violence, this frenzy?

To get back to the womb, they say is what we are all trying to do, supposing that there was comfort there, never realistic, never thinking, because it must have been loud in there, loud and violent. We were trapped in there, trapped and helpless and unknowing and just there.

Perhaps we do keep trying to get back there to where it was dark and falling and noise, this vertigo, this violence.

When Lisa and I make love I want to be doing this always.

It must have been so loud in there, the churning and roaring of our mothers' insides. We fear this and yet we must be trying to get back there and we don't even realize this, that maybe human beings are so violent because their origins were so violent. Does it have to be this way? Who really breaks away? Lisa said everyone hates women really. Lisa said she doesn't want to be a death machine. Contributing to a violent world. These ovaries, she said, containing eggs of violent possibilities.

We moan and press together, our souls screaming or numb, press and press. Let me in we say each to the other without words.

Mothers.

You wondered about your mother, you wondered if when you were conceived was there that second per second delirium that makes people forget?

You knew Mark long before you moved here from California. You have been in love with Mark long before you knew that there was a name for the total inversion of matter into itself. A Black Hole, Mark wrote in one of his journals, is the culmination of people's faith in the big lie, the lie that there is beyond a doubt a mathematical equation that will prove that life is purely a wire mesh screen through which we are all slowly pushed.

Mark has been talking to you for a long time, whispering into your sleep for as long as you can remember. Whispers piercing through the gray clouds of winter; gray clouds that unwind across the sky and descend unnoticed like a suffocating fabric. Covers. Safety. Each time Mark has called you, your senses unravel. As soon as you try to answer him your voice constricts around your body. You are caught at the end of a safety rope only able to see the tautness of the lines above your head.

Are you just supposed to forget what Mark said? Pretend things don't happen? Do you keep it to yourself that Mark knows the secret that explains why sleepwalkers are not afraid?

All this you absorb because it is so much easier to be obsessed with other people's lives, then you don't have to take responsibility for you own. What is yours?

Please to make the pain stop, you say.

How many houses will you have to live in before you can find your own?

How do you really know what is true, what really happened? It is so easy to believe what someone tells you because others' words fill up the gaps and spaces inside.

Mark wrote: A sleepwalker is not afraid because it is without a memory.

You have to remember.

Mark is dead. His words.
A sleepwalker is numb, blind to the feelings of others.

You don't know how to listen. You only hear what you want, what you can to survive. This must stop. How to change?

A sleepwalker is a zombie.

Are you living now in your dream house while wide awake, sleeping and waking the same? All around you people are turning to stone, numb to what is really alive. Are you awake? Are you awake? It's because you yourself are turning to stone and you can't seem to do anything to make it stop.

You sit in this room, all by yourself absorbing Mark's words because you are looking for someone to make sense out of your life, someone to help you understand. It is as you were brought to this place, this house, to read Mark's journals. You have always known Mark. It just takes time to find things.

When I think of sleepwalking sometimes I think that perhaps that is what is happening in people's fear of dying and in their fear of growing. Everyone is afraid to acknowledge the connectedness that exists within all people, that in myself there is a handicapped person, that within myself there is a murderer. This is what is happening, people are becoming walking zombies so that they don't have to be afraid, so that they don't have to feel.

And if it's chemical, these emotions, how a body can bolt upright when it is clinically dead, and if it's chemical, then what are we doing, why care? We must care because the surge of life is blocked up, jarred, ready to self-destruct.

We must then welcome the enemy? To open up to the possibilities within ourselves we must understand these things. How? How can we welcome the enemy when self-survival seems so instinctual? When someone makes me uncomfortable or afraid, I leave, get away, instead of connecting with that part of them that is of myself.

How do we become another, let our energies meet with someone else when we keep distancing ourselves from other people in the self-preserving way of my will over yours? The will is so strong. We have to unlearn how we are thinking because there is something wrong with the way we think, how instead of accepting the differences in others that really do exist within ourselves we try to conveniently fit the other into a very narrow personal framework. We do this with the tools we have, what we are taught is normal. First we deny the differences between ourself and someone else, then we squint our eyes and assign a role to that person, a role from our department of comfortable others. Oh yes, we say, you remind me of my mother, or my father, then we squint our eyes and fit the person into those guises we have picked for them, or if the other doesn't fit we get rid of them, put them somewhere like they were garbage. We may just as well be blind. And I don't mean the blindness where the other senses are working harder, I mean the blindness of all the senses, the senses closing down on themselves, fraction by fraction. Then no one is afraid because everything is in order, just as it should be and we are all sleepwalking. This goes on nice and neat until someone screams no, someone kills the other that doesn't fit, kills the other that hurts them inside, or kills the other to put that other out of their misery.

. . .

YOU knew that there wasn't really a headless horseman but the idea scared you.

You were sure that sometime at night when everyone was sleeping the headless horseman would come. You didn't tell anyone that you thought this. You could picture it so clearly, a man without a head riding on a horse that was frothing at the mouth, a horse with fire-red eyes. You would check under your bed before you could sleep at night, check twice, once with the lights on, and then again with the lights off after your eyes had become used to the dark.

You can see under the bed that there is nothing, nothing but what you put there yourself, the rock collection in the shoe box with the rocks from Pompeii that Grandpa Green gave you, maybe shoes, but mostly under your bed is the green dust from your bedspread and balls of Homer's hair.

Now you dream of a horse but it is a horse's head that you cling to as you fly through cities looking for something, looking for your sister June.

Flying

YOU *are lying on your stomach. There is a buzzing in your ears. You feel your body getting heavier, tingling with weight, as if your flesh were hardening concrete, grounding itself into the bed, a flesh that can take on a form and you are not needed anymore. This stone feeling heavy and porous as if there were water trickling across the backs of your arms, your legs, the top of your head.*

It's like falling, falling backward, and you let it happen, aware that it is happening. This time I will this to occur, you say, pushing out of your body. The only resistance is the thought itself, this is the inability to let go, your preconceptions of what it will be like, of what your body might look like lying on the bed.

You are slowly lurching away and back from the weight of your body. You move out of your body as if you were at the bottom of a deep pool and pushing off the bottom to get to where there is air and sun and clarity. You shoot through this murky suspension. There is a momentary weightlessness, a buoyancy of energy still contained.

Open your eyes, see yourself now. There is a vague shape at first, your body, motionless, muted colors as if the room were filled with smoke. Where you are is somewhere near the ceiling, and on the bed is your body. The corners of the room are lit from the streetlights that throw their brightness down along the edges like melting candles.

You are floating. What if you can't go home again? I may die and never go back again, and as you think this, as fear encases you, back into the body on the bed you are thrust, the body on the bed with the half-open mouth, hands curled tightly.

You bolt upright. There is no sweat on your forehead, no palpitations in your chest.

You account for the setting: Mark's books in the bookcase, desk, photographs, the streetlight streaming into the room, light collecting in the corners like missed dust.

You want to float again, move through the ceiling, see the whole town in which you live.

You lie down again, the heaviness of your body increasing as soon as you close your eyes.

It is different this time, weightless and gray is where you are. It is you dancing madly around your room, moving across the ceiling all directions at once, but not everywhere. There is your body and you don't want to lose sight of it because you are certain if you lose sight of where you are laying on the bed you will never be able to find your body again. You are dancing. What is dancing? There is no body moving. There is nothing containing, nothing to define what is happening.

Back in your body you are, it is this constraint of what you know that brings you back each time.

I will not question, you say to yourself, feeling the heaviness again. I will not be afraid.

It is a complete release this time and there your body is facing you as you hover above the bed. And then you are melting into this body, caressing the figure on the bed, the soft brown hair, the swollen rosy cheeks, the flesh everywhere as smooth as silk or lake water, floating and moving in at the same time an ecstasy of color and taste and flesh all at once. You are caressing your breasts, your pubic hair, the swollen wet folds between your legs. Then your mouth is everywhere, you want to devour this body, its beauty, be enveloped by this woman's body that is yours. When you climax you become aware that it is not you on the bed, the figure before you has transformed, is only recognizable as a young girl. It is young this body on the bed, it is you but it is undeveloped, not yet a woman. Then the figure transforms, becomes luminous, light, arms open wide, a featureless warmth as are you. There is no definition. You are lost.

This is where you wake up.

Alone.

What you think about upon opening your eyes is sleepwalking. What if you leave your body, think that you are leaving your body, walk outside, move through the walls? Once outside you meet other people, other people that talk to you as if you were contained in your body. You were certainly behaving peculiarly the other day, they might say to you. And where do you take this then, how do you define your experience that is real and at the same time marked by your own doubt?

You might never wake up again.

Or what if you were to meet other people this way, other people that had left their bodies on beds somewhere, shapeless energies meeting in the night, or even in the light of day? Who's to know? Who might these others be?

What of evil and being abducted by stronger energy away from the security of your body?

There was a time, a half-sleep dream in your old apartment of answering your door. Let me in, the man with blond hair and laughing, kind blue eyes says. It is cold out here, please let me in. And you fall into his arms, this man who has come to love you. It is momentary the comfort. You can feel the hardness between you and him, his penis, a powerful weapon all of a sudden thrusting you back into the wall. No, you say. No. You tear yourself free and are running back to where the people you rent your room from live. You brush past all the coats in that closet that separates your room from their house, everything is there, the picnic-table umbrella, the broom and metal rake, the boxes, the washer and dryer. You are pounding on their bedroom door, screaming, help me.

Everything is silent. There is no sound of you screaming or pounding on the door. You have no hands, no body. Help me. Where is my body?

You left your body. You didn't lose sight of it on the bed, you were enveloped once and for all into the skin that is yours.

You bolt out of sleep. It is dark. You are sweat-drenched and panting.

Mark. Mark and you were making love.

Mrs. Lorian is hyperventilating in your doorway. She is screaming, Where am I? Why am I here? she screams. The clock says 11:55. Where am I? Mrs. Lorian is screaming. You do not know how she climbed the stairs. In her yellow nightgown her skinny figure is silhouetted by the full moon blaring blue through the window behind her.

Mrs. Lorian lets you hug her. You walk her to her bedroom. She is crying.

Before, love was something that happened like everything else, something that happens to everyone like birthday parties or learning to tie your own shoes. Before, love was Rob, saying don't ever leave me, or your mother tucking you into bed at night, or your father crying after June beat him up, crying and saying he was sorry but he was going to continue to believe what June said, or your father bathing June in the bathtub, or your grandma in Connecticut brushing your hair with an old silver-backed brush with her initials curlicued on it, one hundred strokes she brushed your hair while you sat in front of her vanity, watching in the mirrors where you could see yourself three different ways. Before love was what you were told would happen and it didn't need a name. Now you don't know anymore what love is, what it might be.

In Mrs. Lorian's face, as you tuck her into bed there is something in her eyes that you have never seen before, the way she is looking at you. You are looking into each other's eyes and there is an instant where you forget that you are standing over her, you feel dizzy, you swallow hard. What is it? You see in Mrs. Lorian's face that there are eyes, eyes that are moist, eyes that can look away but don't, eyes that soften, eyes that are clouding with age. As you look at each other what is Mrs. Lorian seeing in your eyes, because you don't see anything that can be described when you are really looking into each other's eyes, it's a feeling. You see in her face that the skin that surrounds her mouth, eyes, and nose is folding away from the bone like how an insect walks out of a shell that is the exact shape of itself, a three-dimensional shadow. These things you see and you don't understand what love might be for, real love.

In school a teacher told the class, don't write about old people because it's cliché. And what is a cliché but a truth that no one knows what to do with, truths that conflict with and at the same time support the fantasy everyone is trying to uphold, that everything is fine just the way it is, and that we all won't die. Isn't this what is really being said?

There is no such thing as ghosts, you say back in Mark's room. You say this into the shadows, shadows that look like smoke or people sitting in chairs watching you.

You are afraid of the dark. You have always been afraid of the dark. Who taught you this? Whose brilliant idea has tricked you into a silence, an inability to explore the possibility of volume that exists within your own vocal chords?

We are dying, Mark wrote. I think of being paralyzed and I think of being dead. I think about fear and being afraid, and this too is being dead. Dying is an idea and like other ideas, is subject to change.

How you and Mark might have loved? Upside down and face to face, your knees holding on for dear life to a metal bar. This is it then? God, how you love him: a slow burning sensation that eventually bruises or blisters.

Mark said, people don't listen to each other.

Mr. Lorian unzips the door to the hothouse. Tonight his prized plant is open. It will be open for the duration of the night. The blossom is pale pink. It is almost white at the edges. There are small white things inside the flower like clumps of talc, like the comet seen through the telescope. The blossom's center is a brilliant red like the back of someone's throat. Your breathing is labored in the humidity. Mark's words fill your ears with the anxious panting of summer.

Summer. Mom calls. It doesn't make any difference. You already know. Mom's voice: Your sister . . . murder . . . prison . . . You hang up. Your sister just killed two people in Clear Lake, in Northern California. In Equinox in the early summer, every summer the hills start to turn purple. The color of the hills is important.

History

I T'S all there in that one photograph. Even now, such a long time after everything has already happened, looking carefully at the Polaroid June had taken on the occasion of her final tragedy it can all be pieced together, the murders, and the endless reasonings, and the stifled yearnings of kamikaze daughters. It's all there as clear as day from night. If only June had shown someone the photograph, things might have turned out different somehow. There is no mystery really, there are no trick endings, people just don't see things clearly, you don't see things clearly, miss the signs that are given, take things the wrong way, and mostly you are and always have been afraid of what you really know.

It's like being able to visualize your own murder, holding that snapshot.

The photograph itself is not spectacular, it's almost stupid. The inscription, pressing heavy into the white border, identifies in June's masculine backhand the subject as Tad Dowd; that's it, no date, no place. It could be anywhere in the world, this picture of a boy from mid-waist to mid-eye seated in a red vinyl booth in a diner. To the left of the frame a virile pair of legs, black leather biking pants, a heavy-handled buckskin knife strapped seductively to purposeful hips, greasing down to combat boots, struts toward the dark outside. His iron-knuckled hand briefly balanced on the wooden doorknob of the half-open screen door. And Tad completely unaware of what is going on behind him; those legs leaving forever just like that.

The expression on the part of Tad's face that is not cropped away by June's amateurish gaze is common enough. Oh, come on, not here, he must have said, curling one corner of his lip and displaying a thick tongue.

It is a marvel how June got exactly half of his eyes into the frame; half of his pupils, only his bottom lashes, half of each green iris, no eyebrows, no upper lids.

But the most interesting part of the photograph has to be the hands. They were moving when the picture was taken and the pinky fingers blur an arc around the tightly clasped knuckles. They are beautiful hands, large and well proportioned. Where the knuckles of the right hand clutch the left, the skin, white as wax paper and taut as a drum, vibrates slightly. Examining the picture long enough you can almost feel the sweat squishing around inside those tightly wound hands.

This snapshot among the things your mother had sent you in a big manila envelope, this snapshot, Xerox copies of all the newspaper clippings, headlines about freak incident, stories of a grieving town, trial updates, as if you hadn't already found out about what June did there at Clear Lake, as if you didn't know.

These records people keep, the only ones people pay attention to, these proofs of existence, the newspaper clippings, the film footage, all that is flat and fantastic but dead, has already happened, and happens again. What is beneath all this really? You must account for all this somehow. This and not someone or something else.

You cross your legs tightly, the dampness of the velveteen sofa itches into your numb thighs. Outside the passing of colors, light to dark and pink once again, languid vinyl blue sky and no clouds. I am leaving, you said into the mirror in Mark's room. Oh please don't, no one says. What if, is.

You. You tried to get inside June, you really did, staring empty into her face, her face in photographs. How could you? Her rosy-cheeked figure is smaller than your thumb. Manageable? There the two of you are, pointedly hopeful eyes and your smiles looking out of that tattered picture.

It was Easter and you are both wearing twin red-and-white patent-leather shoes from Gemco, your little-girl arms poking through the slits in the Kelly green capes Mom sewed, the same, so that you wouldn't fight when Grandma and Grandpa came to visit. There the two of you are with Grandma in between. Behind you, the house in Old Saybrook, the house with the big screened-in porch. There is someone's shadow in the window. Mom? Dad? Grandma is wearing a royal blue suit and she looks as pretty as a magazine model.

Talk to me June, you say. June are you really going to be there? It's been so long since you have seen her. People make things up.

It's 6:30 A.M. and downstairs Mrs. Lorian's wheelchair is moving restlessly back and forth. The toilet flushes. Pipes that take it all away. No one listening to the fact that there is no place for all the refuse, that soon everyone will be engulfed in their own shit.

You go home now, Grandma said on the phone. You go home and then you can come stay with me for a while. You go see your sister and then you get on with your life, Grandma said.

June says, you must come see me. It had been almost a year since she did it.

In a dream your mother tells you that the crossover does occur. In the dream you are watching your mother hold an infant that is you. You are an adult and you are standing next to your mother who is seated holding a baby in her lap that is you. I don't understand, Mother, you say. How does anyone ever know where they really are? The crossover does occur, your mother says, or maybe you said this to your mother.

The shifting rays of sunlight strap mockingly about your sweating body. You wash your face.

It happened in Northern California during what the locals described as an unusually cold spell for mid-August. June had just shown up in Clear Lake in late May looking for work. Then she met Tad.

June got a job working at a game booth at the carnival. She was a change girl for a game called Splash (there was no one to notice that June didn't ever do jobs like everyone else, wouldn't do this, pay attention, the clues). For a dime they give you a white Ping-Pong ball and the object of the game is to throw the ball into one of many miniature goldfish bowls. (Couldn't anyone see the look in June's eyes?)

Tad, described as a loner, fell in love with June. As the story goes, after she had taken a long-handled ax to Tad while they were out camping, she had, upon returning to town, randomly picked a name out of the telephone directory and proceeded to Auburn Street where she had stabbed a seventy-year-old woman and hacked off all the lady's fingers.

I stabbed and stabbed, appeared in one lead paragraph from the *Clear Lake Sentry*. I stabbed her in the neck because if she lived she would report me. The lady was freaking me out, telling me to stop, that she was dying. I told her that she was lucky. When the blood came out of her mouth all of a sudden then I knew she was dead. June saying these things, sensational things like make-believe TV, because that is what people want to hear, not that there is a war inside that won't stop, that there is a mirror moving in and out of infinity.

Underneath, on the back of your eyelids, June, what were you seeing?

All of a sudden? Twenty-eight stabs and the fingers of both of the woman's hands cut off?

People get sick from denying, Miya said.

That trip, a drive across the United States, alone in a car moving from point to point.

Your sister was in jail, she had not yet been put away for good.

All the trips you have made in your lifetime. Why is it that you never can remember the time spent traveling from one place to another?

Each day a remarkable feat of endurance to get out of bed. Each day a conquering of uncharted territory to step out the door. Your horizons are as fantastic as anyone's.

The uncharted territories are inside only.

There was a time when you wished to be the discoverer of alien life forms in other galaxies. There was a time when you daydreamed of walking to the park in broad daylight, unnoticed because you had become invisible. Meet me at the park you told your friend. A plan carefully orchestrated; two invisible girls to meet at a specific place by sheer power of mental force.

Magic.

There was a time when you and June waited on a hill in Sleepy Hollow, just the two of you and the twinkling night sky. Something spectacular, something phenomenal will happen if you just wait.

The sound of the night, there on the hill, mosquitoes buzzing around your heads, crickets, the tall brown grass itching itself in the soft wind.

It would just happen, it could any second, a flash of light, a whirring sound and there would be someone new to meet for the first time, someone new to explain this life to. This is what you and June planned.

Nothing happened but what was going on in your heads. You waited and waited.

The gauges of the car are luminous, everything is operating correctly. The steering wheel is cool where your hands have not been holding.

There on the side of the road, a sneaker or a crumpled paper bag.

You will sit in this seat. You will drive this car until you can't feel your legs.

You must come see me before it is too late, June wrote.

You have to get there.

Why might this trip between two points matter?

As if there should be a point to reach, an end in sight. You have to be inside now.

The earth has been strapped, contained?

It is possible to rocket to other planets.

But what about all that is going on here?

Be here, now, I am listening. I am.

Everything as far as the eye can see, to be subdued, conquered.

There is a hazy voice inside that says, no.

I can't work here anymore Mr. Lorian. My family needs me at home. The postcard in your pocket, the picture cracked where the plastic has been bent so many times. There are poppies on the postcard. Orange poppies in a green field.

Dear Tracy,
    You are still my sister. You can't make things go away. The only difference is that I am in prison for real. I think it is time for you to come see me, there are things I would like to show you. Wake up Tracy. You mustn't be afraid. There isn't much time.
                                             June

Why tell anyone what had happened?
Where do you think you are going? Mrs. Lorian says. She is seated in her wheelchair. There isn't much to pack.
You want to take Mark's journals. Who would notice? Someone would. Someone would.
You think you are so smart Tracy, Mrs. Lorian says, that you can just rush off as you please.
Listen young lady when I was your age I had a bit more responsibility toward the people around me.
The spokes of the wheelchair beneath the shiny brown doorknob move slowly back and forth. Mrs. Lorian's thumbs are circling each other in her lap.
You might take the pages in Mark's journals, the ones that plea what you said, wanted to say so many times. You might take these pages, show them to people before it is too late. You might just take these, tear them neatly from the bound journals into which Mark wrote and wrote.
What will become of all these letters, the time Mark spent carefully articulating his thoughts, sharing all that he understood to be the crucial reasons as to why he had to escape finally?
You think I am just old and that I don't know what is

happening here, don't you. You think that I am not aware that I am dying. Do you think I feel any different inside than I did when I was your age? Where is it that you are going to in such a hurry? Mrs. Lorian says.

I understand if you can't come back, Mr. Lorian says. I hope that you do. I just don't know how I will be able to take care of my mother. It has taken her so long to get used to you. Mr. Lorian talking in the defeated voice which is the tone in which he always speaks. Mr. Lorian not asking you why you have to leave now.

This ceasing to question that comes from too much pain. This mechanism of surviving.

Where were you the day June did it?

Were you locked up tight in Mark's room?

When June walked into the widow Lloyd's house, where were you? Were you out photographing all the people you couldn't be, all the people you didn't know how to listen to?

You can get up now. It's all over, the dentist says. The contents of the room slowly coming into focus, aluminum table attached to the side of the chair you had been reclining in, the window, the silver tools, the white walls.

I want to go home. You had heard yourself crying, feeling yourself to be a gray spot in the corner of the ceiling. I won't make it back to my body. You know this. You can hear yourself crying, I want to go home.

If you want to go home then you had better hold still, the dentist says.

What was really happening, teeth being extracted. Never anything all at once, but one tooth one visit, one tooth the next, holding on to your pain, prolonging the agony. This sickness of the soul that feeds on bodily pain?

Streetlights string past. Is this enough setting to skirt you from place to place?

★   ★   ★

You took the pages, carefully cut the ones you wanted from Mark's journals.

Is there anything I can get for you? Mr. Lorian asked.

What of all the things you might have given Mark? There is no point in asking anyone this. People are just too busy.

Is there something you need for the trip? Mr. Lorian continues, wiping dust from the top of a Plexiglas frame. Indian arrowheads in Plexiglas.

Mrs. Lorian's wheelchair moving back and forth upstairs.

This house is dirty, dirtier than anyone could manage in one lifetime. You stopped trying to clean it. Mr. Lorian didn't seem to notice.

Mark said he understands why someone might just kill:

. . . an outburst, a resolution to the anguished tearing of the insides. When a situation reaches a crux of indecision, this act might provide a resolution. They see what is inside themselves subjectified in a situation. What it is that has troubled or terrified them all along. What is outside can be subdued, stopped, this darkness from within that has no real name, but what it can be likened to and finally stopped altogether. This act, to kill another that lines the interior world, finds a place in what can be seen. Like a period, the act completes what is impossible to line in one's head. How one attempts to conform their internal makeup to an external landscape that becomes so alien to a person that for whatever reason can't adapt.

There are some people that just can't help but be constantly aware of the discrepancy between how they feel and what they are supposed to be doing.

To this you might add that it is somewhere between the greatness of the pioneers that dared to explore new territories and the despised anonymous persons (of which the world is mostly made) that the act of murder can be located.

All the murderous lies to finally make someone angry enough to try and stop it. The lies that one man alone discovered anything.

The people that manned the ships, the women that labored in the factories putting together the bombs that would ensure another victory, the coolies that packed the mountain-climbers' gear, these anonymous people. Among them there will always be someone to pinpoint inequities.

Long silences, the truth will out, finally exploding in a fury of revenge.

These pioneers?

Pioneers to silence the people that allow the same things to happen over and over again.

The last word?

Silence and conquer. The mentality of wars is the mentality of personal relationships. Everyone thinking they are right. It's a messy business. There are so many different kinds of freedom to consider.

Does killing someone bridge the gap between people? Does killing someone knock away the chasm increasing between lives?

Whole towns, cities, cultures, continents of people never admitting that people are connected as is the earth beneath their feet.

A murderer is attempting to silence his own anguish by shutting someone's hypocritical stare, Mark wrote.

Are these June's words?

What kind of a murderer are you?

Your life, an anxiousness between destinations, looking always for someone to order your tangled insides.

It's dark. Two little girls are curled up in the backseat of the van, anxious hands whispering across young bodies, skin on skin, under cover from your father's rear view. Just like in the drive-in pictures, soft airbrushed legs entwined in Technicolor skin wraps, your mother's gum pop-cracking nervously, her face blinking off and on in the front seat as the van moves cautiously through the dozing suburbs. You be

Ginger and I'll be the Professor, you whisper. Two little girls vigorously recreate others' misplaced yearnings behind their parents.

What people want is to embrace what is in the mirror. Who said that?

. . .

DRIVING across the plains through acres and acres of cornfields, you are humming old Broadway songs from *Anything Goes* and *Cabaret* to keep awake. Sometimes June wanted to be an actress. She was always acting she said, that's what people do.

Was there a time when murder was fashionable, something to imitate, something everyone was doing? Was there a time when people didn't have to make things up or pretend there wasn't a difference between what went on in their heads and what they actually did?

You are moving inward now, internalizing, living inside. What is it that you are storing this up for?

June got hooked on drugs. June would be in Bellevue. June would be inside a boxcar winding across the United States, alone, on train tracks, parallel lines that go on and on never touching.

Please let me in. I am thirsty. You gotta let me in lady. June must have said this to get into the widow's house. People do try to help sometimes. There was a girl at your door. You let her in. You were afraid. You didn't want to help her didn't know how. There was nothing to be afraid of.

You gotta let me in, June said.

You gotta let me in, Anna said to you.

I have been here before, you heard yourself saying. This drive. This drive to see June, a drive with a purpose that becomes the aimless drive of some dreams, cars careening through space, no one at the wheel, or cars moving slow down snow-and-ice-covered hills.

How many times will you have to take this drive?

You will drive to see June whether you like it or not, because you can't stop moving from one point to the next even if you wanted to, it was a story that was telling itself, and just kept happening.

June solicited herself. She said most women do that anyway, men too, and that she would just get paid for it and paid good. The soft smell of cool moist flesh rising from the lush plants, the car windows open wide, steel-gray sky transposing the small yellow kernels into the murderous poetry you must recite to keep awake, to keep awake for June.

Humid air, melting air, hateful air, no one's air, bug-filled air, air like heroin, poisonous air, enemy air, spider air, sister air, air to tell lies in, air to be deceived in, crying air, yearning air, moist air, your left temple crushing verbs into stares, the car driving almost independent and crazy like June's shadow disappearing into the fields of corn.

People invite you in, the fantasy says come in, but not really, women say pretty please all airbrushed and dreamy, lying.

You are not yelling this time. You will pretend to be mute then. It's worth $1.50, how you pick at your cuticles, a small jar of lotion to relieve dry skin, all right then, honesty.

A thirty-second film in black-and-white of your fists driving into the creamy faces of all the girls you are not, action-packed silence. The prize: an audience to despise your anger as much as you do. Listen. Is it true that your face has fixed itself into a permanent expression of how you really feel: angry, afraid, numb?

Your film cannot be thirty seconds, ten seconds, a hundredth of a second is sufficient, a subversive advertisement suggesting what the anesthetized unconscious won't catch anyway, a fist hammering into a half-open mouth, a fist hammering at her dazed gaze of invitation, a fist hammering away at the language that appropriates situations, a language that offers pleasant tones to the forgetful.

The applause starts long before this girl with the half-open mouth appears. The tone of her voice is a perfume as she says come in.

Two feet away from her, you can hear each other's breath. You might have whimpered into each other's arms. No one listens. You are mute. Instead of letting yourself fall you take from your bag the plastic measure with which you can see the amount of blood drawn.

This won't work. It all has to be visible in one still.

. . .

June says, watch me when I am asleep. June says, tell me what I look like when I am asleep.

. . .

AND this year on June's birthday the groundhog didn't find its shadow and the winter was so long. Now it is summer and it won't go away, nothing goes away really. You hate summer. You can hate if you want.

You are camping in the woods in Canada. For a test you and June steal away into the woods, up the hill behind the campsite, far enough so that no one can find you and you can't hear anyone even if they were calling. You and June find a secluded picnic bench. You have brought a can opener and a large can of hearty beef stew. Why are you doing this? Because it is a test, a game, something that you and June think to do when you can't think of anything else to do. You open the can and just leave it there, on the bench where no one will find it, maybe ever, you and June think. You are wondering what kind of creature, wild animal or Bigfoot or a child of the woods, will find that can there.

That can screams now, you can hear it. Listen June. Take a deep inhaling breath. What is rotting? That protein an aching terror. June standing on a street corner somewhere in New York, June standing on a street before she went to Clear Lake. June a prize for the economy of spliced automatons, searing help me's, genitals trying to graft innocence. I am a trickster, June wrote. There is a war inside us, June wrote.

In the motel last night you dreamt of June like when you were little. June had clung spiderlike to your back and you had carried her that way forever. June whispering softly into your ear, her silky head resting on your shoulder. June telling you about all the great things you are both going to do in life and pointing out what direction to take, steering you gracefully through forests lit by opal stars. And then standing on a bridge, naked like that with June on your back, your trial had been to account for the number of goldfish planted in the paraffin ponds behind and in front of you. To make both sides equal, you had said over and over. After counting the number of goldfish you held hands and walked into what smelled like an apple orchard, only there were no trees anywhere, only rows and rows of encased mummies. Ancient mummies like the kind in the Egyptian section of the museum. Slowly all the fraying bandages had started to fall away from the decaying figures, revealing the faces of everyone you knew, your parents, cousins, friends from childhood, relatives you had only seen in fading photographs, and ancestors you knew to be yours. You started to run. The smell of rotting apples was singeing your nostrils. Two of the unraveling figures began to chase you and June. Their facial bandages had fallen away completely, exposing two bearded and decomposing images of yourselves. June stopped running and was overtaken. She had lain down on the concrete and shut her eyes. You couldn't stop her from falling to sleep. You were only able to run in concentric circles around her dissolving skull, screaming about the repetition of the veins in everyone's heads and reeling off historic names and all the nightmarish associations they presented. No one was paying any attention and June was dead.

Waking up to the sound of keys fumbling sluggishly in the door, you try to figure out who really had died in that dream. You remember something June wrote on the back of a matchbook cover that had been attached to the snapshot of Tad that your mother had sent you: Today I ran away it was lots of fun.

Where is there to run to, June?

In the murky dusk, sinister landscaped bushes and a few just-planted scraggly trees mark the monotony of Route 70. Somewhere in Kansas you are gritting your teeth against the coming night, wishing you could bite your cheek hard enough to draw blood. Face your fears, Grandma said. This is a game, June wrote.

There is so much that is missing, the parts you can't remember, and even if you could what difference would it make, what?

When a person is gone the space where they were closes up, there is no gap left, not a physical place that screams come back I need you.

Why did no one go and look for June before, why not? It's because of what June knows, what no one wants to hear again. Lock it up.

Locking up the truth, locking up what represents the thought, the one that has to materialize eventually because there are no secrets, none. What is thought has to release itself somehow, what is thought and what is done, over and over.

Dear Tracy,
    The lines on your palm are a map. You can find direction there just as well as reading any map at all. Look at the lines on your palm and you can figure out how to get to wherever it is that you are going.

                                                                June

The night, darkness, a shadow that extends away from the earth into a point. Everywhere else is light.

★   ★   ★

In Equinox you told people you had a sister who was crazy, just that. But secrets can't be kept. Someone always knows what is really going on. You were sitting in a room. There is a man, someone you want, someone you want to touch you, make you disappear. Love me, you are saying in your head, saying so hard that you are lost deep inside, your stomach churning, your skin ice-cold.

Nighttime. It is nighttime and the air coming in through this man's open window is cool. A train cuts through the darkness outside this man's room, a rumbling that comes close then retreats just like your ability to touch anything outside of all that is going on in your head.

There are three trains, no, four really. The first train is the train you can hear now. The second train is the train your father took home, returning across country to see his parents after all that happened. I might not be back, Dad said at the station, this to hurt after he built the new house. People die of broken hearts. What is any one supposed to do with all the things that happen to them? It is a miracle that some people can keep living at all.

When people are asleep they go somewhere else.

The third train is the train that June took, a train she took by herself, many trains that she took because she decided that that was what she was going to do.

How you create your own mythologies, these signposts you hold on to.

The fourth train is the train in your dreams, a train that has been in your dreams since you can remember. It is a train that you are riding on, or it is a train that you are waiting for, or it is a train that you are looking for. You aren't always sure if you will be able to see the train coming in time to get out of its way.

It's easiest to keep moving, to walk, to move through space fast and urgent.

In Equinox the trees outside scratch against the window. There is something happening here. You are sure that the energy that surges between you and this man is love, an overwhelming urge, not from inside but something that presses in on you from all sides. When you look into his eyes you feel like you are falling, not falling away from your body but falling, evaporating really as if there weren't bodies at all, just merging. You bite your tongue. Not to lose control. His eyes trace your profile. There are patterns, histories. This man looks like your father and at the same time he reminds you of your mother. The trees scratch the window glass. You are sitting in this room waiting to be touched. Something is about to happen and you are sure that it is supposed to be one of you, a hand, nervous fingers, reaching across the room that is eons of space, and a roar like putting your ear to a conch shell.

I keep a scrapbook, he says, breaking the silence, this man with hair the color of fire. This man you don't want to give a name to because names spoil things. You want this to be different. Just red and blue to purple. Simple.

I'm not morbid, he says. I just collect murder trial stuff, he is saying. June Hawkins, I have been following her trial, he is saying looking into your eyes. There isn't a tunnel. There is a wall then. A wall that you have to figure out what to do with. The same last name. Coincidence. What is this man thinking? Why is this happening? This man with a scrapbook filled with stories about your sister. You didn't tell anyone. You were trying to make it go away. This is supposed to be love. This is supposed to be love (echo like calling your name down a well). Do you know about this? he says, sitting down next to you on his bed. Your face. His face. Knowing without words. Knowing without knowing. Whose game is this? The life-size wooden puppets, the set burning red behind them, signs? Not touching when nothing is hidden anymore. Something else, this surging between two people. Hold me, you want to say but don't.

Here look, he is saying. And there she is, her brown eyes piercing out of a page in his scrapbook. I started keeping this stuff after my brother died, this Bax is saying. Yes, everything, everyone, with names eventually. He liked that kind of stuff, Bax is saying, turning the pages to more and more pictures of June. My brother said it is important to understand these people, then you'll know what to do if you ever come across them. My brother had three whole scrapbooks of Manson.

You are sitting on Bax's bed. His hand is so close to yours that you can see the patterns of the veins beneath his flesh. You are matching his veins to your own. Your hands are cold. Bax's hair is red. Tammy and Teddy had red hair. The room is walls and carpet and shelves, shelves heavy with antique toys and vintage paperbacks, the covers of these books showing voluptuous women, their eyes always looking sideways.

People collect things.

Bax collects things, a visual interpretation of all the baggage you carry around inside of yourself, all the lies and half-truths, all the fantasies, all that you can't let go of, try to control and at the same time be contained by. Bax's shelves are covered with these things, small statues, movie stills, antique objects of desire really. Is this how you have learned to live? Shelved and shelving.

What is a dream then? What you can't see, can't even hope to see here, like how a sunset just keeps going when the sun disappears over the horizon, keeps being a place that is fiery as the sky was before the dark.

It's the mechanics of distances you can't measure that you need to understand (what is inside), because you can be with people in so many different ways.

When someone you love is gone you are sad, grieve with your entire being.

You want to hold on to things, touch them with your hands, touch with your heart.

When you sleep you touch people and this is everything, these dreams in which you touch so many different people in so many ways.

All in red before, everything knocking, a shadow, and you imagine who it might be at your door. It's a picture, something important that makes it either impossible to stay awake or impossible to go to sleep, something else. You see this picture from all angles, even upside down and blindfolded. The picture is of two figures. The surface of the snapshot is shiny as a tongue. You are trying to figure out the relationship between the two figures. The picture wants to be understood, wants to be as simple as a postcard, a small colored picture of a place. This picture the one you see, want to be like a postcard, is in black and white, teasing and uncertain as someone else's ghosts. The picture is not a candid before picture, or an airbrushed after the fact. You do know one thing about the picture. It is of two figures holding hands, left hand to left hand, right hand to right. It's all knowing that to be facing each other this way their arms must be crossed. You just want to know where to position yourself in regard to this picture. Your picture and not the snapshot June took, the snapshot June took of Tad before she killed him. You aren't looking at this snapshot yet.

Sometimes you look at someone and see in their eyes your own anger, a hatred that fluctuates between wanting to hurt someone and wanting to hurt yourself.

You can see this in someone's eyes, in their face, in their paling skin, the eyes sharp and needling or blank and retreating deep inside.

When you see this look in someone else's face, you are frightened because you don't know what to do. You know you should help them but you can't, are afraid. Mostly you see your own murder in their face and then you just want to get as far away from that person as possible.

June is listening to Tad's snores coming from inside of the tent. June can see the veins bulging in her moonlit wrist. The lake is behind the tent. The moon is behind the lake casting a splitting ray of light across the water's dark surface.

June lifts the tent flap. She is balanced on the balls of her feet steady as someone moving through a forest undetected, a woodsman or an Indian. June's back bends as she enters the tent. The only sounds now are Tad's breathing and June's heart pounding in her chest and the brushing of June's hair against the nylon roof of the family-size tent.

Tad's eyes are open because this is how he sleeps.

Behind June's back her left hand holds the wood ax handle.

The moment before Tad heard the crushing heaviness, felt his skull split he saw the heavy wooden ax handle like a gangplank suspended above June's forehead.

It is wet and warm inside the tent then nothing.

How you give of yourself, is there any such thing really? How you give of yourself, or think you are giving of yourself, but you never really are. These acts of kindness you perform, always expecting something in return because you are always looking for something outside of yourself to right what is inside. What is real giving? How does a person ever really give anything when they are so afraid?

Might giving be finally admitting that you are the same as everyone else, that these things you keep, what you try to hold on to, what you know, these things you call yourself are really only layers of other people's voices, layers and layers of other people's wishes, what everyone has always hoped to be true. What you know inside to be true, that people leave, go away, but that everyone, what is inside of everyone, returns. What you keep and hold on tightest to are lies, the lies that keep you afraid, the lies that you fight to believe in, to believe that you are different, important, that somehow there is a you, a you that can be likened to something concrete, something true and dependable, as if a photograph of two people, any two people were alive and in the moment, not a photograph at all, but something stone maybe, unlike memory.

There are just no words for what you really are. What you know to be true between fitful dreams, how your body tosses and turns, and you think of passing from sleep to waking, think this while you are dreaming or while you are asleep. Somewhere in between, this is where you really are. It's the place where you really know yourself that is the brief space when you first wake up in the morning and for a minute you have to think of who you are, it's awareness but it's empty of self. And it's this waking into self, the self of other people's voices and fear that says this is frightening, it is scary to not know who you are and so you make things up, begin to remember what you have been told.

Then there is all that you know without knowing.

Nighttime, think of nighttime. Trains and night time. Your father first; hating his immobility, then hating all men because there has to be someone to blame. Men get off the hook so easy, your mother said. What don't I do? your father said. Perpetrators and victims. Nighttime and trains. What cuts through what? Dad, you said wanting to talk about something, wanting to get inside of him. Think about the night sky, you said. I went water-skiing for the first time Dad, you say. You don't talk about June. It is done already.

Did you ever try riding in the sun? Dad asks. It is a special secret thing, he says. Some guys kept trying to get me to do it up at Clear Lake. The lake has to be just right, the water just right, the time of day, it has to be late in the afternoon. The sun in the late afternoon makes a reflection on the water the same as the moon does. With your skis you ride on the trail. The water reflects the warmth of the sun. On the phone, always on the phone. A safety device? Crossing distances that perhaps shouldn't have been crossed. Things were different then, Grandma said in letters.

The shadow of night extending away from the earth like a pointed cap. Dad, we have missed each other. This melancholy after so much anger. What does it mean, touch? I am no longer a little girl, you say but not to anyone. It is safer to play a little girl, safer for everyone. There are prisons for people that don't belong. Love gets confused, parent to child, goes brittle sometimes, hardens into distance because there is always a right and wrong way to do things, moralities and structures that can smother or warp the possibilities of basic love, fear that smothers the possibilities of basic love, and the deep hatred that pain can cause because nothing can be so contained. Let me out.

Other summer nights. There are so many ways to see the same scene, always your body, what is inside, the real measure.

What you know? You yearn for a meeting that will go beyond this, a meeting of souls to defy boundaries, the ones that are and the ones that you have made up. Something to go beyond the many ways you can view a summer's night.

What you see near the train tracks, a church, the roof of the church, a wooden owl adorning the church roof beneath the steeple. How many ways can you see this same scene, moment to moment, with memory and emotion dictating your vision? The sky behind the church might be the same shade of gray, for an instant this gray is seen through the eyes of acceptance, a passion for what is. How many seconds is it before the sky behind the owl is too heavy, abruptly engulfs the church, the wooden owl, squashes it?

Trains don't pass here anymore.

In his room, in Bax's room, the train rumbled past, shaking the foundation of the house. Nighttime it is nighttime. Bax reminds you of your father. There is a pattern to all that is and you will make sure that it continues. You want to get inside of someone.

In the Exploratorium there was a double-sided mirror so you and June could sit in chairs on either side of the mirror. On the mirror you could see what both of your faces would look like combined into one.

This the desire to possess something you can't have.

Outside at night the bats skim the surface of the water. These bats fly in patterns, so many of them zipping back and forth, a few feet above the water, never running into each other.

You watch mesmerized. You forget that for a while there are things to do or that you are doing anything at all. Seeing.

You are amazed by the flight of these bats, creatures that can't even see flying in such intricate patterns, never crashing into each other.

At first you think you might die. You have known about what June did. You had been pretending. At first you wanted to leave, go away, anywhere at all, just not to have a sister that killed two people. You stopped reading Mark's journals.

Every day became the same, taking care of Mrs. Lorian, going through motions as if by moving fast enough you might
wake up and find that none of it had ever happened. It was,
it really was Bax, this coincidence and not the ones you had
been making up in your head. The coincidence that he knew
about your sister, this knowing without knowing. How
intricately connected this all is. It's just that you had been
reading the signs wrong. There really is such a thing as fate.
But you have to want to be alive first; not narrowing down the
choices.

*Dad, you say, Why is June talking to herself out in the yard? When
you talk to yourself it is because you are playing with dolls or telling
yourself to do this or that, or that you don't deserve to be in trouble.
June talks as if there were other people with her when really it is just
June alone in the yard with a dress on that's too big, black velvet on top
and a white skirt with big black polka dots on it. Where June is sitting
is in the tall grass in front of the chicken coop. The skirt of her dress
looks like it is coming out of the grass.*

It just seems like there is just no real order, no rhyme or
reason to the memories that come and go.

I am going away now Bax, you said. June is my sister. I need
to be alone now, you said.

Bax says, don't go away.

You just can't speak.

I love you, you say but not with words. This, to love
someone because they allow you to see who you really are, to
know where it is that you have to be going.

It's when you decided to really tell the truth, admit to the real
picture you saw of the two people, because when you admitted
that it was a picture that you saw and not the picture that
belonged to you in any way, then you knew you would go see
June.

Yes June is my sister, you said, not any Hawkins but this one,
the same as my own name, you said.

Hold me, you say in a dream. You and Mark, or you and Bax, or you and Miya, all that is dead this looking for your parents, this trying to right what is inside, the man and the woman inside of you that must be nurtured can't be contained, or defined at all.

The sound of your breath, the moans and cries and whimpers, is a child's urgency (no, never innocent).

I think that from between my legs I am going to lose my mind, you said.

The real picture you saw of the two people, the one you were trying to get inside of. The picture that you knew you couldn't fit into, wouldn't and still you tried. This picture that really referred to your interpretation of how you were to relate to this life at all, a picture of your own doom, an apocalyptic pairing of a man and woman, walking together into the trap they set because they were too tired to turn around. This picture you don't ever want to be in.

Listen you finally said to yourself, June is my sister.

You have been quiet for so long as if you had done it, as if you had killed two people.

You could hear your voice saying, can't you see the patterns in things, how fated this all is? And then you became your voice the real one inside that said, no.

It's safe to see signs—coincidence, believe in fate or believe you know what is about to happen to you or that in your dreams there are clues, because then you narrow the possibilities don't really have any possibilities at all. Mark said this. There are so many ways to see the same scene.

The horror, the sounds of your parents' passions(?). You just wanted to envelop them both, then disappear.

It's a trick you thought. Everyone lying.

Because what you really fear is nothingness.

Is this all there is, this coupling?

You want to belong.

You want to not be dead and dying.

In Equinox when you were leaving the hills were purple.

This is what was important to remember when you were leaving, purple hills.

As far back as you can go in your head, the first time you remember that is whole, with a place, people, a situation, is being at a hospital.

First, right before the hospital there is Mom's leg, her short skirt, beige jacket with leather buttons, and then her leg.

Into the car you go after Dad has covered up June on the backseat. Dad carried June because she was asleep and then you climb in next to June.

Mom gets in front pulling her leg in but it doesn't go in all the way before Dad shuts the door and Mom is screaming because the door shut on her leg.

Please Mom don't scream. It is too loud. You cover your ears. You don't want Mom to be screaming because June starts to scream too and Dad says, Oh God, Oh God.

You put your face into the back of the seat.

The car is driving fast through the night and there is blood up in the front seat on Mom where her leg was stuck in the door. It is bleeding. You don't want the blood to be filling up the whole car.

There are rows of beds. Bright lights. Blood after Mom as she walks on the floors that are slippery.

There is a stench, bitter as an abscessed tooth. It clicks, what that awful smell is. You pull over onto the shoulder of the highway. You remove from the backseat a brown lunch bag of molding something. You pull the cellophane off the food. The plastic wrap cringes in your palm. You check the map. The map that you have marked carefully to show yourself the quickest way to get to June. This map that can't really show you where June might be really. A jet plane crosses overhead.

In college the biology teacher had told your class about male primates. He had said that once when he was doing fieldwork, he had seen a male chimpanzee, in a fit of violent rage, seize an infant from the arms of its mother, swing it around by its feet and dash its fragile skull against a rock. The mother in her attempts to retrieve the chimp was herself severely beaten. The teacher had concluded that of course such cases were extremely rare, but that the potentiality of its occurring is the main reason why primate mothers keep their infants away from the males as much as possible.

Awake or asleep the drama of your family's sickness, of your helplessness, went over and over and over as if you were a rotary card catalogue and the cards just kept turning and being shuffled.

There are things that June could do, what you could do, what you learned in school. June could name the types of minerals, tell the difference between organic and inorganic matter, tell how old the earth is thought to be.

June writing these answers on paper, the blue of the ink that smells sweet and sour at the same time, or the gray marks of pencil, a dusty smear where you rub your fingers across the page.

It is about falling and falling, and trying to stand still.

June could multiply fractions and mixed numbers. June could punctuate sentences correctly.

June could also inflict pain on herself for no apparent reason.

Please stop it June, you said. What can I do? And then you would go into your room and close the door leaving June in the hallway banging her head against the patched plaster wall that is greasy and finger-marked from so much human pressure.

June what is in that box you keep under your bed?

It's none of your business.

In the box are bits of broken glass, aluminum-can pull tops, pieces of crumpled paper.

What is valuable anyway?

Can you please stop that June, please, and you hold your

hands over your ears, digging hard into your flesh with your fingernails, a focus against all this screaming.

June will eventually return to her room, sit on her bed, looking at her hands again and again as if her hands might have changed since last she looked.

A church billboard flashes by. More innocent children are killed each year because of abortion than all the fatalities of the World Wars. Everyone is always trying to pass off the blame. That billboard grates like barnacles.

What of all the babies that June didn't have, babies that could have been seen on a sonogram screen, facial features in miniature, dotty motion, then gone.

And the livingness that June took away from others, what of that?

So full to the bursting, a bud ready to open, uninhibited passions expressed with hands and eyes and words, words that don't spill from lips like a dam overflowing but words that are spoken as something done for the first time, or something done as if this chance may never come again. It's this joy that gets lost, must be relived. Is this what makes people so crazy then?

Your sister took the lives of two people. Was it supposed to be that way?

You are afraid of what you will find.

Start and stop, start and stop how you tried and tried to get inside of your sister. Start and stop, the clicking of anything that is alive.

You just want the truth.

The sun is slinking through the oily gray sky. Concentrate. Stay awake. Drive.

I don't care. I don't care. That faraway drone humming into your ears as you look at June for the first time in almost a decade. That rhythm always throbbing hypnotically through June's body, drawing everyone toward her. Everyone holding June too tightly against their own fears. This is a game, June wrote.

★   ★   ★

Fences, gates, bars, people in uniforms, long hallways, these things you must pass before you get to June. These are real metal bars that won't move, can't be sawed or filed away like in movies.

It's back and forth, back and forth, the grating of helplessness and possibility, a whirring sound.

The mechanisms that operate the doors to the hallways, the mechanisms that operate the bars in front of each cell; gears, silver, solid and persistent, a huge machine that needs no eyes.

What you know already and what you hope to know go back and forth.

The prison takes up lots of space.

So when you walked into the jail that October morning it was everything all over again.

June is in front of you. This is not a postcard. And are other people's fears not your own? This.

Listen to me June, you want to say.

What June needs is . . . a million voices with all the answers echoing through space. Guilt pours into your stomach.

Mark said, people don't listen.

June is just standing there behind the glass working her hands into her thighs and smirking away in the queer yellow light, like she has this big secret that no one is ever going to find out about, this in her face, because there are no secrets anymore.

You can't feel anything. Please feel something. Please not to be numb, to be sleepwalking.

But you can't feel anything. June is standing there in the fluorescent light looking at you. And you want to hurt her, slap that vacated face, scream at her mangled little head, your mangled little head (demolish these bodies that fall prey to these thoughts, these thoughts). The head, which one, whose? The head that has haunted, still haunts your dreams. Always will? The head that falls from your mother's paintbrushes, slow and slippery as IV fluid, possessing all your mother's "cityscapes." Your mother's paintings of gaunt and fixed people in poses as uncomfortable as their averted eyes, hands always in motion, contortionists milling and tangled in various poses of discomfort. Always waiting. Tension flicks off of these paintings, deep purples and sharp greens, the colors of an unbearably hot southern evening, or the calm before a catastrophe. Viewing these paintings for any length of time strains the neck muscles, the sinewy faces begging, tantalizing, offending, drowning at the bottom of an unsettled pool.

Research was done on the dreams people have right before they die.

It is said that the dead come to fetch the dying.

It is said that it is a dark passage from life to life.

There are two common themes in these dreams of the terminally ill. People that believe that death is a part of life and a point on a continuum of being dream of light, of wholeness. People that believe that after death there is nothingness, that there is no magic, no place to go, these people dream of a place where everything is gray, where crowds of disbelievers are shuffling aimlessly about with their heads down. Despite the two categories, the terminally ill dream vivid dreams of another place, they all dream.

You have been dreaming of your own death for a long time, because when someone is lost and when there is something that you can't seem to find you die over and over again.

The lights of the room she is in bounce sluggishly against the purple glow on your own skin. June bugs. June your sister, a muscle pried from craggy rocks just twitching there before you. You aren't playing make-believe. You are twitching. Look at June, how she really is here in front of you. This inability to sort at all, to figure out who you are and who June is. Was it you who killed two people, which two? Who is visiting who in prison?

Anything is possible.

Denial reverses the order of things.

June is grinding her hands into the pockets of her issued jeans. You don't even need to wonder at what she is thinking about, you know. June is staring at your purple face through the soundproof glass. She knew you'd come, wearing duty in your nearsighted eyes like the poorly needled tattoo on her left thigh: Tom 79, in india ink, tinged green and blue.

It's the scene with the butcher knife. That dulling blade crashing into the sink of dirty dishes, your face looming, monstrous and frothing as a rabid dog. That hatred, useless and consuming. How you see yourself then. When was there not seeing yourself?

It's a foil. It's that before, you really wanted to kill your parents, to kill the man and woman inside you, and June killed a man and a woman for real. These different prisons, the one you made for yourself and the one that June is really in for life. You have to make an equation because that is how you can live.

June came to you in dreams. June is in front of you now, separated only by the soundproof Plexiglas.

In the dream, June says, you lie, and she is trying to kill you because of how you touched her. Look at me, she says. She says, tits, see them. She says, pee-pee, vagina, cunt, suck it OK. Then June presses up against you and you know that she is going to kill you. It's you who are about to be killed, not your parents, not the two people that really are dead. It's a dream.

Are you awake yet?

Guilt is not the shiny edges around a portrait. This is the real picture.

You have been trying to kill yourself for the longest time.

People are afraid to listen, Mark wrote.

And you have to listen now, reading nothing on June's face except all the neon half-expressions in Mom's cityscapes, and it's insane, all these partitions and rules, seeing a body going through motions and not quite being in that body, and you can feel the blood on June's hands, know what June is saying without words. You can feel the blood, clotting menstrual tissues screaming from somewhere deep inside those pockets of hers. There is a hunger in June's face. No, there is a hunger in your face. See what is really there now.

Your eyes dodge, glances breaking badly like a pointless game of pool, each sister refusing to fall in any pocket, refusing to touch. June's eyes are giant marbles just balanced there on her face, lids as thin as rice paper, dark circles just smudged across cheekbone. Now. See now. Not dream to dream.

Your father's face flashes into your brain like a metal plate. You fall standing.

Wake up.

Stare if you want, June says. You are in here too Tracy.

Is this a question?

You know I had it right down to the minute, the date, the exact hour that you would come. It's true Tracy. Does that frighten you?

June, you say, about to tell her something important that slips away as fast as trying to stay in a dream, to not wake up in the morning but to stay in the good part.

Tracy, it's all right in here, actually this has been the best year of my life. It's a city in here, a secret society just the way we want it.

June does look good, more beautiful than you have ever seen her. Her eyes sparkle. When she looks at you she is seeing you, not something behind you or in front of you, but where you are. Always someone else to see you, find you? The calm in June's face is a calm you have never seen before, at least haven't seen for long enough for it to have not faded from your memory.

Why did you do it June? you think, but don't ask. Questions as redundant as the veins that run beneath everyone's flesh, veins that can be broken down (to reason?) beneath microscopes, finally seeing what is invisible to the naked eye now, how a highly ordered network of energy fields, not matter, pulsates, movement and not stillness.

This is where it starts then, because seeing your sister there before you, you see your whole life pass in front of your eyes. Dying. There isn't anything you can do to change what has happened, what she did, not anything.

315

★   ★   ★

June is in prison for life.

It's all there in that one photograph, those legs walking out of the frame, Tad's halved eyes. All that is missing in the picture is a girl named June, seated anxiously on the other side of a red vinyl booth, nervously snapping photographs of nothing in particular.

The Rapture of Christmas and Summer

THAT picture of your mother and father holding you, holding June. This picture that Grandma has in a small wooden frame on the nightstand next to your bed here, this picture that you looked for so many times before, and couldn't find for the longest time. This picture really happened. This picture of a family. And now you can't even believe one corner of that clown embrace, Mother's arms, Father's arms, wrapping around you, wrapping around June. The snapshot pose that covers the real feelings, skin walking over bone, breezy as a shirt on a wire clothes hanger. The framed blur of hands flicking over found shoulder blades, the mark of clipped wings? You float anyway.

How far away that landscape seems from here, quilted in your grandmother's bedroom (I'm over here, your father says. I'm over here, your mother says). Your parents' voices, just two distant specks pulsing on the horizon, the perspective prairie-flat.

You are attached to this earth by a string as delicate as a

thread of silk, as delicate as aging skin draping loosely over facial bones.

Can't someone see this, that passion can drive a person mad, mad enough to want to take away from others what one doesn't have?

You think you know what it is like to die, a slow squelch of feeling, nerves ceasing to register sensation. It's the slow tickle of an arm numbing, then legs, until finally what you are just slips away, but not quietly. And where do you go?

You don't want to fall asleep and never wake up?

Is this what you are supposed to be doing in this life, sleepwalking?

You can feel yourself lunging upright from horizontal, a slow-motion clicking against the heaviness of your body.

Wake up. Wake up.

What is it that makes daily motion worthwhile? How do you learn to face nothingness when there are so many battles going on inside?

Let me out.

If you could dig down to China, see the back of your head, be everywhere at once, then does it stop being nighttime, nighttime this place of grayness, this place where you must live, a place that is real that will always be there, a place where your sister is in prison forever and forever? It has to be this way this time, in this lifetime.

How you can live now, how you can go on, continue, is to believe and believe that there are real reasons for you to be here, real reasons and not just ideas that you have to be numb to understand.

It is a given where June is, where her physical being is at this very moment. Is this all that you can keep track of, what you lock up? What you control? In the telling of any story isn't that what you are doing being in control, commanding an audience, the you that told this story, the you that are reading it, and the you that was telling the story all along.

Ghosts, the ghosts in the eyes of photographs, the ghosts,

that found this place where you were born, a place that was taken. This is what everything up to this point in your life has been about; what is taken away from others and what is left in the place of that loss, a grayness that haunts and haunts.

You wish for this, your own death, an afterword to this story, what would finally take care of what it is you cannot seem to do, to accept what has happened and move on, to accept what your sister did. And get on with your life. Your life, because really that is what you have to work with.

How it would be, this fantasy:

Postscript—June Hawkins

This book is printed as it was found in my sister's room. I am certain that it is not finished.

Tracy wanted desperately to be able to give a voice to June. Tracy wanted to be able to show what made me do what I did. But I never have given anything away. I am a taker.

I find it ironic that I ultimately have the last word. My sister Tracy just like myself was a very violent and selfish woman. Unlike myself, Tracy was a good actress, a real good chameleon and a liar. Unlike myself Tracy saw hope where I saw none.

There is not a lot to say. I am sorry that my sister is dead. I am also sorry that she had the gift of knowing how she would die. If you go back in the story you will see that Tracy knew she would die in a car crash. Orion look for it, her dead friend said to her in a dream. And it was in winter, the car crash.

So you tell me, what we are supposed to make of this life?

I wanted to kill my parents. I failed. Tracy wanted to understand murder, an accident took her life. You tell me what anything might be for.

I am in prison. I have the last word. Take it or leave it. There must be something in all this, some sign or warning, maybe some sort of hope, somewhere in this story.

I am finishing this story. I am sure you are curious about me, a murderess. What kind of girl takes the lives of others? What kind of girl would burn her parents' house down, yes in a premeditated attempt to kill her parents?

I am a girl much like the kind of girls you know, the girls you love or hate or abuse or worship or put on pedestals or don't listen to. I could be your daughter or sister or lover.

I am just as crazy as anyone you might know. I am just as crazy as you yourself perhaps.

I don't think it was an accident that Tracy was killed. I think it was an act of God.

Because the bottom line, at least what I have had time to think about here, the bottom line is that people don't learn anymore. I mean how creative does a person have to be to get people to admit to the fact that we are all inherently violent and it is because we can think that we can change?

I have always thought that life is only hell because hell is what most people understand.

God, the God that Tracy believed in, the God that is inside of us all knew that the only way to get people to pay attention to the fact that they had to change, change or self-destruct, this God that knew that the only way people would listen to what Tracy was trying to say about herself and about me and about being alive, was to die, become a lesson. This we all understand, a young life halted in its prime.

Whose crazy notion is this, this sacrificial knowledge, the martyr incarnate, the self glorifying, you'll miss me now? Baby Jesus. People never growing up is all. This fantasy of yours, these fantasies we have to live in instead of being awake. To tell a story and then disappear, a perfection of not needing to account for what you are and what you see, as if anyone really needed anything different. So you fantasize your death because this is what happens to women's voices, especially their anger, it must be killed. But you are still here. Now what?

Say it then, just say it:

This story I am writing, well it must be assumed that the narrator is dead, that any resemblances found in the story to a living soul are purely coincidental, a fiction of the narrator (i.e., existing in her mind and your mind alone).

You must learn to accept responsibility.

It just won't do, you never really will disappear, there will always be someone else to contain what you now call yours, this energy, this life. This story, there is no one to blame except yourself, no one to finish what you have set out to do, tell a story about what is lost and what you have found in the place of that loss.

Each idea, any idea at all about how you might save the world is something to hang on to.

So many times in the course of a day you feel betrayed and it's all related to the ideas you have of how you might save the world, ideas of how you think that other people should live their lives.

Words on a page tilt because something inside cries, no.

Whole nights pass and there is nothing that can be done about the anxiousness of these truths already known. The truth about your sister and the truth about you. You are not dead and neither is June. Being dead is about going away and never coming back, not ever. Being dead is about being lost. Are you lost?

The birds' songs that press into the dark, marking prints of sound into who you are, into the anticipated dawn, not a hum these songs, but a cry.

Stop it you want to say. You are not ready for another day to start. The birds' sounds, you don't know the word for their sounds, the sound of digging down to China, this place that is past the innocent slit of the dead sparrow's eye. Mothers tell their children that if they try hard enough they might be able to dig down there. Fathers say of course, of course you can't dig down to China. What you keep hearing now in the nighttime, in the same way that you are ignorant of a form into which you might shape your (story), (idea), (thought), own voice, what you keep hearing in the night from the ghost inside, the ghost that is what you have to believe in, the ghost of others long gone, is that yes, yes you can dig down to China, and even though you might not get there for others to see, this is not what is important. You can dig down to China God says.

The form is just to distract you from the story you are telling, the story that will tell itself anyway, a story that is the sounds the birds make, the sound of a plastic shovel scratching at moist earth, a fury of energy and being alive.

You think better at night. Alone in the dark you claim what is yours, what can't be locked up.

As soon as the light of day appears the monsters sleep.

The bird's song, two notes, high then low, a sound like a V marked into flesh with a sharp object.

It is meant to pierce the flesh or the night or other people's perceptions.

Quiet now.

Sometimes when you look at your hands they become what they are and you are shocked out of your indifference. These hands, the ones that remind you of the animalness inside that is always there. Hands that are at once claws for grabbing, climbing, holding on to things, defending your life, (or taking the life of another), hands that are for caressing yourself or someone else, wiping yourself, picking and scratching, hands that can steer a car or a pen or a paintbrush, hands that can guide matter to express what is inside.

The monster tosses and turns.

The truth that is between light and dark, the gray area that is the blood that seeps from the cut skin that holds it in is what you know. The truth is that making love is with and without definition, a passion for transcending a life of bound silence, a life of stone. This gray area is what you know, action and inaction the same, motion, everything, yourself included, whoever or whatever you may be to God, the gray area that makes you see your hands, makes you know without knowing that you will return and that the only thing there really is to be afraid of is not being afraid or angry or scared or in love or sad or filled with wonderment, alive.

It is tedious work to let the monsters rest at night or be awake for whole days at a time, of facing all these things that you must face alone.

The naked trees, spindly as bones, lash at the sky because you keep blinking, blinking and moving.

But you don't move. Your body stays in North Carolina.

Grandma is in the kitchen. There are guns in the attic. If you kill yourself this is control. If you kill yourself that doesn't make other people go away. If you kill other people things just happen again, repetition. In the attic Grandpa Hawkins's guns are lined up against the wall like vials of blood.

There were restless afternoons before dinner, your mother in the kitchen, your father on his way home from work, you pressing yourself against June. June pressing herself against you in the bedroom. What is dying?

Now you can't breathe. You used to be afraid you might swallow your tongue. Out with sickness June. There are boxes for people to be put in, real boxes that go under the ground. How do people know then when someone is really dead?

What is it that you did June?

This grandpa sewed people up in the war, sewed their limbs back on like they were dolls. Putting things back together.

There are pictures of your grandpa when he was overseas in the war, whole scrapbooks filled with these pictures. A real war then? Not this war you make inside yourself. Sometimes it just seems as though there were nothing at all and you and everyone else just makes it all up. Let me out. Which voice is saying that?

Are you beginning to remember that how you have come to perceive the world is through a distorted perspective of select memories? These memories that are scarred by what you are trying to understand, this braid of violence.

If only you could give it all away. This is what you want, to purge yourself once and for all?

But there is no one to give it all to. This is what you must change, this taking and giving away of all that no one knows what to do with.

You are telling this story to yourself.

You are listening.

Men and women don't like each other really, June wrote. Your mother is working with people that are dying of AIDS. What is love then? Don't touch me, the voices say, we are drowning. There are boxes that go underground. Your mother says, these people, when they are really dying, when there can be no denying that they are really dying, then they start to live. Lessons? All you need to know is on the back of your eyelids, June wrote. Everything people try so hard to name, to order, to control, just disappearing, exploding into what can't be named anymore. Panting.

The man that flew the plane that dropped the first atomic bomb on Japan went crazy, he did. The real history. In Tinian, where the Enola Gay was before the flight, your Grandfather Hawkins knew this man. There are pictures of your grandfather standing in front of bodies, bodies mounded up like compost. There are palm trees. There are naked native women. These things in scrapbooks your grandmother carefully put together. On the back of the pictures of the native girls your grandfather had written in his hard-to-read doctor's scrawl: look at the eyes on her; this on a picture of a woman with huge breasts whose eyes were in shadow.

There is a picture of your grandfather peering over his surgical mask like he was at a costume party, his gloved hands hovering over the exposed organs of someone's open body. My organs are functioning in total darkness, Mark wrote. The organs in these pictures are visible in a snapshot that is maybe an inch by three inches in size. Organs that stopped functioning decades before now.

There is a picture of your grandfather and the man that flew the Enola Gay. The two men are smiling. They have their arms around each other. The men are standing knee-deep in the ocean. On the back of the picture is written: This man dropped it.

In daylight, the mirror across from your headboard threatens to swallow up the room.

There is an empty porcelain pitcher in a bowl on a wooden washstand. The spout of this pitcher points north. Equinox is north. You will have to straighten out your life, Grandma says. There is a carefully painted rose on the inside lip of this porcelain pitcher that overlaps another rose, two roses on the inside of the spout. A pitcher in a bowl, its calm emptiness, not urgency to make such delicate roses with a fine pointed brush. You wonder how anyone might make something so beautiful.

Tomorrow is promised to no one, Grandma says.

But Grandma there might not be a tomorrow.

Divided souls, the war to kill the real God and not the one people make up. June.

The fantasies people have, what is used to make people sleepy, forgetful, afraid. Divided, divide.

You are sure that what you think about the thoughts that you have, the ones that concern your pain, wishing someone dead, telling someone that what they do is not important, evil thoughts. You are sure that eventually thoughts turn to action, must materialize somehow.

There are also things that you do that can't ever be taken back, damage done that is irreparable, situations, people that are irretrievable; saying something that you shouldn't have, not doing something that you really wanted to, violating someone's right to be a person, to say yes or no (these impositions of the self). There are the things that can't be taken back that you can't seem to do anything about, an arsenal of weapons, a magnification of your stubbornness.

You can't take back these actions, the crimes you commit or help to commit.

It's true that once there is a thought at some time (and maybe it won't be you but your offspring) at some time this thought will materialize become an action.

Thoughts have to take shape sometime, nothing can remain contained.

Please go away. Please go away.

Do wounds really heal?

Does anything get better?

These thoughts that seem to appear out of nowhere, the urge to murder, a poison inside, a drive to make up for what has been lost, what you can't control. This outburst from a seed that has been gestating. Your thoughts. June's actions.

How can these thoughts be exorcised?

You must control what you think, be careful about what kind of thoughts you have.

Sometimes it is best to never leave the house at all, to stay in bed and practice thinking about nothing at all.

You wish for this day:

Nothing happens, nothing at all, no one is born, no one dies, no one is killed, no one makes love, no one moves, it is very quiet.

This day picture-perfect frozen like the displays in the Museum of Natural History, likenesses of animals and Indians that will never move, not ever.

Even the weather is perfect. There are three shades of gray hanging above everyone's heads from dawn until nightfall, a canopy of stretched felt that hovers three feet above the top of everyone's sedated skulls. Rest.

When this grandpa was a little boy for mind control his father used to hold a knife to his head until your grandfather could show his father, show him in actions that he was no longer afraid. Behave, Great-grandfather must have said. Your great-grandfather would make your grandfather squeeze a live snake into a glass bottle.

Your great-grandmother loved violets.

In the mirror the yellow-stained wallpaper drips slow and sinister down the wall, the walls that are pushing in then out. Breathing. You stare at your own distorted head in that mirror.

.   .   .

WHEN you wake up in the morning the first thing you do is locate yourself, set a context, remember who you are and exactly what it is that you are supposed to be doing.

When you wake up it takes a while to locate this self.

What can you do? You dreamt you had glass in your hands, glass that is thick and hard and cracked like ice. The flesh on your palms is cracked in the dream. Your hands are transparent and glittery like mica.

It's time to get up, Grandma says.

June gets up every day. June sees days and nights, mostly hallways from a cell. June sees through bars, vertical parallel lines, a half-finished grid. People do things when it's really something else that they wanted to do.

It is dangerous to wake a sleepwalker.

It is time to get up now Tracy Hawkins, Grandma says.

.   .   .

GRANDMA tells you about her neighbor Dionne, and how Dionne's mother went insane shortly after Dionne was born. There's a memory: looking at your face in your father's eye, trying to explain to him, trying to make him understand. Do you love me? he asked. Why is that always such an impossible question?

Out the bedroom window Tammy and Donna are playing what looks to be a game of house. There are dishes lined up along the porch. Tammy is wearing what looks to be her father's fishing pants. Donna is wearing an apron. Two sisters playing in a yard.

If you blink your eyes they are still there.

Will this story stop?

When will you see things as if you were cradled, seated comfortably in the middle of a clean white room with windows on all sides through which light is streaming in wrapping your body?

Is this what you really want?

Grandma is smoothing your bedclothes, telling you how when Dionne's father died, Dionne's grandparents had locked up the house that Dionne was born in, the house Dionne's father couldn't live in after Dionne's mother was so sick, went crazy. Grandma tells you that it is rumored that Dionne's parents were really brother and sister.

What is love? What might it really be for?

Tracy you have to get up now. Face things head-on, nothing goes away you know. Grandma's soft voice telling you these things.

You can get in that house you know, through the back, Grandma said.

Your father's mother telling you to face things head-on.

It's done, Grandma says, over. You can get on with your life, she says.

That this really happened, that while you were away loving a man long dead and preparing an old woman to die, June killed two people, a young man and an old woman. There is a man and a woman inside of us all, June wrote before.

In the dream there is a gigantic wheel, a large spool the kind that is used for telephone wires or anchor chains. This spool is a giant rolling wooden cylinder.

Strapped to this wheel are many women. They are tightly roped onto this spool, close so that they are touching, their shoulders and calves. Some of the women are so close that they are almost overlapping. They are all facing forward. Their heads and feet reach the edges of the spool.

The wheel is rolling toward you. The women strapped to the spool flatten with each revolution. New women take the places of the flattened ones so that they too can be flattened. Silent and accepting you can only watch.

All right then I will look, you say to Grandma, and to your reflection in the mirror and to Donna and Tammy playing so hard outside your window, laughing, oblivious to all that is going on in your head.

The world is what you make it, Grandma says. You have choices. You can sit in this bed and mourn away your life for what June did or you can get up and do something. Bad things happen. Life goes on.

You have been asleep for a long time.

"I can feel my body waking up."

Are you awake?

. . .

THERE was a Christmas when your Mom made all the gifts she gave.

There was a Christmas when your Dad stepped on the stereo because Big Herb lived in the house and Dad came for Christmas anyway.

There is this Christmas alone with Grandma.

You hadn't really wanted to see it, but one morning after helping Grandma take down the Christmas tree, you had found yourself in Dionne's parents' abandoned house thinking you might take pictures.

The sickbed is intact, surrounded by funeral bouquets of thick discolored plastic flowers and huge velveteen ribbons. The smell of rotting wood, suggestive of outdated newspapers and the dust, pungent as antiseptic, pierces your nostrils with others' long-ago illnesses. You can't ever run away, not really.

The dimly lit air, dense as emphysema lungs, rasps harshly where the drapes allow the daylight to enter the room. The sheets and bed pads are crumpled on the floor like a child retching horribly from the oppressive stench.

In the living room, the darkest room of all, only a crucifix of light slices through the thick drapes, just barely wrapping one worn crushed velvet corner of a mildewed armchair. Next to the armchair are pamphlets about faith and healing with the Lord. The paper of this wisdom fading dull and useless, like things that cling; lint or bad dreams or the sensuous wrap of a young child, legs open spiderlike and blind.

It is too dark to take pictures. On your way out through the bedroom you see it. Tacked above the night stand cluttered with medicine bottles is what looks to be a valentine. On closer inspection you can make out the delicately drawn outline of a human fetus sketched on a heart cut out of binder paper, the faint blue lines going diagonal behind the childlike scrawl: Happy Birthday to my loving daughter Dionne, Love Mom.

Grandma said that Dionne's parents might have been brother and sister.

People get sick from denying.

There are so many ways to love someone.

. . .

DIONNE hemorrhaged yesterday. She had to be rushed to the hospital. Your grandmother says it's because Dionne doesn't take care of herself. Dionne has three kids, Tammy and Donna go to Bible school and Baby John is four months old. Dionne's husband Curtis Allen owns the fish house. Curtis Allen doesn't go to church. Grandma says Curtis Allen married Dionne because she was pregnant. Dionne tells Curtis Allen that she will leave him if he doesn't go to church but she never will. Curtis Allen spends most of his time running the fish house.

Last week before Dionne hemorrhaged she had taken you to a revival meeting at the Pentecostal Holiness Church on Harker's Island. A revival meeting is for saving people, for letting Jesus into your life.

Dionne is singing in the choir, her round face singing, her heavy body swaying: soon and very soon we are going to see the King. Dionne's mouth shapes these words.

The evangelist is foaming at the mouth, screaming, I am asking you in God's name, in the name of Jesus Christ to come up to the altar. . . . We'll do this together. I want all you young people. Will you come? Will you come? Times are tough and young people, you young people, need all the help you can get to lead you away from all this temptation and sin. His face is swelling. I'm going to tell you about child abuse, he yells. His face is frothing green around the eyes and mouth. Child abuse is when a fetus gets sucked up into a billion pieces, he yells.

Sucked up real good, you think, like all the young women you saw when Grandma took you to Atlantic Beach. These young women, girls really, walking along the shore, picking up small shells, their stomachs swelling tight like an eye with the lid pulled back.

Dionne sitting next to you in the pew keeps saying, Amen, Amen. You saw her mother's sickbed. Dionne.

Driving home from the revival meeting, Dionne had explained what Rapture is.

Well you see it's like this, she says. We must suffer for what we did back there in the garden.

Baby John's formula bottles are clanking around in the backseat.

You see, when Jesus died for us on the cross he made it so that we could get to heaven if we believed.

Grandma rowing you and June around in the harbor in Old Saybrook, the harbor down the road from Grandma's big white house. The oars dip into the glittering water like someone splashing in a bathtub. Grandma's eyes green, her strong tan arms. June trailing her small hand in the blue-green water.

Tammy is eating a Tasty Dog, watching the shadows blurring by outside the car. Donna is asleep. Donna has diabetes and at church the preacher tells her that Jesus will make it go away if she believes. Donna is eight.

Father Stellehy said he woke up in the ambulance, heard the sirens and thought he was dreaming.

★   ★   ★

It's going to be like the ark when God gave everything a chance, Dionne says. Well Rapture is going to take us to heaven. God is going to give the world to the Christians, those in the grave that believed and me, and Baby John, because he's innocence, we'll just disappear and then those that don't believe will see God's power, but it will be too late for those that didn't believe. It won't be like skeletons or anything, God will have given bodies back to the dead for heaven, only better than before, and we'll just go to that big mansion in the sky. Let's say we were driving like now and God said it was time, well you'd just see my clothes and Baby John's and Donna's because we'd been saved. Tammy is not listening.

That's Rapture, Dionne says, and it's going to happen soon. If you ever hear the voice of the Lord, you'd better take it as a sign.

You'd liked to be saved, but you wanted to save them first.

When Dionne came back from the hospital you went to visit her.

She is lying on her bed. Her fleshy arms look like the satiny white puffs that line a coffin lid. She is covered with her wedding band pattern quilt. She is listening to gospel on the eight-track.

Tammy don't sit like that when there is company, Dionne says. Tammy pulls her legs under her dress, tightly squeezing her knees together. Tammy's long hair is greasy and uncombed. Tammy and Donna as Holy Rollers can't wear pants or cut their hair.

Ten percent of the girls in Tammy's graduating class are pregnant, Dionne says. Dionne is unconsciously fraying the hem of her left robe sleeve with her massive hands. It's not being able to deny the devil that's all, she says.

Baby John starts crying. Tammy picks him up out of the crib. She takes him to the rocking chair to feed him his formula. Baby John stops crying. His eyes are set too close together.

You know, Dionne continues, there's been a lot of fathers

messin' with their daughters like the preacher said. One girl in Tammy's class had a baby by her father last year.

Hearing this, Kelly, the neighbor girl who has been folding laundry on the floor, turns and says to Tammy: U done av to wuwuy about dat Dammy u badder wunt duch u.

Tammy says, rocking Baby John on her knees, yeah and you better shut your door tight tonight Kelly because your badder be on the prowl.

Kelly's speech impediment gets worse as she gets older, your grandma said. Kelly lives down the street in the trailer park with her father and his mother.

In this setting you see these people acting out your life. You are Kelly folding the laundry on the floor, doing what you can to be in another's family. Is Dionne your mother? The beast and good queen all in one? You see your own fate in this scenario. You are unable to separate from your mother. Are you Tammy now? The mother's voice, your voice becoming one and the same, just as you see Tammy becoming Dionne because most likely she will be unable to see any other way. As you are listening to Dionne talk you start to believe what she is saying as will Tammy. Tammy will do what her mother's words dictate as the small voice inside of her, the voice that she might call hers, that says, No, I don't want to, translates helplessly into a fat body into oily skin. That's it, people can kill each other while they are living, smothering one another into an immobilization of souls that just need to breathe.

The mother no one knew about, Dionne's mother, insane, crazy. Where did she go?

There are scientific explanations in books, many different ones to explain such mysteries as people who disappear, vanish without a trace: void spots of universal ether that can completely destroy solid objects, magnetic fields that could disintegrate a person by rearranging the atoms in a body.

But this doesn't explain Dionne and her situation, wanting to deny the devil, her body disintegrating before your eyes. The voice of Dionne's mother inside her still. Let me out. These voices that can't be denied, the voices that make up each person, the longing really, the fighting to be alive.

Even the scientific explanations for disappearing persons can't explain the truths reported by the loved ones of the vanished, the ones who can still hear the voice of the disappeared body calling out, whispering from where they were last seen.

Dionne just lying there like she was going to be raptured tomorrow.

You are trying to think about that.

Grandma says, you have to go back now, get on with your life.

. . .

WHAT about all the bombs Grandma? you say, so angry you have to hold on to the faucet of the sink as if it might support you as the room shifts. I wish that all the bombs would just go off now Grandma, you say.

Grandma shifts only slightly in her chair. Grandma continues to chew.

Please sit down now, Grandma says.

Words and paintings and a child's embrace, and automatic cameras and diseases, control, what there is to hold on to, disappearing all at once, exploding into a thousand pieces.

Look at me, Grandma says.

Mother's eyes looking far away.

Don't go away Grandma, please stay. Preparing Mrs. Lorian to die. Miya wanting you to hold her. Your eyes in the mirror. June straddling a dead man. You, in love with a man long dead, his words.

You can't forget.

Sometimes when you are in another's gaze for a long time and they are in yours, eye to eye, this feels like dying.

You just can't accept this, a spider's life, of killing a part of yourself or a part of someone else, this livingness in each other that people seem to be unable to nurture. You just won't accept this, a giving of life, the leaving, the going away.

Mark tried to love women, he did.

Women say, yes, then no, with and without words.

Lying.

Your mother makes you look down because she knew that she couldn't tell you and that you wouldn't be able to tell her how you must come to hate each other finally.

This order?

You don't want to hate.

The giving and the going away.

June won't go away either.

This fear that makes you look away.

Your mother didn't mean to make you look down.

You think you know more than your grandmother.

Your grandmother is still alive. Your grandmother gets up with the sun every day, every day.

Please sit down Tracy. I don't know where you got your ideas, or who taught you what you know but it just isn't right. Your grandfather if he was alive he would talk to you. Things you can't understand are a part of life, awful things do happen. Your grandfather and I knew from the start that June couldn't make it. Sometimes these things happen. She was a very sick child. Your answers are narrow Tracy. How you want to see things goes against nature. These homosexuals, your mother, it's not that she doesn't love you it's that they are mad with the way the world is and instead of trying to change it everyone is trying to end it. No I can't explain the bombs. I don't really think that anyone wants to use them.

There are cancerous cells in your grandmother's body, real ones. You think about this, Grandma's house that is immaculate, cleaned daily, Grandma's body that has leukocytes multiplying and multiplying in her veins, the cells that fight disease that are to ward off cancer multiplying out of control. What can't be held in finally, ordered, ignored.

All of a sudden you want to tell your grandmother about Miya, you want to tell her how much like your mother you really are. You want to shock your grandmother.

As you think this, just as your mouth starts to open you realize that this is what you have really learned, to hurt others in an attempt to make all your own pain go away.

This body of yours that it so often seems that you are just glued into.

Balance.

Grandma is still alive. Your Grandma is seventy-one. But she doesn't look old at all. Her eyes are still green. Her hair is soft brown and has never been dyed. But this is not what's important, even though of course this is how you measure things without thinking sometimes, by how they look. It's what's inside that is important Grandma always says.

I am a fighter, Grandma says, wiping her mouth. I face life head-on. Tracy if I could I would give my life for you to wake up, for you to understand. Sometimes I think that the reason I am still here is to guide you.

You see yourself. You don't want to be seeing yourself anymore. You are seated at a table, a small table for two, the table that your grandparents felt to be adequate as a kitchen table when they retired and moved South. You are seated across from your grandmother. Your grandmother is old, but not a body that is decaying around a diminishing life. Your grandmother is alive, there is laughter behind her green eyes, eyes that are fiery, that are sharp, that are clear, the eyes of acceptance, passionate eyes that don't look away, like you looked away when you looked in your mother's eyes.

Grandma says she would die for you to understand.

Your mother said she was sorry it hurt, sorry she couldn't listen.

You don't want to be seeing yourself anymore.

Grandma please don't go away, please don't ever leave me, you say. I just don't know what I would do without you.

Grandma says she is thankful for every day she has on this earth.

This earth and not another one.

Come here Tracy, Grandma says, and into her arms you go as if you were a child and Grandma holds you and the tears start and stop, start and stop and finally you are crying, sobbing, a wave that jolts then pulsates through your body releasing what has been inside for such a long time.

Grandma holds you and there is nothing else but the holding, her arms around your body, her cool hands along your forehead.

I love you, Grandma says, and you know that she won't go away.

Grandma's fingers wipe at the drops of water on her iced tea glass. The patterned swirls of water rushing to fill the space after Grandma's fingers leave the surface of the glass. Then Grandma's hand slides up and down the whole surface of the glass. Grandma's palms glisten with water.

Grandma reaches across the table and picks up your glass. She wipes the wood surface of the table. I wish you'd use coasters honey, Grandma says. See there's a mark here now. Grandma fingers the faint ring on the table where the glass was. Tracy you are going to have to learn to respect other people's things.

What matters.

The last words, things to matter, the urgency to create something, life, or a porcelain vase, or a photograph in the face of what looms over everyone, the truth of where you are, everywhere and nowhere at the same time.

Grandma believes that there is healing. Grandma says that love, real love is a powerful thing, that it gets inside of you, catching you unaware.

Grandma says that at night, sometimes at night Grandpa comes to her, wraps his arms around her filling her with a warmth that sustains her.

Grandma says she is not afraid to die. Grandma says she is just glad that she can't see into the future. How could you live with knowing when you are going to die? Grandma says.

You look at your grandmother. You wonder how it might feel to see things from where she is standing, from her vantage point, the things that have happened to her, what she has wished for, what she dreams of at night.

If you could get inside of another person, be in their skin, their situation, have their history, their perspective and understanding, then (it's true) you would no longer be able to judge their actions.

Grandma's perspective.

June's actions.

Each to their own life. No one to save anyone here on earth unless you save yourself first. This is what Grandma knows. This is what Grandma says.

I am always in your heart, Grandma says, remember this.

Double Solitaire

THERE is no dust in here, none. This room is really yours. I told you before when Grandpa and I first moved here in 1980, I distinctly remember telling you on the phone, not to be sad because we were leaving the house in Old Saybrook, and that we had a room for you here when you came, your own. Grandma said this to you, she did. Grandma says you always have been like a daughter to me. This is important. Why shouldn't a twenty-three-year-old have her own room? You are never too old to be taken care of, Grandma says. Grandma says things like this and Grandma doesn't have to be drunk.

In this room that is yours there are pictures of your family, small snapshots in frames, gilt frames like the kind that can be purchased inexpensively at Woolworth's. These are pictures to look at. On the floor in your bedroom there is a round rug that Grandma says belonged to and was made by your grandfather's mother, your great-grandmother. This rug that is patterned with roses, big blossoming pink flowers, has been so well taken care of that there is nothing worn about it. The rug is still soft to step on, soft to run your hands across it because each piece of yarn was placed close together, so close together it must have taken someone with the patience of Job to make it, Grandma said, reminding you to put it on the chair if you are going to do exercises or whatever it is you do in there with the door closed.

To make a rug like this takes time.

You are lying on your bed, the chenille bedspread is bumps, clean white bumps that smell like Ivory Snow and hanging on the line outside. This smell you associate with the parts of your life, parts of your life that have been suffocated for a long time. You put your face against the cat pillow that your Dad sent Grandma for her birthday when he was living by the freeway. The cat pillow which is blue and hard, a stuffed toy really, smells like jasmine. Everything in Grandma's house smells like something fresh and clean.

My house doesn't get this way by itself, Grandma says.

The time spent grieving.

The time spent making a house clean and lovely, a place to be comfortable in, a place in which to live.

The time spent making a round rug with roses.

The time spent getting sick enough to take what doesn't belong to you.

Everything takes time.

After you saw June you stayed in Equinox for how long?

What were you doing?

Time spent being dead.

It takes a long time to get so numb.

I am fine Grandma, you said before on the phone, you don't need to come see me. I am fine, you said to Grandma. I am working on a project. My job is going well. Your job? Taking care of Mrs. Lorian, being in love with a man long dead, a job?

And you kept writing to Grandma convincing her that everything was fine. The letters you wrote are here to prove it. You can read them if you like, Grandma says. You can read them if you want to.

It is the last day of 1985. Grandma has a calendar in her kitchen to prove it. Grandma has three calendars in her house and four clocks and a barometer in the living room next to her violets so she can tell when it is going to rain. Grandma likes to be in tune with what is going on. There are magazines, *National Geographic, Smithsonian, Yankee, People, Time*. Grandma reads all of these magazines, some like *People* she reads cover to cover. June was in *People* magazine. How to account for that?

You might brush your sneakers off before you just toss them all muddy on the floor, Grandma says from the kitchen.

I'm sorry.

You say that but you keep doing it.

The phone rings. I'll get it, and you stumble catching your foot on the rose rug.

Grandma is standing at the sink.

With one hand she is rinsing the soap from your underwear and bras and with the other hand she is leafing through her field guide, looking in the bird section, as if she didn't already know them all by heart anyway.

It is Aunt Vickie on the phone. Aunt Vickie is Grandma's only surviving sister. There were twelve kids of which Grandma is the oldest. Now there are only two brothers left plus your grandma and Aunt Vickie. Aunt Vickie was one of the main reasons why Grandpa decided to retire in Raynes, because he wanted Grandma to be near her sister.

Hi Aunt Vickie you practically yell into the phone.

This is a joke you have with Grandma because like clockwork Aunt Vickie calls every evening to ask if you would like some dessert or if you have been to the dump yet, because if you had been to the dump did you notice if there were any new cats there. Aunt Vickie and Uncle Ellis Raynes never had any children but are a lot like children themselves, the innocent part of children that is amazed by anything new, likes to eat and is afraid of things like that someone might be listening in on the phone conversation. Aunt Vickie and Uncle Ellis have ten cats.

Keep your voice down. Maybe I should just come over. I think someone might be listening. Aunt Vickie is talking in whispers now.

Grandma's blue sweater that is hanging over the back of the chair is reflected in the shiny kitchen floor.

No one is listening they just don't do stuff like that anymore, Aunt Vickie, you say.

I don't know Tracy. They keep track of a lot of things we don't know about.

You cover the mouthpiece and whisper to Grandma who is wringing out her slip in the plastic washtub in the sink, Who are they?

Grandma shakes her head.

I am going to have Uncle Ellis bring over some doughnuts. We stopped at Hot and Crusty on the way back from More-head. Ellis had to go to the doctor's but he is fine. The doctor said that all his walking has practically given him a new heart. Ellis walked five miles yesterday. Aunt Vickie practically shouts this.

I'll see you tomorrow then Aunt Vickie whispers.

Happy New Year, you whisper into the phone.

Happy New Year Aunt Vickie whispers back.

You might help a bit more with all this work that needs to be done, Grandma says when you hang up the phone.

Really I didn't think it possible to have such lazy do-nothing granddaughters. I . . . I . . .

Grandma stops.

Did you ever? she continues. I am sure that I know what that was all about. Uncle Ellis is going to bring his beady Indian eyes over here to ogle and stare at you, no doubt on the pretense of bringing some delectable dessert?

Doughnuts, you say.

Those two are like children, Grandma says. Only much more

340

predictable. Pizza Inn for "spaghetts" in that dark cave of a restaurant and then right to Hot and Crusty or Greasy and Powdered for some lead balls, I swear, and all this after going to see Ellis's doctor. That man is lucky to be alive at all. If I hadn't been home that day when that man called me from Harker's Island Ferry to say that Ellis was all white and clammy and having difficulty breathing and would I please come get him, he would have died. I raced his drunken self to that hospital and just in time. He is what sent Vickie to the hospital before. She called your grandfather when she first fell in love, asked your grandfather for his advice, that she had met a man where she was stationed. Of course she didn't listen to Grandpa and I still to this day don't know why she called. Well it wasn't four years before she had a nervous breakdown you know. Oh I know they need each other like plants need water. It's certainly a funny world.

Hot and Crusty, my lord. Here Tracy would you please hang these things on the rack that is in your closet?

Aunt Vickie and Uncle Ellis don't know about June. No one in Raynes does.

Sometimes the process of thawing is as simple as seeing new things, Grandma said.

Aunt Vickie had a nervous breakdown. You would like to talk to her, but it is not something that is talked about. Aunt Vickie has a hunched back, her body bends toward the earth as she walks. Her hair is gray and she looks much older than your grandmother even though she is in fact twelve years younger. Grandma said before that Aunt Vickie and Uncle Ellis were quite wild in their younger days, before Uncle Ellis's drinking got out of hand.

Aunt Vickie has a cane, a clunker as Grandma calls it. Aunt Vickie has kind eyes. She was in the Marines. She drove a bread truck. She won awards for selling the most Avon products in Eastern North Carolina. Aunt Vickie and Uncle Ellis keep a garden, take care of their cats as if the cats were their children, feed all the stray cats in town and live right across the street from their church, the Free Wheeling Baptist.

It is hard to see it at first but Grandma and Aunt Vickie really need each other, thrive on their differences. They are sisters.

There are pictures of Grandma's family on the nightstand next to your bed; pictures of Grandma and her sisters when they all lived in Massachusetts.

There is a picture of Aunt Vickie sitting in a big truck, a milk truck. She has a dress on and high heels and she is driving a milk truck.

There is a picture Grandpa Hawkins took of Grandma. In the picture Grandma looks about your age, though she is probably older because Grandma didn't marry until she was in her late twenties, twenty-eight to be exact. The date on the back of the picture says 1944, so Grandma was thirty. It is a candid picture. Grandma is in her bathing suit, stepping into a motel pool. Her mouth is open wide as if she were about to scream.

There is a picture Grandpa Hawkins took of Grandma. It is a small snapshot, black-and-white. Grandma is in her bathing suit. She is holding her stomach in because the water she is stepping into must be very cold. Her mouth is open wide as if she were laughing hysterically.

There are so many ways to see the same thing.

Grandma told you that when she left home it was the most important decision she ever made. Grandma was only fifteen. Grandma left home because as the oldest of twelve and with her mother getting sick she knew that if she didn't just leave she might never be able to. Her mother didn't believe in doctors, denied for the longest time that her swollen belly was a sign of something that needed immediate attention. She got so sick from bearing all those children, and never taking care of herself. When your Grandma was fifteen she left her family and went to another where she was paid to be a mother's helper. Grandma finished high school this way, sending small amounts of her paycheck to her father to help with the hospital bills.

The choices people have to make are never easy. It is always hard to leave.

Your grandma was a fighter from the start.

All that Grandma has, what she takes pride in, what she worked so hard to have, is all that you have always felt you just deserved to be given. It's a funny world, Grandma says.

Life is about hard work, Grandma says, and the reality of it all is that if you don't take care of yourself then no one else will. That is just the way things are. Don't get me wrong, I mean this in the most basic sense, of course there are so many people that need help, but the point is you never really can help anyone unless you are right with yourself first.

These simple truths that Grandma illustrates by how she conducts her time here.

Life is about hard work, and life is about suffering. You take the good with the bad, and you keep moving and you face life head-on because that is the only way.

How much suffering? How much?

There is no dust in here, no holes in any closets that need to be plastered, no greasy floors that it would be best to always wear shoes when walking on. There is no dark basement beneath the house. There is earth beneath this house, earth and a history you can find out about if you want to.

These things that are here in North Carolina or anywhere, houses that are equipped with convenient places to dispose of what no one wants to see. It is hard to keep up with new developments for some people, not everyone can do it. Your grandmother can.

I've worked hard all my life. I was never handed anything and don't you forget it, Grandma said.

Grandma let you keep it there in the window anyway even though it was a difficult thing to do, to just allow you to leave an orange on the windowsill for over a month.

It's a test Grandma. I promise I won't let it get too out of hand, you said.

Here at least put it on this, Grandma said, handing you a carefully cut square from the green Styrofoam tray that the pork chops had come on. It's washed, she said. I just don't want any of that orange to start molding on my windowsill.

The smooth white windowsill.

The round rose-patterned rug.

You understand, Grandma said smiling, my baby Tracy. Is this some sort of project? Oh never mind.

That was three weeks ago when Grandma asked you how come the orange was still on the windowsill, and why were you wasting food?

Your Mom sent the orange for Christmas, sent it from California, the orange, and some sprigs from the bay tree, and some walnuts, these things loose in the Christmas package your mother sent you.

How nice, Grandma said opening the present that your Mom had sent for her, an aqua-colored silk scarf with small sea horses and shells and red beach umbrellas on it. This is really very nice, she said again.

How nice, you said, fingering the white tissue that was wrapped around a bizarre little doll that the enclosed note said was made by June when she was ten. A doll made a long time ago, out of a sock. A doll with no arms or legs, just a stuffed tube really. The face is delicately painted for such a strange shape; small rosebud lips, and pretty-lady eyes, each felt-pen blue eye framed with long lashes. This your mother sent you for Christmas.

You felt drunk all of a sudden, drunk and maudlin holding the strange tube doll June had made.

Now that's quite a disturbing gift, if I do say so myself, Grandma says. I just never thought to send someone a dirty sock stuffed with who knows what for Christmas. I really wouldn't care if the president's wife had made it.

Also in the package, a picture of your mother, her eyes looking steady into the camera, and a blank journal and a fountain pen.

"There are all kinds of doctors," your mother had inscribed inside the cover of the journal. "Healing comes in many forms."

Grandma's Christmas trees are always magnificent, the fullest and greenest. If only they didn't have needles, Grandma says, sweeping them up as they drop. Lint from towels, this bothers your Grandma too.

Grandma has so many ornaments on her tree, ornaments she has collected throughout the years, each with a special story. There is the tin star that you made when you were five. There is the porcelain angel with real hair and a golden horn to her lips that goes on top of the tree, just as it went on top of Grandpa's tree when he was a little boy. There is a bamboo cane that Grandpa painted red and white and sent to Grandma when he was overseas. There is also a small wooden horse that your father carved in Boy Scouts when he was thirteen.

Your grandma tells you these stories or is saying, remember this or this and you start to remember things in a different way.

This orange that has sat in the window for over a month, its skin drying, the bottom going soft where it has rested on the green Styrofoam, this orange is the way you have been remembering it for too long now.

The wind is whistling through the trees, pressing against the side of the house.

There is going to be a big storm tomorrow.

In the kitchen Grandma is cracking pecans. You can hear the metal of the nutcracker on the shell, the splitting, the shells dropping into the silver tray Grandma uses for this.

What are you doing in there? you ask from the bedroom, even though you know perfectly well what Grandma is doing in the kitchen, doing what has to be done? No, doing what she has to be doing.

I am cracking nuts, Grandma says, it has to be done sometime, it's psychotherapy, I can't have all these pecans just sitting around in my house.

OK Grandma I'll help you in a minute, how about we play a game of double solitaire?

It's New Year's Eve, the last of 1985.

Simple things to work for this year, returning to Equinox, making amends with the people you just walked out on.

Syzygy is what will happen tomorrow. On the news the weatherman showed using plastic models how the sun and the moon and the earth will line up, causing unusually high tides that will be exacerbated by the northeaster that is working its way up the coast.

You cut, Grandma says.

Two decks, two piles, these cards that Grandma used to play bridge with in Old Saybrook. Just tell me when they are gone Grandpa Hawkins must have said, I'll be in my office, hiding. His arms about Grandma's middle. Tell me a riddle Grandma might have said then.

Grandma lays out her cards so fast and even, her fingers handling each card like a real pro. You forget about your cards for a minute and just watch.

Wait up, slow down Grandma, don't start until I have all my cards lined up, you say. Yes, Grandma this is the absolute best way to spend New Year's Eve.

Come on we don't have all day, Grandma says. I think a little wine might be nice, Grandma says her green eyes meeting your gaze as Grandma has met everything in her life. Grandma pours two small glasses of white wine from the bottle in the cupboard that has been there since Christmas. You have laid out your cards.

You aren't sorry you didn't call your Mom? Grandma says, sitting down and taking a sip of her wine. I just think it is best. What is there to hear about? I know she is your mother. I just think that this once why don't you allow yourself to stay in the present? Are you sure that you aren't angry about that? It's not too late you can still call if you want. Hey don't start yet.

But you have your cards all laid out.

It's just not card etiquette to start until all the players are ready.

No Grandma I think it is best not to call.

Well then let's go.

Red and black, mostly diamonds and clubs, Grandma mostly hearts and spades. 6–5–4. Grandma has a nine on her ten. No aces yet.

You know Tracy, Grandma says, starting to chuckle, your grandfather always did say it is never too late to give some people a spanking. I am talking about both your parents right now. You can wish that you know. It's funny to imagine isn't it? Just deserts. She continues moving her cards. Put your ace up.

Oh sorry.

I used to have tantrums about the house and it seemed that there was dust everywhere some days, that I never would get everything done, it all piling up and I was so stubborn on the landing I would wait and Grandpa always did come and you need to be tied why I think I might just have to hold you down for a few minutes Pat, he would say.

You take a deep breath listening to your grandmother, it is nice to listen to her voice. She is moving her cards.

Phillip, your father, wasn't too old to be spanked so many times. When he came home with your mother and of course they were looking for handouts a young bride not even seventeen and her stomach was swollen and I knew what your grandfather was thinking. Too young to be raising a family everything unplanned and sporadic I don't know where Phillip got that from, that everything will just take care of itself attitude, and it's really too late to bring all that up. You can put your two of spades on my ace. You know you look so much like your grandfather. You are a lot like him you know. It's in the eyes, and those thick eyebrows. It's wonderful. I am sure that Grandpa is watching over us this very minute, Grandma says. I must not have shuffled very well, I don't believe this hand. Nothing to turn up. How's your hand?

King of hearts ace of spades. Grandma we should start over because this hand is going nowhere I can just tell.

Your grandfather didn't have the patience for cards, just like you. No, keep going you never can tell though I do seem to have all the high cards in my hand.

I am really on a roll now, Grandma, look.

Let's see what you have going there, because I can't move. You can put that seven on the eight there and move that five up, see?

Oh cut it out let me just play my way.

All right Miss Card Queen. I'll just watch now until you run out. Who knows maybe you'll go all the way this time you know you never have beaten me yet. This beginners luck.

Hmmm.

Pay attention Grandma you might miss something.

It must be the wine so warm, did I close the car windows? It will rain soon.

I am going to win this time.

Well I didn't exactly have a fair hand. This we'll consider a New Year's present, Grandma says.

At midnight you stand on the porch with Grandma. The wind is howling. The rain has started; a slow rain that prickles your arms and face.

You dream of June. She says, come in here quick get out of bed, hurry.

It's so obvious June says to you still talking to you as you are sitting up in bed. Oh, it's all so obvious. It doesn't even have to be what you have been thinking Tracy, that the two sisters were somehow magically safe and sound nestled cozily in the backseat of the car having been found finally in the woods after having been lost for such a long time.

Some of the nails are tin nickel nails and those are the ones the two sisters had to find, June is saying. You see Tracy, the stairs kept going up and up, and somewhere in the stairs were the nails that were different. Those nails, the ones holding the stairs together, the tin nickel nails were the ones that needed to be found, it's all really quite simple, isn't it?

. . .

On the first day of the new year the sun and moon and the earth stand in a straight line. On Grandma's kitchen sill, above the sink, three tomatoes are ripening.

Be careful Grandma says. Her green eyes twinkle. Where Grandma lives her house is only a few feet above sea level.

Because of the alignment of the planets, on this first day of the new year the ocean is crashing up onto the land. People in nearby towns have had to evacuate their homes because of the flooding caused by the extremely high tides. Grandma's eyes twinkle. Grandma's arms are tan. Grandma is in the window. You are outside. There are three ripening tomatoes above her head where she is standing over the sink peeling vegetables and singing.

The tide is so high. Down by the fish house if you put your head to the ground the ocean is flush to the earth.

In Grandma's living room next to the grandfather clock that stands as high as the ceiling there is a glass table with eight violet plants in different colors: pink, white, lavender, deep purple. These plants always have blossoms, always. Your grandfather's mother loved violets. Above the violets the face of the grandfather clock has a small window in it where a sun and moon rotate changing places once a day because Grandma winds the clock every Sunday at 12 P.M.

Grandma, you ask, what's the process of cells, when they divide per second, per second?

You ask Grandma this but what you are really thinking about, what you really want to know is what might anything be for, Grandma will go away, can't just stay forever and ever. This is what you want. And what of all this, this list you write down because it gives you something to look at:

Niagara Falls, chicken wishbones, bumblebees, cashmere sweaters, the discovery of new planets, pick-up sticks, varnished wood, sculptures, the feeling that you have known someone that you just met for your whole life, books, records, sunrise, sunset, the space between two tightly held hands, cowboys, museums, zoos, the space between whatwepretend-toknowandwhatwepretendtonotknow, CPR, ambition, the Book of Job, sex or friendship, your head in someone's lap, Chinese silk, birthmarks, bay trees, kangaroos, Helen Keller, the stars at night, thank-you notes, Doppelganger, when heart transplants are perfected it will be possible to put a woman's heart in a man's body and vice versa, gloves, the orbit of the planets, romance, blue balloons, poetry, chocolate, anatomy, black-and-white, love letters, Xerox machines, giggling, bad dreams, hopscotch, harmonicas, motel soap, Christmas cookies, lines from your favorite song, clotheslines, what does it mean to be in love with someone's mind, ideologies for everything; love, music, writing, planets, cooking, fashion, Queen Anne's Lace and hemlock look almost the same but one is deadly poison, formulas to power, 102 elements, that vocal chords allow for sounds that are rarely used or needed?

Grandma reaches for her dictionary. It's not osmosis, or is it diffusion, cell reproduction? A piece of Kleenex dangles from Grandma's watch band, that tissue unconsciously tucked there, waves over the wine-colored pattern in the Persian rug, like a signal flag.

There are so many questions you want answered.

Grandma gets up with the sun every day.

At Pamlico Sound after lunch you and Grandma take a long walk, each heading down the beach in opposite directions. It is hard to walk in the wind. Storm clouds are moving fast overhead. The ocean has covered what is the actual beach. Grandma is not afraid. Grandma is excited when Mother Nature gets the upper hand. Where you walk is in the dunes. You look behind you. Your footprints in the sand, where you have been these footprints are being covered over, erased by the wind.

There was an article you saw once, four paragraphs, filler. The blurb was about a woman an older woman found on the beach. She was covered with seaweed, her nose was bleeding. She couldn't remember how she got there and she didn't know who she was.

Over and over in your head you are thinking about these lines, lines that you aren't sure belong to you or belong to Mark or belong to anyone:

Lapping across acres and acres of abraded sexless stone
Fossilized zygotes wrinkle colorless and tired across the back of my brain.

The back of whose brain? Wrinkle colorless and tired, or don't wrinkle at all like what? Lapping like a swimmer or a dog?

You walk along the beach. There are so many footprints going back and forth. There isn't a print into which your feet go. You walk. In grade school with potatoes you made ink prints on paper. Ink prints. Footprints in sand or snow. With dull kitchen knives you carved into the potato, making shapes and designs. You dipped the cut potato in colored ink and pressed the design as many times as you could until the ink ran out. You would dip the potato in a new color or use the same.

Back at the car Grandma's hair is standing straight up on end as if she were hanging upside down. Grandma looks at you. She is laughing so hard that she is crying. You can't think of what could possibly be so funny. Grandma looks as if she has seen a ghost. Grandma laughs and laughs. Your hair is standing on end, Grandma says. Overhead the dark sky lights up. Hurry get in the car, Grandma says, the air is charged with electricity, it is dangerous to be outside now, Grandma says.

Heading back toward Grandma's you are both laughing so hard that Grandma has to pull the car over to the side of the road. The rain is coming down hard. This, Grandma's laughter, your laughter, a music that pierces through the fierceness of the storm outside like a fine silver thread that wraps your bodies together. The car might as well be a toy boat drifting through space, because the only thing that matters now is this laughter.

What is and what is, the reflection of each other's faces in wet laughing eyes that belong each to the other.

How to make the pain go away without causing more?

You have to go back, Grandma says.

. . .

You haven't turned on the light yet. You are still awake.

. . .

A dream moves through a grandmother's sleeping body.

The woman who is sleeping soundly, Patricia Hawkins is the grandmother of the young woman, Tracy Hawkins who is at this moment standing near the foot of her bed.

The bathroom light, she had left the bathroom light on and when she woke up some hours later she was certain that if she went in there her grandfather would be lying on the floor again.

"If only I hadn't gone to the store that day. When I came home he had been dead for only a short while. I know that God arranged for me to be out, because had I been here there would have been nothing I could have done."

How someone would look, how they would be, gone, on the bathroom floor or anywhere when the time comes.

The bathroom is the way it always is, sparkling white porcelain, thick blue towels, a braided rag rug in front of the toilet. Tracy looks at these things and goes to her grandmother's room.

Tracy thinks to wake up her grandmother. The urgent feeling that words must be said now. What to say? "I can't sleep Grandma."

The untied café curtains move in and out with the warm breeze. It is not dark. The light, that of dawn or dusk, is from the almost full moon casting its glow in Pat's room.

On Pat's nightstand is her clock radio that she listens to every night before she goes to sleep, or late at night if she wakes up: the news or the weather. There is a picture next to the clock radio of her husband Jonathan, a very distinguished-looking man seated at a desk smiling, his pen poised. Jonathan was a doctor.

Tracy stands still at the foot of Pat's bed so as not to wake her. She can't remember what it was that brought her in here in the first place.

It's always hard for a person to remember their selfish motivations.

There is a dream moving through a grandmother's body like the slow roll of earth tremors.

Is this chemical?

Unable to assume what she doesn't know, a simple action might be fraught with ideas. Ideas as farfetched as being afraid of seeing a real ghost, or being afraid that the gap in the earth that stretches for miles across California might split open any day dumping most of California into the sea. There are just some things that there really is no point in being afraid of.

How is it that nothing stops?

It really is impossible to believe in anything when an end is always perceived. Nothing can grow this way, not anything.

A small fragment of any person's dream might be enough in regard to the truth that no one asked to be born.

What Pat saw today. What Tracy saw today. A young girl with long blond hair flying a kite on the beach. The young girl, Donna, called out, "watch this, now it's gonna go," to her father who was sitting on the pier smoking his pipe and watching her. "Reebut, reebut," Donna says running down the beach, the bat kite moving up, its long red tail sputtering. "I think there is a frog on the beach," Curtis Allen says.

It's a pretense of answers to ever think one knows what is best for someone else, unless they first know what is best for themselves.

If trust, like love, like death, is just ideas, then it's nice to be able to see them in a context.

The kite line stretches from Donna's hand. "Watch this Daddy," she says tugging the string so that the kite goes up higher.

"Isn't this the life," Donna says, "reebut, reebut."

If the kite eventually tangles in the pier or dives into the green water, if someone decides one day that they just won't get out of bed, if nuclear waste floats invisible through the air, in Donna's wrist, at least now, there is a sensation that defies all this.

A dream moves through a grandmother's sleeping body.

Christmas is really over. Before you know it summer will be over too.

Christmas in North Carolina was warm. And at night the sky blackened so quickly that, like a charcoal drawing, you could have smudged it out if you wanted to.

Grandma's cool hands pulsing along your forehead, her fingers running through your hair. Her face showing the delicacy of your own passions; skin draping loosely over bone.

The Story

IT is in the kitchen. June is sitting in a chair first of all. Her feet are not touching the ground because her legs have not grown long enough yet to be able to reach the ground when she is sitting in a chair, not just in the kitchen but anywhere. June is kicking her legs back and forth, one then the other, fast or slow as she talks. June is excited. June is excited about the story she just wrote, a story all written out on paper, paper that she holds in her hands or puts in her lap. When June puts the paper in her lap her hands become animated, are fluttering about her face or her body, hands that talk, talk better than words, but she hasn't started telling her story yet. These hands of June's, yes hands as light and strong as wings.

Mom and Dad are watching June. You are watching June. You and Mom and Dad are sitting in the yellow wood kitchen chairs that are lined up in front of June's chair because you and Mom and Dad are being the audience.

June's eyes are wide and she talks in the voice of a child. Yes June was a child.

The story June is telling and maybe it was on her birthday or Mom's birthday, no it just seems that way now because when June told the story it was a family celebration, yes that is how you remember it, as a celebration.

June starts. Her eyes are wide. June's eyes move slowly from listener to listener, a real storyteller, big brown eyes open wide into the eyes of those watching her, the family.

June begins:

There is a King and a Queen and they have lots of kids.

June is holding her paper but she is not reading from the paper because she has memorized the story.

And their kids have lots of kids and they live in a big palace that is in a forest.

June is telling the story she made up and you are all listening.

And they live this way in the palace doing things and being happy or sad or mean but mostly just having fun and playing until one day ivy grows all over the palace and grows more and more until the palace gets all covered up and it looks like trees and then it is winter and ice covers all the ivy on the palace and everyone in the palace dies or goes to sleep for hundreds of years, the children too.

June stops talking and gets up out of her chair and goes to look out the window. June is looking into the neighbors' yard, looking at the fence. Behind the fence is the neighbors' swimming pool. There is ivy on the fence. Through the cracks in the fence the water in the pool is glittery.

Are you going to finish the story, or is that the end? Mom asks June this.

June turns back from looking out the window and goes to Dad and climbs onto his lap. She does this. June always went to Dad. Dad has big blue veins in his hands. You see the blue veins in Dad's hands disappearing into June's hair and then you see the blue veins again, blue and brown.

June finishes the story:

The castle is that way for hundreds of years, and then one day it is spring and the castle has no more ivy or frost or ice. There is a new King and Queen and they are getting ready for the children to come back.

Rowboat

THERE is nothing supporting you. You are floating as if on Houdini's magician's table except there is no table, no illusion.

What has left trails away from your body as if swords had been inserted, pierced all the way through, marking the holes through which it all has left.

What has left, is leaving, all that you can't control, viscous threads moving farther and farther away.

Each thread leaving your body from where the flesh has been pierced; threads that don't disappear or detach but become longer behind you, are slender like threads of silk.

In the darkness with your eyes shut or open you can see these people finally (yourself among them) Mother, Father, and sister and all the people that you have longed for, loved (?), now too you are seeing all the people you don't know, in the darkness all becoming threads that have left your body.

There is nothing supporting you, all here, a network of dreams like the fine tentacles of a jellyfish dangling beneath its darker shape that is slowly rising to the surface.

Medicine

LAST night you dreamt of your Grandpa Hawkins. There were three parts to the dream.

The first part: There is a bird, a large black crow and it is banging and banging against your window. Oh no, Oh no, an omen, this, and then you are at the beach, you are walking out in the ocean, moving across the surface of the water on a bridge that is made of dark brown cork. The bridge, a carpet supports you. You can see the others, people you know on the beach. There is a man in the water, a boy and then a man and then a boy, like how in sex sometimes a person's face does this. You just stay away from me, you say, starting to run. The man is smiling. You know who I am and why I am here, he says taking hold of the edge of the bridge and flipping you into the water so fast. This man with hair the color of beach sand is who? We know each other he says. It is your mother and then it is Bax. The shock then acceptance that this is not your mother but you and your lover. You are not angry anymore to be in the water. It's an in-between feeling this, where you all of a sudden feel yourself pushing and pulling, your hands clawing to get inside, but this is only the feeling, there are two separate people in the water.

The second part: You are sleeping, trying to sleep and you can't because Grandma is outside of your door crying. Please go away Grandma, I promise that tomorrow I will help you clean the house. No, she says, you promised that today you would and it is today and I am tired.

You roll over facing the window, pulling the covers over your head, hoping that she will stop soon. The crying just gets louder. Donna and Tammy are at the window and they are smiling in at you.

You get up march to the door and swing it open, furious that you can't get any sleep. You yell, all right Grandma where do we start?

Grandma is gone and the house is empty.

There is a note on the table, not a note that Grandma might write. This note is on paper that has been used many times before, is stained with food, greasy with fingerprints.

The note which is typed says: I have gone to the hospital to wait out the thunderstorm. God wouldn't allow a hospital to be struck by lightning. You make the arrangements. The letter is continued in handwriting, yours; I just had to leave, I hope you understand, this is where the road must end.

The letter is stamped, twice, the same red-ink stamp like those that postmen might have. The stamp says: God knows, he will know, God knows we are going.

You are holding this letter, this dirty piece of paper. You realize that it is wrong, that there are too many things wrong, out of character. First, the letter is written as if this had occurred a long time ago. Second, Grandma is not afraid of storms. Third, is that it is you who wrote this note.

All of a sudden it is very funny, so funny that you start to fly around the room, leaping and turning this way and that. Out the window you go and you are up so high you can see the world below you, a place where everything is so dreadful and urgent. But you are flying, you are above this laughing and turning as your body would be in deep space, weightless.

The third part of the dream, what stays with you all day:

Grandpa Hawkins is standing knee-high in a mountain stream. The bottom of his yellow hunting suit is dark where the water has touched it.

There are fish jumping in the part of the stream where your grandfather stands, your father's father, Doctor Hawkins.

Grandpa Hawkins's eyes twinkle and he says come join me, I have an extra pole here. You have to start soon he says, before the sun gets too high.

If you write to your grandfather I won't speak to you, your mother says from behind you, taking back the lavender stationery she had just given you.

It's a long hike down the mountains and when you get there your grandfather is gone.

You are sitting by the stream crying.

When you wake up you are sitting in bed. There is light streaming through the windows and your face is wet.

You can hear Grandma in the kitchen.

The clothes washer is going. Coffee is perking on the stove.

Out in the garden Grandma is bent over the tomato plants. Drops of dew, pinpricks of light are miraculously arranged, glistening over the lawn and the trees.

There are towels and sheets almost still on the clothes-line.

This hour, a momentary coolness as important as Grandma's

reason for being in the garden weeding between the rows at 6 A.M. before the heat of the day begins is what matters.

There are scallops of light prickling across the water. The gulls are congregated on the pier, fighting amongst themselves for the remnants of the day's catch. The sound of the men walking down by the fish house, their heavy shoes on the weathered planks of the pier, the sound of an engine starting, the ocean bubbling, frothing, this is what you hear, now.

Grandma has to swim, every day she can.

Grandma is out farther than you might go, her body moving steadily through the green-blue Atlantic. This picture, bigger to you than it really is in the scheme of things. Still this picture is important. Your grandmother, her arms, her breath, her feet, a rhythm . . .

Of course I won't let you go, Grandma says, holding your feet as you dived under.

There has to be someone holding, and someone to hold on to.

The truth of the matter at hand, of any matter at all, this touching, soul to soul that enables the continuing of all that is.

Grandma waves and smiles.

This beach chair, the one you are sitting in now, a beach chair that is made of white plastic, the weave loosening with the heat of the day.

After you saw June you went home. June had given you the key to the locked metal box that your mother has kept. In the locked metal box were the scrapbooks that June had made.

In the basement, the same basement, the same stone foundation that was beneath the old house is where you found June's locked box.

The lock rusted.

June said please. June said, I want you to read my journals, look at my scrapbooks.

It just didn't matter which house was overhead, the old white house, the one that June burned down, or the new house that was built on the old foundation. The basement was the same, damp, musty and pervasive with the sense that it was an intrusion to be where it is so dark and mysterious.

The box is heavy.

Someone has to keep track of what is happening, June said.

It isn't stifling to stand beneath a house. There is a door through which the sunshine caves in like laughter after a long silence.

The dream house collapsed and in its place stands a woman, a strong woman, with kind green eyes that don't look away, cool dry hands that caress or hold or dig wherever they please. There are bits of dirt, rich black soil beneath her fingernails because the woman that dissolved the dream house likes gardening as much but not more than swimming whenever she can.

After you went to see June Grandma said you come stay with me.

There were seven scrapbooks inside the box, not one for each day of the week or anything as symbolic and seriously wrong with making something out of what isn't really there. There are seven scrapbooks inside the box because the other scrapbooks are lost.

The scrapbooks: pages and pages of collages, of articles cut out of newspapers, pages and pages of detailed descriptions of actual events that occurred between the years 1976 to 1980, before June burnt the house down. Events that affected the community at large, catastrophes that befell people other than June. There are very few references to June herself. The only reference to June is that these are her scrapbooks. June arranged these pictures and these articles in this specific way. That is for the most part the only reference to June.

These scrapbooks, something to look at always or something to not look at at all. The information June had compiled from newspapers and magazines, and cut and pasted together, a myriad of subjects. This, the key, June's ordering of events that occurred and her juxtaposition of these events. Precisely what most of the pages in the scrapbooks consisted of, randomness, chaos. Nothing was revealed, there were no real answers as to why June did what she did.

There were notes, specific notes meant for a future reader. June had planned for that, a future analysis of what she was keeping track of.

What you took with you for no other reason than to have something of June's to hold on to, look at some other time, is a couple pages that June had torn from a journal she wrote when she was in the hospital in Seattle. You take these pages:

Barbara said write a journal for her to read, she said it is important to try and remember certain things. Here it is. Hi Barbara. Here is my attempt to keep track of my thoughts and express my anger.

Go to hell I said at first. GO TO HELL.

Why did you burn your parents' house down? You might have killed your parents and your sister. Why no remorse? You can't hide forever.

Hide forever. Where were you? In a damp basement.

There used to be windows in here. There used to be boxes in here, boxes you put here, boxes you had put the different phases of your life away in.

I see you June. I'm going to get you now. It is a game in the woods behind middle school. New bikes. You and June got new bikes. The trails behind middle school are perfect for riding bikes on, bumps and hills, a roller coaster in places.

What was in the basement besides June's box: a half-finished dollhouse Big Herb had started to make for your mother. A dollhouse for spiders to nest in. The plywood of the dollhouse aging in the basement, as anything ages that is locked away. Rotting.

It was Tracy, she did it really. You all don't understand. People can possess other people to do things for them. I know this. People can get other people to do their dirty work for them by concentrating really hard.

Fuck I said I did it. I did it I screamed to my father.

My father doesn't listen. My mother looks away or says she is sorry.

I don't want anyone else in my mind. All of you leave me the fuck alone. Stop trying to get inside of my head, all of you just leave me alone. My head, my thoughts they are mine. MINE. I'll tell you why I burned the house down I burned the house down because Tracy possessed me to do it.

It just started to happen. I wasn't actually there you see. There was my body doing it and I was kind of like just watching it all happen. I was dousing the hedges first with gasoline, then the stairs and then I was on the roof.

I saw her, a young woman. I guess it was me doing it. She looked like me. It was one of those out of the body experiences. My body possessed by the angry evil thoughts of my sister Tracy.

Out in the yard in the dark of the night there is a young woman and she has a handful of kitchen matches.

It's an old house, an evil and rickety house. There is poison in the wood. Maybe the house is possessed by the people that live there or the ones that lived there before.

I had a dream. I was carrying crosses up a long mountain trail. These are special crosses because someone is going to get married, and then they are going to take their lives in front of everyone.

Tracy is in the dream, Tracy and her sickeningly perfect self. She is even dressed like a cheerleader. She is marching in the front holding a baton that is lit on both ends. My mother is marching next to her. My mother is naked and she has a huge erect penis.

In the church which is miles and miles up the side of a mountain there are all the kids I have ever known from schools except their faces aren't the faces of kids their faces are the faces of lizards, slimy newts and some have insect faces, eyes that bulge, millions of eyes on each dark orb. Everyone is holding these crosses.

You'll do it June, Tracy said.

This is a dream I had Barbara. I am not sure if it was before or after I burned the house.

This room is a cavity, a hole in my tooth or a strand of hair

off of my head. The strand of hair is looming over the bed like
a vein pulsing in a magnifying glass.

Then there was the letter you found in the pocket of the jean
jacket the prison sent to Mom at June's request. I won't be
needing these things anymore June must have said.

A box of June's things in the basement of the house your
mother is selling. What June won't be needing anymore, a jean
jacket, a large black leather bag, empty, a small pair of men's
cowboy boots (too big for June but she wore them anyway) the
heels worn down on the outside because June walked like a
ballerina with her feet turned out, June's things.

The jean jacket used to be Mom's. It is faded. Embroidered
on the right side of the collar are forget-me-nots and two small
ladybugs. Ladybug, ladybug, fly away home, your house is on
fire . . .

You remember when Mom embroidered this jacket. She had
just quit smoking and needed to keep her hands busy.

Around the buttonholes are thorny vines and leaves. On the
back of the jacket is a brilliantly colored bird as big as life, in
gold and turquoise, fiery reds, purples and all the colors of the
sky or the ocean. Mom always drew from her head. There is no
bird that looks like this.

June stole this jacket from Mom.

Drawn on the sleeves of the jacket with indelible markers are
numbers and names, and on the inside of the left sleeve it says,
Medicine Man in red paint. June didn't mark up the jacket
where the embroidery is.

The letter is in the inside pocket, still in its pink envelope. 896
Bitzel Street, New York, New York, in Mom's curlicue
handwriting. A letter June kept with her.

This letter written two years before June was in Clear Lake.
You were in Equinox, in college.

Did you go home that year? For Christmas? Mom never told
you she wrote a letter to June. Each member of the family
pretending away the pain.

February 2, 1982

Dear June,

I hope this letter finds you on your eighteenth birthday. Your father gave me this address, he said that this is where you could be reached. He also said that you and Mick were on the methadone program. I am glad. I hope it works out for you.

Happy happy birthday, daughter of mine.

I don't know what you might need. Please use this money to buy yourself whatever you might like to have on your eighteenth birthday.

I miss you June. I hope that you are happy. I hope that you are doing the things that you really want to be doing.

June I never could understand you. I only wish that there might have been some way of knowing what you might have needed. I am sorry. I was not a good mother.

When you were born it was as if in a dream. Your Grandpa's car racing through Old Saybrook. Your father panicking, breathing for me, then remembering he would say deep-breathe slow, take it easy Vi. Your head was pushing its way out in the backseat of Grandpa's car. It was a cold night but I had the window rolled down, the smell of saltwater and everything so clean outside, the snow and the damp bark of the trees, and I wasn't cold. I wanted to be outside. The lights out the window, stringing by so fast, like Christmas lights.

I had been in labor the whole day. I just didn't want to go to the hospital, lie in the bed for hours and hours and just wait. So I stayed inside, played with your father. We were like two kids that day.

You were born within two hours of arriving at the hospital. So much hair you had June, and your tiny hands and rosebud lips, straight from heaven you had arrived all nine pounds of you.

In the hospital I had a dream that I still think of as vividly as if I had just woken up. With you asleep at my breast I dozed off.

I was an Indian woman living in the mountains, alone with a pack of wild dogs that took care of me as if I were their child.

Where I lived was in a cave. Inside the cave was always lit by torches. The dogs kept the torches going by breathing on the flame each dog breathing on each flame one by one at sunrise, midday, sunset and midnight. The walls of the cave were

364

covered with elaborate drawings that in detailed diagrams showed me how to live alone in my cave without speaking. I don't know how I communicated with the dogs, we just understood each other.

There were other Indians. I was part of a tribe. Each person in the tribe lived in their own cave, except for the men, the fathers as they were called who all lived at the bottom of a deep red lake, unable to ever leave unless the dogs wanted them to give birth.

You see the women all of them lived alone, each in their own cave. I only knew this because the dogs told me this. We have been living this way forever the dogs would say. It is best.

The wolves were the babies. This is where I woke up.

I can still smell that cave as if I was just there, eucalyptus and a smoky smell.

I don't know why I wanted you to know about this dream. It's just that I clearly remember that when the nurse woke me up I told her that I had just had the most magical dream. I told her that you would be a child who would do great things in life. This is what I told her.

I am at work right now, have a precious moment between rounds to sit down and write this letter that I hope finds you. So I will tell you a bit of what has been going on at home, in my life and with the kids.

I wish that you could see Pearl and Paul. They are just so wonderful, fill my life with the constant excitement of their new discoveries. It is a strange thing to have twins, a boy and a girl to boot. They both do well in school. Oh never mind I really want to talk about you, talk about how I miss you, how I regret so much, wish that I could have known somehow what you needed.

As you grew up June, I don't know exactly when, every day seeing you, and the things that you did and your anger and rebelliousness and wild imagination, every day I was seeing myself growing up, a painful reminder of how difficult my own childhood had been. Certain times I would look at you and it was as if I was seeing a ghost. I would pinch myself sometimes to snap myself out of the vertigo, a helpless feeling that it was all happening again. I just had such a difficult time talking to you, just as my mother had a difficult time talking to me.

When I was growing up June things happened that I could not
tell anyone about. The only thing I could do with all that I had
to keep inside was to rebel and I got in trouble, got pregnant,
was sent away to have an abortion, an unheard of thing at the
time. I never can be certain whose baby it actually was. I just
don't want to think about it. Straight to a Catholic school I was
sent, further inside all my anger was forced to go, and then I met
your father, a man from a well-off family, a man with dreams
about the world that seemed so much like my own, that people
would be so much happier with everything out in the open. And
this was starting everywhere, a new hope, a feeling of freedom
and breaking down the old structures that seemed to be suffocating everyone. Your father was practical as well as being a
dreamer and in many ways he provided what I had never ever
known, an unconditional love, a safety from hurt and violence as
well as having an open mind. My mind at the time was so raw
with emotion and anger. You are the most passionate person I
have ever known, Vi. Yes he loved me your father as I suppose
I loved him. But it is so hard to love another human being when
you don't love yourself. All I knew of love was hurting the
person you were closest to, and then of course there were no
boundaries that I had ever known, not real ones anyway, just the
boundaries that were always being imposed on me.

My therapist said that she thought it would be OK to tell you
what I am about to tell you. I don't know why but my first
instinct was to wait until sometime when we could talk. Of
course I don't know when that might be.
Part of my healing has been being honest about what has
happened to me.
My father, your grandfather sexually molested me when I
was growing up. There is no other way to say it.
My denial, my keeping quiet about this has ultimately taken
its toll on you kids. It has been hard. I am sorry June.

The rest of this letter, words swimming out from the center
of where a liquid was spilled on the paper is illegible. There are
drawings that are blurred, small stick figures dancing, running
and holding their arms out, something always missing.

You don't need to read this letter anymore.

There is a lump in your throat, a lump that disperses through your eyes. You cry a lot now. Simple things make you cry. Donna and Tammy playing on the beach; the sound of their feet in the sand, the smell of the salt water that sneaks into this dark basement you are letting go of. Simple things make you cry, what you once thought of as false, ugly, what you hated the most before. These things make you cry now.

In the basement is where you were and it was damp and humid in there.

These words in your hands, words written by a human being that is your mother, words written by another human being that is your sister.

There is a rawness about the world, a tenderness that amazes you.

In the basement as you read, the urge to leave Sleepy Hollow forever and never come back was so strong. To leave forever and be in Equinox, or at Grandma's.

But to go away from anywhere forever would be to fall asleep again, that's what happens, going away and going to sleep, the same as being lost, an escape of body only, removing yourself so completely that your pain is only amplified.

Sleep was torment then, because the truth will out, it just will.

You can leave and come back.

You are not your sister.

How long it has taken you to separate yourself from anyone, to see yourself as a person capable of making your own choices.

People do dream of one another at the same time at night or awake, this powerful surge of aliveness that comes from stepping across the space that exists between people, blood-related or not, a space that requires listening.

Your understanding so hampered for such a long time because you and June are still alive.

There is no way to escape really.

Each person a complex organism, a miracle of flesh and

feeling and ideas. Each person a complex organism here for specific reasons. This isn't really so hard to understand. If you look around you there is so much work that needs to be done.

This is what there really is to behold.

And now and now. Everything is done that was before.

Your grandmother is swimming in the ocean.

You are here. It did happen. While you were away your sister killed two people, an ugliness that is a part of you must be contended with. This that is a part of you just as Donna and Tammy playing breathlessly at the edge of the water are also a part of you.

It is hard to say when exactly it was that you really woke up.

One note, a note that appears at the end of one scrapbook says:

I hope that you are not disappointed that I have not provided any answers for you.

Sometimes people just know what they are going to do in their lifetime and there is really nothing that they can do about that knowledge.

· · ·

AFTER a while you had numbed to June's story, so entrenched were you in your own grief, a solitude of helplessness. After a while you had just numbed to pain.

You weren't surprised at first that your sister committed murder, what surprised you was that June was still alive. For so long you had assumed her dead. When someone is dead are they gone?

June didn't go away any more than you did.

After a while you couldn't have cared less about Tad's aunts who had holed themselves up in their Clear Lake house refusing to talk to anyone, saying only that God would have the last word, saying there would be justice even if June was still alive.

After a while you couldn't have cared less because you were so busy trying to figure out your own life. But it didn't work.

You kept getting sicker, more and more numb, unable to acknowledge your own part in the crime, in any crime, how much of an accomplice you had become in your denial of what had happened.

How to account for a helplessness that nurtures a denial of responsibility?

Somewhere in the taking from of what belongs to others is where you can find a glimmer of an answer, an answer that will somehow have to be unearthed if anything is to really change.

How to account for your final acceptance of an order of life that had numbed you into forgetting how frequently and with such ease you are able to take what is not yours?

This life that you are living now.

This is what you were taught?

There are pictures to draw in class, pictures for Thanksgiving, pictures drawn in crayons as waxy as the faces in the books you read in school. There are Indians and Pilgrims to draw with these waxy crayons, brown and orange, green and yellow.

On this day we are thankful.

What was it that you were being thankful for?

Were you thankful for the ghosts that had been subdued, thankful that beneath your feet was a shiny floor onto which your shoed feet could step?

You were being taught that it is OK to take from others.

You learned this, to be afraid that if you didn't take from others, then others would take from you.

These places, Equinox, Sleepy Hollow, North Carolina, for such a long time backdrops that you moved in front of unable to accept what had happened.

It is amazing how people can survive.

It is amazing to be alive at all.

Why don't you come in for a swim now? Grandma says.

Donna is sitting in the sand next to you. I'll bet ya can't swim as far as you, Gramma, she says, pursing her lips to one side.

I'll be in, just a little longer, you say.

You come in Donna, let's continue with your lesson.

This summer your grandma is teaching both Donna and Tammy how to swim. They are wearing old dresses. They can't wear bathing suits because of their mother's religion. Donna has a plain sundress on. She has unzipped it in the back. Tammy won't swim lately with Grandma. She is sitting down by the dock where she is watching from a distance what her father is doing over by the fish house.

The smell of souring olives permeated the air, the purple olives, the ones that fall off the tree because no one bothers to do anything else with them. These olives, their seeds adhering to the street, the gravel in the drive in front of your house. You can see where each seed is, as if they are points on a map. What was vivid at the moment, standing face to face with your father, your own father and not any other, what was vivid then, the smell of the souring olives.

You were standing face to face with your father in front of the bay tree, in front of a house that never really belonged to anyone, a house bought for kids that didn't really care.

What is the same, the foundation, the concrete structure onto which a new house was built, a new house that wood had weathered to look rustic and modern at the same time, and fits right into this suburb. Your Mom is certain that she can get a good price for the house. She wants to sell it, move away from this place now.

Nothing moves in Sleepy Hollow on a hot summer night, this is what you are remembering now sitting in a white plastic chair, nothing moves, not even the smell of rotting olives, a glue on the summer night pavement.

There will be fog in the morning.

Face to face with your father, there will always be gaps, something missing. Please Dad, please tell me something that might make a difference. Blood to blood. Are you really my father? This can be proved if ever there was a doubt. Are you really my father? What does that mean? The smell of olives and heavy air that doesn't move here. Everywhere as damp as a sponge. Is that smoke I smell coming from the basement? Is it?

There are so many questions to have and that doesn't mean you have to ask them or forget about them either.

Dad? Your mother says there is a time for everything. You didn't say this.

Your father's eyes, his face, that of a young boy, someone who has been hurt and can't seem to shake it. His face. Your face. Some things can't be seen?

There are just things that you never will know, and even if you could know these things it wouldn't matter now. What difference would it make to know if there was a reason, a specific incident, a specific person or group of people that made your sister June commit murder, try to kill your parents before? What difference might it make to know, to know the real history of the Greens, the real heritage and not just this garbled train of events that has shaped you. This a child's game of telephone operator, how you learned about your mother's family's history, the facts changing as they were passed from person to person.

You get out of the chair and put the towel on the sand, your head facing the water.

How you want to love and will, not when you are alone in bed at night, or running aimlessly on back roads sweat dribbling down your heaving chest (of course you think of love at these times too). How you will love is when someone is telling you something face to face and you are lost in their eyes hearing with all that you are what is being said.

You have to laugh sometimes. It is so easy to see someone in a special light, but for some reason or another their eyes are closed or the light is something you made up. And the person isn't seeing you in the same light at all.

You have to laugh sometimes.

No, what matters is now, is any moment, the one you are in and the ones to come. You move in and out of a dream house that is how you yourself make it, a dream house that is yours, yours and separate from what is happening, separate and at once intricately connected to being awake. Nothing to be denied or forgotten except the lie that there is an end, an end to fill you with fear, to make you afraid, so afraid that you go numb, can't move or grow at all.

Dad?

Yes.

This will happen again if we let it, if we don't grow up now.

Your father's eyes were watering behind his glasses. He didn't seem to care if you his daughter could see this.

It was a hot summer night in Sleepy Hollow.

If people had porches they would be out on them, enjoying the cool night air and listening to the sounds of a summer night.

It's amazing how people go on.

To say goodbye and mean it, to know that God is the gray area between all that is alive, a fullness of understanding and acceptance that is living in this world awake, to know that making love is not so much of the flesh but of souls balancing together because through ears and eyes they listen each to the other, seeing what is really there, eyes shut or open.

To know these things is to know the first and last line of any poem that is beneath the language of the orders you cling to as a child clings to an adult that may not be alive at all.

You are not a child.

It started at night, the haunting of your ghosts and it continued into daylight jarring reality because you had been dreaming with your eyes open but you weren't really seeing what was going on around you.

It was the ghosts of those that had been taken from that haunted you. Will haunt you again? The ghosts of yourself, your family, girls like Anna, Mark, ghosts that said and will keep saying that nothing can truly be contained but what is dead, that everything keeps moving that is alive.

Ghosts that will keep reminding you that you did not erupt from where you stand, that there were others here before you, that it is your job to ensure that others will be here after you.

This is the whole point then, you are not entitled to take what isn't yours. You cannot claim as yours everything you see. There are others.

These ghosts that will keep reminding you that it is a lie to pretend you ever brought yourself to any place, that there weren't so many others that enabled you to be here at all, so many others that enabled you to survive.

This story? The one that had to be told?

No one wants to be given everything, told of the future, really know what others are thinking. Because then you have to admit your ultimate fallibility, a powerlessness that does become powerful when accepted.

You had only wanted to see a future that you wanted to see. You had only wanted to read others' minds to hear what you wanted to hear.

But if you only want glimpses of the truth then you will continue a life where a claiming of the self only comes at night, alone in bed. This existence to keep others alone too, alone in the dark claiming bodies and thoughts because this is the only place where a semblance of safety is ensured.

You thought this.

To want only glimpses of the truth, to be seduced by forms and not shown the whole of anything, this is what you thought you wanted, afraid that if you saw the whole picture you would want to stop altogether.

Just don't give it all away an ominous voice of learning might have said. This when talking about good rhetorical skills, painting or appropriate behavior.

The truth, that you could only see the whole picture slowly, a piece at a time.

It's also true that you wondered before what it would be like to kill someone, to make life disappear.

The real battle that goes on inside, to understand this mechanism that seems so deeply instinctual somehow, to want to stop what can't be stopped at all. Even if you blow yourself up, this universe will continue.

This murderous mechanism inside, why you or anyone might take it upon themselves to decide why anyone might live or die? You do think that some people would be better off dead, better off unborn.

How to account for this?

You looked back, wanting to find a specific reason to explain why anyone might take it upon themselves to decide who will live and who will die.

This story is about grief, about losing something never to get it back, not ever.

There are mechanisms for survival, many of which you are not aware of that are the magical stuff from which the best dreams are made.

The one mechanism that astounds you is how your body could ensure its survival by taking in only what it could.

What are you looking at? Donna says, the you sounding as ridiculous as your face must look, a zombie on a beach towel just lying there while there is water to swim in and shells to find . . .

Donna, hands on her hips, her dress stuck to her body, shakes her head and goes back to Grandma in the water.

It's true that for the longest time you have wanted to be taken care of even before you were so lost, and sometimes you wanted to be taken care of so desperately that you considered putting yourself in an asylum where the attention would be ensured. You wanted someone to take control of your life, someone to tell you what to do, and what to think about.

Just let me sleep, please just let me sleep. This when the house in your dreams was light and airy, a place to meet people, to do whatever it was you felt you couldn't do in your life, fly or touch the bodies of the women in magazines, the women offered as something other than what they were, than what you are.

But this house became dark and terrifying when you tried to stay there. The fantasies unraveling.

When did you let go of the dread that pulled at your dreams? There is a difference between what is dead and the ghosts.

Thoughts becoming actions.

You can imagine the world you want to live in.

Awake is where you realize there are so many others imagining too.

Asleep you wanted so desperately to be loved, seeing love as something that would right your grief, seeing love, Bax or James or Miya as people to take control of your life.

You wanted to be loved as if love were a sweater to wrap yourself in, as if love were a coat of armor, as if love were a behavior to learn, an object to admire and not what it really is, to care for others as you care for yourself when you are really awake.

Out of all that had happened before you came to Equinox, out of all that had happened while you yourself were trying to understand how one family might contain so much hate, how you could contain so much hate. Out of all this you tried to make sense, to order, to control all those battles that were going on inside pressing to get out and at the same time you were trying to order other people's battles. All that was outside pressing in.

What else?

You finally had to allow the doubleness of your nature to just live.

Mother.

Father.

There is man and woman inside us all, June wrote.

You really did know this all along.

This, what makes you human, this that doesn't need definitions or rules but is in and of itself as pure as water that is at times rough or mirror-silk calm.

You wanted to exorcise all this before.

Your life for so long, an anxiousness between destinations, leaving one person's opinion, and when you left all you were really doing was looking for someone else to order what had become so tangled inside.

There were fourteen yarn God's eyes in the living room of the Mountain View Care Home. Each one carefully made with the colors of yarn the residents liked. Around two pieces of slender wood that made a cross the colored yarn was wrapped.

What Mark didn't say that you know now to be true is that parents might want their children to continue where they left off.

The same things that used to disgust you, scare you, what you saw before as monuments to something pathological, amaze you.

What is truly amazing is that you are here now. Your body has kept growing. There has been nothing you could do to stop this.

There is this skin that holds you inside; skin to rub, touch, hit, scrub, behold, skin to scrape, burn, restructure, skin that isn't impermeable but lets things in and out of, skin that can be cut.

It is no accident that blood moves away from where it has been released.

You have to go back now, Grandma says.

You are going back to Equinox. You have worked your way into the present. It is the summer of 1986.

What you can and can't take with you:

What you can take with you: your ability to question, to imagine, and the knowledge that June is alive. The only thing that can be locked up is her body, not her thoughts, not yours, not ever. Your dream house, you take this with you.

What you can't take with you: a denial of who you are and from where you have come, your Grandpa Green's rock collection, fictions about your family, any fictions at all.

Fates can be sealed in a lifetime, possibilities that just won't be. There are things that can't be changed.

Are you coming in? Grandma is holding Donna's arms. Donna, face down in the water kicks furiously, brings her head up, laughs, spurts water, starts again.

Come on Tracy, Grandma says.

You are standing in front of the ocean in North Carolina. In the water there are rocks and plants, minerals and oxygen, and all forms of sea life.

The sand burns your feet as you walk to the water's edge.

The water is cool. A line of foam crosses your toe as a wave retreats.

You don't walk in slowly, you plunge right in because Grandma says this is the best way to do things.

The dream that goes back. This is what you are thinking about as you wake up. You can continue now. As you wake up, objects, acts, situations evade you, slip away, and you only know that in the dream you went back.

Clear Lake

IN the daylight, in the woods that surround Clear Lake there is a resort town. In this resort town there is a place where people can go to be naked. This is a special place, where people go to be naked and it is fenced off from the rest of the town, so that people in clothes can't spy. At night people are naked in their cabins. It is dangerous to go outside naked at night.

June plays in the mud. You swim or draw. You play with June in the mud. Mom sunbathes and helps the women with the meal preparations. Dad reads, or works on the book that he is writing or thinks about bills.

There is a boatride on the lake at 2 P.M. and your family is going.

You have your shoes off, socks off, and are sitting on the floor picking your toes. The shoes didn't feel right so you took them off.

Tracy we are trying to leave, your Mom says. Why didn't you think of this before? Mom isn't really angry. Mom is frustrated. There are lots of other things to be thinking about, not just being at a nudist camp, not just getting kids dressed to go on a boatride. It is becoming an ordeal.

June has a hood on, a blue hood. June is wearing a blue windbreaker.

The boatride is not a trip to be naked on. Naked is for back at the camp.

The camp is like a club. There are fourteen cabins. You and June are the only kids. There are mostly couples, not pretty couples like on TV. There is nothing to imagine when everyone is naked. Naked is white and lumpy for real when you first see it, not shiny and smooth like TV. The women have breasts that sag, and the men have weiners that look sad. Men don't look like how you imagine Captain Kirk, all special like a king when pretty ladies press up to him on TV.

Are you kids ready? Dad asks. Dad has on plaid shorts and Indian sandals.

You don't want to go on the boatride anymore. You have your shoes back on but they still don't feel right. You have a purse. In the purse are paper dolls, some gum, and three pennies that shine. Your grandma in Old Saybrook gave you the purse and the three pennies before you left there to move to Sleepy Hollow. This vacation is while the house in Sleepy Hollow is getting ready to be lived in.

The wind is warm. The family walks down the gravel road between the fourteen cabins. This is your family.

At the boat dock there are three other people plus the man who drives the boat. A husband and a wife have on matching outfits that look loud and nasty against the gray sky and green lake. The wife has white sunglasses on and her hair is frosted. She is staring at you and your family. You can tell she feels sorry for people that don't have her pretty things, like her pearl necklace or her long pink fingernails.

Your mother doesn't wear makeup and wouldn't frost her hair to live. Your Dad has rich parents. Your Dad likes to be poor. Your Dad's Mom who is the best lady in the world has a thousand times better everything than this lady and her mustard-colored shorts that match her husband's mustard-colored shorts.

When you want to you can look like a big lady just in the way you can make your face go. If your shirt is bunched up right you might just as well have big titties in there. Who's to know? Sometimes when you are alone and it is just you and your father, you bunch up your shirt and make your lips go a certain way, like a big lady's. You hope when you do this that people think you are your Dad's wife. You especially hope this when you are in a car together. It's best if you have your Mom's dark glasses on and you hold your purse up high on the dashboard where people can view it.

The other man going on the boatride is the one who is always at the pool. When he is at the pool he is under the water for a long time. When he is out of the pool he is always looking like he did something wrong and might be caught at any minute for doing it. Or he just looks through his binoculars out across the lake.

Down by the lake there is a big fence that separates the nudist camp from the rest of Clear Lake. At the entrance to the camp there is a guard who sits in a booth.

The man with the binoculars is looking down through the pier at the water.

Well, I guess we should be going any minute, the lady with the mustard-colored shorts says to her husband in mustard-colored shorts. She is pulling at her pearl necklace. I don't particularly know why we have to take this trip today, or any day, she says.

Her husband scratches his head where there is hair, and breathes deep with his eyes narrowing. Honey, he says. You can't think of how mustard looks like honey. June has a booger.

You just wish you were at Grandma's. Grandma has a rowboat that she takes you and June for rides in.

Honey, this vacation is to relax. We are having such a nice time, he says. What else do you want? he says in a Dad voice.

What are you staring at girlie? the lady asks you. You would bite her or tell her that her frosty wig looks about ready to fall off but you know better now.

Mom's best friend in Old Saybrook, Beverly, is the fattest woman that ever lived at least. One day she was in the kitchen, sitting in a chair that her butt was hanging over the sides of like she was extra people and you asked Beverly if she wasn't ever afraid of breaking chairs and especially the one she was sitting on. Beverly told your Mom that her children were wild and rude. Beverly talked about you like you weren't there.

Everyone is on the boat. June isn't rude. June is smart. June can read lots of things and she is only four. The motor is loud. You are glad everyone is wearing clothes. There are people in a speedboat and they go by and stare. They know that you are from the naked camp.

Huge clouds cover the sun. The water gets gray. The clouds move by fast and the water is greener again.

With Grandma in her rowboat, the water sparkles and the paddles scooping at the water sound like splashing in a bathtub.

The man with the binoculars is sitting next to June. June looks pale and her brown eyes look mean, then nice. June is prettier than you and people always say how pretty she is when the family goes places. June looks like a doll because she is so little. June is not a doll. Dolls can't read.

At the camp you wear your bathing suit. You stay in the pool. You hold on to the warm metal, and with your hands you move your body around and around the edge of the pool. You don't know how to swim in this pool because there is no shallow end, just deep. Sometimes you splash water onto the edge and watch the water evaporate in the sun.

You wish for things to be different. What happens is that finally everything ends just where it begins, in darkness. There are no longer any guidelines, nothing to hold on to. It is true that if you look at anything long enough it will disappear, no not disappear but transform, and there is no longer a language for what is before you.

★   ★   ★

What you see driving away, a highway stretching in front of you like a zipper opening.

What you know is that there is a real space that exists between people and that everyone goes away finally, has to, and if you listen really carefully you will know where they are, its smells really, sensation, the environment embodying emotions, enabling you to recognize a place as your own, the real place inside this flesh that you can call yours if you want to.

Names and blood. How people can be related. The complicated design of a family tree. The complicated decision, the time spent figuring out what to name a child, what to name anything. The truth of blood-related similarities, a sameness of physical features, voice tone maybe, the unresolved issues and the truth of what you are really here for, to continue as does everything.

You know how to say goodbye now and mean it, a tremor that rushes through your body. The earth hasn't exploded yet.

Things do change. The woods you brought yourself to, woods marked over and over again with leaves, and breath and rocks, smooth pebbles or jagged stone. These rocks that understand the water of the river that flows around and over them. Just as you have finally come to understand the futility in denying that you have been trying to fit yourself into a fantasy of a life with others' specific boundaries and orders, a life that for you could never be real. Your sister really did kill two people.

I am afraid that if you touch me I might disappear, is also what you meant to say before, when you felt yourself falling, letting go.

June is my sister, you said.

I have to speak now, you said.

The picture of doom does get smaller, a photograph that spins into deep space getting smaller and smaller, the two people in the picture you have seen for so long (or is it three people?), voices that whisper but not nearly as strong as your own voice, the one that says, I am here now, this is important.

The pulse in another's wrist beneath your open palm, the pulse of another's heart beating, this is what really matters.

At Clear Lake, in the summer, the shores are dotted with families, mostly poor. The town attracts a certain type of people: mothers and fathers wanting to show their children the great outdoors, wanting to escape the suburbs for a weekend, and just wade or float unbothered in the algae-speckled man-made lake in the mountains. Algae and microscopic life just floating there in your cupped hands.